Interpersonal and Group Dynamics

A Practical Guide to Building an Effective Team

SECOND EDITION

Bruce Bjorkquist

2011
Emond Montgomery Publications
Toronto, Canada

Emond Montgomery Publications Limited
60 Shaftesbury Avenue
Toronto ON M4T 1A3
http://www.emp.ca/highered

Printed in Canada.
Reprinted August 2014.

We acknowledge the financial support of the Government of Canada through the
Canada Book Fund for our publishing activities.

Acquisitions editor: Bernard Sandler
Developmental editor: Sarah Gleadow
Marketing manager: Christine Davidson
Director, sales and marketing, higher education: Kevin Smulan
Supervising editor: Jim Lyons
Production editor: Andrew Gordon
Copy editor & typesetter: Debbie Gervais
Proofreader: Nancy Ennis
Indexer: Paula Pike
Cover image: M-X-K/iStockphoto

ISBN 978-1-55239-397-0

The Library and Archives Canada CIP record for this book is available from the publisher on
request.

To Kathryn, problem-solver extraordinaire

Contents

CHAPTER 1
Member Roles: Participating Effectively in Your Group

CHAPTER 2
Leader Roles: Leading Effectively in Your Group

CHAPTER 3
Norms: Establishing Effective Rules in Your Group

CHAPTER 4
Goals: Setting Clear Targets for Your Group

CHAPTER 5
Dialogue: Speaking and Listening Effectively in Your Group

CHAPTER 6
Conflict: Resolving Disputes in Your Group

CHAPTER 7
Cohesion: Building Your Group into a Unified Team

CHAPTER 8
Critical Discussion: Generating Ideas in Your Group

CHAPTER 9
Decisions: Solving Problems in Your Group

CHAPTER 10
Evaluation: Improving Your Group's Performance

APPENDIX A
Meetings: Conducting Business Effectively in Your Group

APPENDIX B
The Experiential Model: Teaching and Learning Group Skills

APPENDIX C
The Experiential Exercises

Preface

Some 30 years ago I taught my first course in interpersonal and group dynamics, a new course offered within a nursing program. Nursing educators and practitioners had long recognized a need for leadership and group skills studies for nursing students, and college nursing programs responded with a variety of offerings designed to assist students in this area. Today, virtually all college programs require group work in their curricula.

My first attempt at teaching group dynamics was something of a disaster, both from the students' point of view and from mine. I did what many a college teacher has done. I selected a textbook, prepared and delivered lectures, planned and directed exercises, and developed and administered tests. In this rather traditional way, I tried to teach group dynamics. The students were kind but clear in their course-end evaluation, and I learned two important things from their review.

The first thing I learned was that students do not develop practical group skills by reading about groups, listening to lectures about groups, talking about groups, doing exercises in groups, and writing tests about groups. In short, I learned that my initial approach to teaching group dynamics was sadly inadequate, providing students with a "head trip" but little in the way of practical skills. I remedied the methodology problem the next school year by developing a learning model that has proved most effective.

My experiential model for teaching and learning group skills was a most important part of the first edition of *Interpersonal and Group Dynamics*, and remains so in this second edition. It is described in both Appendix B of this text and in units 2 and 3 of the Teacher's Guide. The inclusion of the model and its attendant resources is an expression of my now long-standing commitment to skill acquisition. That commitment began with the student feedback on my first attempt to teach interpersonal and group dynamics many years ago.

The second thing I learned from the student feedback on that first course was that the textbook that I had selected was also focused on theory and, for the most part, unconcerned with practice. Moreover, it was too difficult. Written by a university professor for second- or third-year university students, it was undoubtedly an excellent text for students at those levels in that setting. The text was composed almost entirely of theoretical explanations of various facets of group life. The theoretical orientation, technical terminology, and conceptual complexity, however, hindered access to the practical fundamentals of group work.

Although I was able to remedy the teaching methodology concern almost immediately, the textbook problem took me close to 20 years to address. The first edition of *Interpersonal and Group Dynamics*, with its simple style and its focus on practical skills, remedied that long-standing problem. It provided a clear and concise presentation of the basics, while including significant, practical strategies for skill development. It was a practical manual for building an effective team. In summary, it gave a simple account of the essentials of interpersonal and group dynamics.

This second edition of *Interpersonal and Group Dynamics* retains the same basic approach as that of the first edition. However, thanks to years of student and teacher feedback, this edition adds new material, eliminates some dated items, and offers revised presentations throughout. These revisions have resulted in a clearer and more manageable text for students and teachers alike. Supplemental resources such as the Teacher's Guide and the PowerPoint presentation also reflect the various improvements that have been made to this edition.

Part of the book's simplicity is to be found in its style. I have written the book in the form of a training manual rather than a traditional textbook. It employs, for example, the conversational tone of a coach. Moreover, it is light on theoretical analyses of group dynamics, and it is heavy on basic "how-to" explanations. The text also takes a personal approach in its presentation, a feature that makes the material easily accessible to students. It is a practical guide written in a simple style that is both conversational and personal.

It is also a simple book in the sense that it attempts to present only the essential concepts associated with interpersonal and group dynamics. In educator terminology, I have included the "need to knows," consciously avoiding the "nice to knows." Without question, much more could be included. Many teachers who use this book will, no doubt, supplement these essentials with additional materials of their own choosing.

Throughout, I have also tried to keep the language simple. Where technical terms can't be avoided, I have provided clear definitions and many simple examples. All in all, this book in its second edition remains a simple manual that covers the essentials of group work. I believe that it will continue to serve college students well as they prepare themselves for working in groups in their chosen career fields.

FEATURES OF THE TEXT

Guide for Conducting Successful Meetings

New to the second edition of the text is a powerful guide for conducting successful meetings. Appendix A, "Conducting Business Effectively in Your Group," provides students with a clear and simple guide to holding meetings that are both productive and satisfying. Meetings often fail because attendees lack the knowledge and skills that can make meetings rewarding experiences. In this appendix, students will learn the essentials for conducting business meetings effectively through an exploration of topics including room selection, meeting notification documents, meeting agendas and minutes, rules of order, and participant roles and responsibilities (chair, recorder, reporter, attendee). Students will know what to do before, during, and after their meetings, whether those meetings are held face to face or are conducted electronically.

The Experiential Model

In Appendix B you will find a description of five student teams that teachers can use to teach interpersonal and group dynamics in an exciting and practical way.

The model includes an Executive Team, a Lesson Review Team, a Teaching Team, an Energizer Team, and an Evaluation Team. Teachers can choose to use one or more of these teams depending on their circumstances and preferences. The more teams that the teacher uses, the more that teacher functions as a consultant, coaching the various teams as they plan and carry out their tasks. Appendix B describes the experiential model, providing detailed job descriptions for both teams and individual team members. Units 2 and 3 of the Teacher's Guide also describe the model.

The Experiential Exercises

Appendix C provides detailed instructions for conducting experiential exercises that are keyed to topics in each of the ten chapters of the text, as well as the new appendix "Meetings: Conducting Business Effectively in Your Group." In the experiential model, the Teaching Team, a team of students, has responsibility for teaching the lesson of the day to their classmates. Their lesson is always a two-step lesson. First, they lead the class in the assigned experiential exercise. Second, they provide an explanation of related concepts from the assigned chapter. The exercise provides the class with an experience of chapter topics *before* they receive an exposition of the topics.

Note that teachers who choose not to use the experiential model can still use the exercises of Appendix C. They will conduct the exercises themselves rather than coaching student teams to conduct them. Note further that unit 8 of the Teacher's Guide provides resources for use in the experiential exercises. Resources that the class needs in order to do certain exercises (role-play instructions, for example) are ready in the Teacher's Guide for duplication by the teaching team or the teacher.

Practising Your Group Skills

In the section of each chapter called "Practising Your Group Skills," students receive specific team assignments pertinent to the chapter or, in the case of the Lesson Review Team, to the previous chapter. The Executive, Lesson Review, Energizer, and Evaluation teams get their assignment in its entirety in this section. The Teaching Team, which always has the major responsibility for a class session, gets its basic assignment in this section but is also directed to Appendix C. There, as we saw above, they get further details regarding the experiential–exercise portion of their lesson assignment.

Mastering the Material

Each chapter includes a section called "Mastering the Material." The items in this section are intended to assist students in learning the chapter material, checking their comprehension, and preparing for tests and exams. The items focus on *recall* of information, not *recognition*. The goal is mastery of the words and ideas that are fundamental to a basic understanding of interpersonal and group dynamics. Students who can complete the worksheets without looking up the answers will be well prepared for test situations. The Teacher's Guide includes correct responses to all items in this section.

Presentation of Chapter Content

Each chapter begins with a statement of chapter objectives followed by an introduction to the chapter topic. The detailed presentation of chapter content follows and the chapter concludes with a summary.

The inclusion of many examples enhances the exposition of chapter topics, assisting readers with comprehension of the material. Moreover, the conscious repetition of key concepts within and between chapters contributes to coherence throughout the text. This repetition should enhance learning overall. Chapter summaries give readers detailed reviews of the key ideas in each chapter. In addition, summaries can serve as additional introductions to chapters for those readers who choose to use them that way. The chapter summaries should assist readers as they prepare for both classes and tests.

New to the second edition are various boxed items that appear throughout the text to help with study, to prompt reflection, and to provide samples of key documents. Some boxes are included as *study aids*, capturing key ideas of the unit in a brief summary that will help students retain the material. Other boxes offer noteworthy *quotes* about group work that are intended to stimulate interest in and discussion of the various topics of the text. In addition, other boxed items provide *samples* of key documents (such as agendas and minutes) that are set off from the main text for easy reference.

COURSE CONTENT ONLINE

A chapter-by-chapter slide program of all course content is available online to teachers, who can use it in their personal class presentations and discussions. In addition, teachers who employ the Experiential Learning Model in their classes can make the slides available to their student teaching teams, who can use the slides, as assigned, in their student-led lesson presentations.

The Sequence of Chapters

The sequence in which chapters appear reflects my preferred order of study. However, each chapter has been written so that it can precede or follow any other. The actual course of study, therefore, is at the discretion of the teacher.

Teachers who choose to use the experiential model in its entirety may wonder about the wisdom of leaving the assessment of team performance (Chapter 10) to the end. In the model, performance evaluation (not to be confused with grading!) is a regular part of every class session. I continue to follow the sequence of chapters in the text, but I require all evaluation teams to study a portion of Chapter 10 before they facilitate an evaluation session. You will see this requirement in both Appendix B (the job description for the Evaluation Team) and the "Practising Your Group Skills" section (the instructions for the Evaluation Team) in each chapter.

With the addition of Appendix A in the second edition, teachers have another option for setting their sequence of learning experiences. "Meetings: Conducting Business Effectively in Your Group" will strike many as an excellent place to begin their students' exploration of interpersonal and group dynamics. The unit has many practical applications for college students, who frequently find themselves working in groups.

The Teacher's Guide

A Teacher's Guide supplements the text and is available to teachers who adopt the text or consider it for adoption. Unit 1 introduces the guide, providing an overview of its contents. Unit 2 gives a general description of the experiential model for teaching group skills, and unit 3 describes the model in detail. Appendix B of the text and these two units of the guide together provide a thorough description of the experiential model for teaching interpersonal and group dynamics.

Units 4 and 5 provide forms for duplication by the teacher for use in class. In particular, unit 4 offers communication forms that can be used by Leaders, Recorders, Reporters, and Participant-Analysts in the experiential model. Unit 5 also contains forms for reproduction by the teacher. These are grading forms that can be used to calculate scores for various skills taught in the course. Both types of forms will, no doubt, be of interest to teachers who use the experiential model and those who opt for a more traditional approach.

A test bank of over 250 questions with answers is found in unit 6, and the correct answers to all "Mastering the Material" items of the various chapters are given in unit 7.

Unit 8 of the guide provides detailed instructions for conducting the 10 experiential exercises that are assigned to teaching teams in the "Practising Your Group Skills" section of the various chapters of the text. Unit 8 also includes resources necessary for conducting the exercises, including items that can be duplicated for handout or other purposes. The materials in unit 8 are most effective when used in the context of the experiential model described in units 2 and 3 of the guide and in Appendix B of the text.

The final unit of the guide, unit 9, provides teachers with sources of additional experiential exercises that can be used in Interpersonal and Group Dynamics classes that employ the experiential approach to teaching and learning group skills.

Acknowledgments

Over the many years that I taught interpersonal and group dynamics at Conestoga College, I worked with students in the fields of nursing, recreation, engineering, security, and policing. In all of those years except for one, all of my students worked on their group skills using the structures of the experiential learning model that is incorporated into *Interpersonal and Group Dynamics*.

The development and successful use of this model has been one of the most rewarding aspects of my professional career. I frequently tell colleagues, with all sincerity, that my students taught the best lessons ever taught in my classroom. To all—dare I say it?—the thousands of students who embraced the model, worked with me, learned from me, and taught me so much about teamwork, I express my sincere thanks.

I am grateful to many colleagues who did administer and those who still do administer programs and coordinate activities in the best interests of Conestoga's students. In particular, I thank Joe Martin, Greg Burns, Don Douglas, Carolyn Harrison, Bill Jeffrey, Eric Dahlin, Tony Martinek, Jal Wadia, Bob McIver, Mark Derro, and Gordon Greavette for their collegial approach to our common tasks at Conestoga College. Your teamwork in the offices of the College makes the teaching of teamwork in the classrooms of the College more effective.

Four colleagues deserve special mention and special thanks. At one of the busiest times in his career, Bob Bamford joined me in teaching interpersonal and group skills to Conestoga's first class of degree-level students. He mastered the experiential model in record time and brought his considerable interpersonal skills to bear on this new challenge. Thanks, Bob, for the courage to jump in and for the very valuable contributions that you made. You are an important part of this text.

It was an easy transition, I believe, for Geoff Johnstone to add to his traditional roles as professor of sociology and soccer coach by becoming a consultant and coach within the Interpersonal and Group Dynamics course for degree students at Conestoga. Having taught successfully at the College for many years, he enthusiastically took on the added responsibility of teaching Interpersonal and Group Dynamics. His previous teaching and coaching experience prepared him very well for this new assignment. From all reports, he did a superb job, and that's not at all surprising. Thanks, Geoff, for your contributions to the ongoing development of the experiential model.

I also wish to thank Jean LeForge for her many contributions to the development of this text. She has used the experiential learning model successfully with students in security and policing, and she has adapted it for use with human resources students as well. Her classroom experience is very much a part of this text. Thank you, Jean, for securing essential resources, for sharing your teaching strategies, for reading and rereading the manuscript, for providing valuable feedback, and for encouraging me in my work.

In addition to teaching security students and policing students, Maureen Murphy-Fricker has taught welding technicians. Maureen has successfully employed the experiential learning model with all three groups of students, adapting it to special circumstances where necessary. Her experience in the classroom has contributed in important ways to this text. In particular, her creativity shows up in experiential exercises that she has personally developed and kindly permitted me to use. Thank you, Maureen, for your enthusiasm, your creativity, your support, and your generosity.

When Conestoga College began offering degree-level programs, all students in those programs were required to take the course Interpersonal and Group Dynamics. College administrators saw the value in this practice-oriented course and ensured that students received training in teamwork before they engaged in teamwork within the various other courses in their programs. The professors assigned to teach this course have done an exceptional job, first receiving training in the experiential model, and then employing it successfully with their students. In this regard, special thanks go to Ken Brooks, Barbara Hall, and Barbara Primeau.

I'm confident that teachers and students who use this new edition of *Interpersonal and Group Dynamics* will find it to be an extremely helpful resource, one that is easy to read and one that gives solid guidance regarding the knowledge and skills required to be an effective team player. I'm most grateful for the thoughtful reviews of the first edition that were provided by professors Patricia Kimmerer and Margot Murray of Durham College. You offered specific suggestions for the improvement of both the content presentation and the sequencing of chapter materials, and I trust that you will recognize some of your valuable contributions in this second edition. Your work is now an important part of this work, and I believe that students and their future employers will be the ultimate beneficiaries of our efforts. Thank you.

Finally I would like to express my sincere appreciation to the congenial, dedicated, and professional staff at Emond Montgomery Publications. For their encouragement and assistance in getting this edition to press, I especially thank Bernard Sandler, Sarah Gleadow, Debbie Gervais, and Jim Lyons, and the editorial staff at Emond Montgomery for their many contributions to this project.

Bruce Bjorkquist
Waterloo, ON and
Fort Pierce, FL
February 25, 2011

Member Roles: Participating Effectively in Your Group

Individual commitment to a group effort—that is what makes a team work, a company work, a society work, a civilization work.
—Vince Lombardi, football coach

INTRODUCTION

To begin our study of the roles that members of small groups play within their teams, consider Hollywood actors for a moment. As you know, an actor is a person who portrays a particular character in a story. You also know that some actors are better than others and that great actors often capture the hearts of millions of people with their outstanding performances. Each year in Hollywood, the best actors are rewarded with an Oscar, the top prize for performance in cinema.

Now, those of us who aren't Hollywood actors also play roles, but not the kinds associated with movies, television, or plays. We play various roles in our families and in society. However, we don't really *play* the roles the way an actor does. Rather, we *live* or *fulfill* the roles that family and society require of us. Within our families, for example, we live the role of son or daughter, husband or wife, brother or sister. Beyond our families, we fulfill other roles that are often work related. For example, we are technicians, nurses, office managers, and personal counselors.

Like Hollywood actors, we can do a good job or a poor job in the many roles that we play in society. This book is designed to help you do an excellent job in the roles that you will fulfill now in college, and, later, in work groups in your professional life. This chapter, in particular, focuses on the roles associated with effective participation as a member of a small group. While winning an Oscar is out of the question, contributing to the success of your group, earning the respect of your teammates, and enjoying a sense of personal achievement are not.

CHAPTER GOALS

After completing this chapter, you should be able to:

- Define the terms *goal* and *role*.
- Define the terms *task goal* and *social goal*.
- Describe the difference between a task goal and a social goal.
- Define the terms *task roles* and *social roles*.
- Name the six helpful task roles that promote task completion.
- Describe the task skills that define each of the six task roles.
- Name the six helpful social roles that promote social cohesion.
- Describe the social skills that define each of the six social roles.
- Name and describe six harmful group member roles.

All the world's a stage, and all the men and women merely players. They have their exits and their entrances, and one man in his time plays many parts.
—William Shakespeare, *As You Like It*

In this chapter we'll first discuss the relationship between your group's goals and the roles that members must play in order to achieve those goals. We'll then discuss task roles and social roles—the member roles that help a small group get its work done and build relationships among members. We'll conclude with a look at certain actions that are harmful to both group productivity and group unity.

GROUP GOALS AND MEMBER ROLES

To get a clear understanding of the relationship between goals and roles, let's use the example of a heart transplant operation. The goal of the operation is to remove an unhealthy heart and replace it with a healthy one. To accomplish this goal, several individuals must successfully fulfill very different roles. The surgeon fulfills one role, the anesthesiologist fulfills another, and a nurse fulfills yet another. Together they must play their respective roles successfully in order to achieve the transplant goal.

All groups, large or small, set goals and assign members to fulfill roles that will achieve their goals. This chapter is dedicated to helping you and your teammates develop the knowledge and skills to successfully fulfill key roles that are essential for achieving your team's goals.

role
a set of expectations associated with a particular responsibility

As you know, a goal is a target that you aim for. We'll have much to say about goals in Chapter 4. Now, however, we'll focus on roles. A **role** is a set of expectations associated with particular responsibilities within a society or group. For instance, society has a different set of expectations for each of the heart transplant team members in our example above. So, too, our society has sets of expectations for parents, teachers, students, and others as they fulfill their roles in society.

The expectations that society has for a particular role amount to a set of rules for properly fulfilling that role. Nurses, for example, are expected to live up to the standards that their profession has set for the benefit of society. Because roles are really sets of rules for behaviour, it's natural for us to judge the performance of other people in their roles.

When someone fulfills a particular role well, we commend that person. In contrast, when people fail to live up to the expectations of a role, we find fault with their performance. In the first case, the individual met society's expectations. In the second case, the individual did not.

In our society, then, we have good nurses, good parents, good teachers, and good students who meet the expectations associated with their roles. Unfortunately, we also have bad nurses, bad parents, bad teachers, and bad students who don't fulfill our expectations. As we will see in the next sections, there are roles that help small groups achieve their goals, and there are roles that hinder, or prevent, team success. In other words, small-group members—just like doctors, nurses, parents, and Hollywood actors—can be good or bad at what they do.

HELPFUL AND HARMFUL ROLES

There are a number of helpful roles that you as a member of a small group should fulfill within your team, and there are some harmful roles that you should avoid. In the rest of this chapter, we'll describe regular *member roles* that you should fulfill within your team to help make it functional and successful. In Chapter 2, we'll focus on special *leadership roles* (leader, recorder, and reporter) that are essential for your team's success. In both chapters, we'll describe specific skills that you can and should develop to help your team reach its goals.

TASK AND SOCIAL GOALS

Every small group has two basic goals. The first is the **task goal**, the goal of getting the job done. The second is the **social goal**, the goal of building good relationships among group members. When a group functions as a team, members are productive. They get the job done. In addition, members respect one another and they develop a sense of unity or cohesion. For example, the team of nurses who not only get the job done but also respect one another is a team that functions effectively. They are a successful team because they are both *productive* and *cohesive*.

TASK AND SOCIAL ROLES

Task roles are roles that you can play on your team to help your group achieve its task goals. The successful use of these roles within your group will make your team productive. Similarly, **social roles** are roles that you can play within your group to help your team achieve its social goals. As you will see shortly, each role is characterized by a distinctive skill that defines that role. The skills directed at task completion are called **task skills**, and those directed at social development are called **social skills**.[1] The key to becoming an excellent team player is to fulfill your task and social roles by skillfully taking the appropriate actions at the appropriate time.

To help you become an excellent team player, we'll first look at the six helpful roles that you can play to assist your team with task completion. After that, we'll examine the six roles that you can play within your team to build and maintain good relationships among members. Lastly, we'll look at six harmful roles that excellent team players do not engage in.

SIX HELPFUL TASK ROLES

The helpful task *skills* associated with the six task *roles* of an effective group member include sharing your ideas, asking others for their thoughts, checking to see that everyone understands an issue, summarizing the progress of your group, suggesting directions that your group might take, and motivating members to get the job done. Let's look at each of the six roles that employ these skills to promote task completion. To help you remember these roles, we've given each one a memory-friendly name.

task goal
the goal of getting the job done

social goal
the goal of building good relationships among group members

> The way a team plays as a whole determines its success. You may have the greatest bunch of individual stars in the world, but if they don't play together, the club won't be worth a dime.
>
> —Babe Ruth, baseball Hall of Famer

task roles
member roles that enable a group to get a task done

social roles
member roles that help to build and maintain a cohesive team

task skills
the distinctive skills that characterize each of the six task roles

social skills
the distinctive skills that characterize each of the six social roles

---

1 The concept of task roles and social roles has a long history. Benne and Sheats (1948, pp. 41–49) were among the first to discuss them, identifying 13 task roles, 8 social roles, and 8 harmful roles.

1. The Idea Sharer

Idea Sharer
member who is skilled at sharing his ideas about team tasks with other team members

Effective group members contribute constructively to group discussions. The **Idea Sharer** is the member who is skilled at sharing his ideas about team tasks with other team members and does so regularly. In doing so, he helps his team achieve its task goals. The Idea Sharer is essential for team success, and the most successful teams are those in which all members are Idea Sharers. When a group has many ideas, it has more possibilities for task success. To help your team succeed, share your ideas regularly with your group.

2. The Idea Seeker

Idea Seeker
member who is skilled at asking others what they think about a given task

Effective group members want to hear what others have to say about an issue, and they seek the opinions and views of their teammates. The **Idea Seeker** is the member who is skilled at asking others what they think about a given task. Idea Seekers are effective group members because they consciously seek information and opinions from other members of the group. If you want your team to succeed, then regularly ask others for their ideas.

3. The Comprehension Checker

Comprehension Checker
member who is skilled at ensuring that the group has a common understanding of an issue or task

Effective group members take the necessary steps to check that all members understand one another regarding group tasks. If group members are interpreting things differently, communication will fail and the team will waste time in confusion and misunderstanding. The **Comprehension Checker** is the team member who is skilled at ensuring that the group has a common understanding of an issue or task. To ensure that members of your team are "on the same page," check comprehension regularly. In Chapter 5 we'll examine several communication skills that will assist you when you serve as Comprehension Checker on your team.

4. The Progress Summarizer

Progress Summarizer
member who gets the group to stop and reflect on the progress being made

Often when groups work on their tasks, members get confused and head in different directions. This, of course, can be frustrating and counterproductive. It is the **Progress Summarizer** who gets the group to stop and reflect on the progress being made. She is skilled at compiling the various ideas and decisions of the group into a brief and clear summary. Summarizing progress is a useful way of getting everyone back on track. If you regularly help your team to summarize its progress, you will make a valuable contribution to its success.

5. The Direction Suggester

Direction Suggester
member who is skilled at making constructive suggestions about the options that the team has at a given time

When trying to achieve their task goals, teams often find themselves wondering what to do. They just don't know how to proceed. The **Direction Suggester** is the team member who is skilled at making constructive suggestions about the options that the team has at a given time. She helps the team by suggesting a course of action to take. You can contribute to your team's success by suggesting that it proceed in one way instead of another to achieve its task goals. By doing so, you'll help give direction to your team as it pursues its goals.

Getting the Job Done

The Role	The Skill
Idea Sharer	Offering own point of view to teammates
Idea Seeker	Asking teammates for their views
Comprehension Checker	Ensuring that everyone understands an issue
Progress Summarizer	Giving summaries of team accomplishments
Direction Suggester	Offering ideas on how the team should proceed
Group Motivator	Encouraging teammates to finish team tasks

6. The Group Motivator

Among other things, effective group members are motivators. They are the "movers and shakers" within the team. When undertaking a task, group members often have different levels of interest with respect to that task. In addition, it's not unusual for team members to get sidetracked. The **Group Motivator** is the member who is skilled at encouraging others to direct their energy to completing the task at hand. Groups form in order to get tasks accomplished, and you can make a major contribution to your team's success by constructively motivating others to complete your team's tasks.

Group Motivator
member who is skilled at encouraging others to direct their energy to completing the task at hand

When members of your group regularly fulfill all six task roles described in this section, your team will be well on its way to success. As an individual, you may feel more comfortable in some roles than in others. This experience is quite common. To become an excellent team player, however, you should regularly do all of the following: share your ideas, seek the opinions of others, check comprehension, summarize progress, suggest directions, and motivate teammates.

SIX HELPFUL SOCIAL ROLES

Just as there are six roles that help a group accomplish its task goals, so there are six roles that contribute to the achievement of a team's social goals. The social skills that define each of these social roles include encouraging others to participate, supporting them when they do so, facilitating communication, observing the group's emotional climate, relieving stress in the group, and mediating conflict when it arises. We'll now examine the six social roles that help a group reach its social goals. Once again, we've used memory-friendly names to label each role.

1. The Participation Encourager

Effective group members encourage others to participate in group discussions and activities. The **Participation Encourager** is the team member who is skilled at stimulating all members of the group to contribute to the group's effort. Frequently, more assertive members of a group take the lead and make decisions for the group. When this happens, less assertive members may feel left out or ignored, and the team's sense of cohesion will suffer. If you encourage all members to participate in discussion, you will be a powerful influence in your group. Others will understand that you value their opinions and that they have a part to play within your group.

Participation Encourager
member who is skilled at stimulating all members of the group to contribute to the group's effort

2. The Participant Supporter

The best team players support those who make contributions to the team's life. The **Participant Supporter** is the team member who is skilled at showing support for others when they make a contribution to the work of the team. A little praise, for example, can go a long way in motivating members to contribute their ideas and opinions. It enhances self-esteem and strengthens the sense of belonging, contributing to the team's cohesiveness. By supporting others when they share their thoughts, you contribute to the achievement of your team's social goals.

Participant Supporter
member who is skilled at showing support for others when they make a contribution to the work of the team

3. The Communication Facilitator

Effective group members facilitate the communication of feelings within the team. Earlier, we saw that the Comprehension Checker works to ensure that members understand their jobs. In that case, communication skills were directed at task accomplishment. Here, we see communication skills being directed toward the group's social dimension. The **Communication Facilitator** is the member who uses communication skills to build good relationships among members of the team. Communication Facilitators focus on the emotions and mood of the group in order to foster positive feelings among members. In so doing, they promote their team's social goals. You will contribute to a positive team spirit in your group, when you facilitate the communication of feelings. As noted above, communication skills will be explored further in Chapter 5.

Communication Facilitator
member who uses uses communication skills to build good relationships among members of the team

4. The Process Observer

Effective group members regularly observe the dynamics within their group with a view to strengthening relationships among members. The **Process Observer** is the team member who is skilled at noting the emotional interactions among members as the group goes about its work. When hostility is observed, for example, she can help to defuse a potentially harmful situation. When "good vibes" are observed, the Process Observer will reinforce them with appropriate words and actions. By being attentive to your group's emotional dynamics, you can be a strong influence in the creation of a supportive, trusting environment.

Process Observer
member who is skilled at noting the emotional interactions among members as the group goes about its work

5. The Stress Reliever

Excellent team players have, among other things, a calming effect on their teams. It's inevitable that people working together will experience stress and tension. Team success or failure depends, to a large degree, on the team's ability to manage this stress effectively. The **Stress Reliever** is the team member who is skilled at taking steps to reduce the emotional tensions that groups inevitably experience. A reminder to "lighten up," an appropriate joke, or a call for a time-out are often enough to relieve stress. When your group gets stressed, you will make a valuable contribution to team spirit by being a stress reliever.

Stress Reliever
member who is skilled at taking steps to reduce the emotional tensions that groups inevitably experience

6. The Conflict Mediator

Effective group members are ready and willing to help manage interpersonal conflict in constructive ways. The **Conflict Mediator** is the group member who is skilled

Conflict Mediator
member who is skilled at using the best conflict management strategies to assist members in dealing with the inevitable conflicts that arise between and among members of a group

Building the Team

The Role	The Skill
Participation Encourager	Inviting teammates to be socially involved
Participant Supporter	Showing appreciation for the efforts of others
Communication Facilitator	Encouraging teammates to share their feelings
Process Observer	Noting the social interactions among teammates
Stress Reliever	Taking steps to reduce emotional tension
Conflict Mediator	Using conflict management strategies

at using the best conflict management strategies to assist members in dealing with the inevitable conflicts that arise between and among members of a group. The Conflict Mediator may, for example, use tactful private conversations with individuals to deal with interpersonal conflicts. Or, he may employ confrontation strategies with the whole group present to achieve a healthy resolution of a dispute. One of the most important things that you can do for your group is to help mediate conflict when it arises. Conflict resolution is the subject of Chapter 6. There, among other things, we'll describe both peer and professional mediation strategies in detail.

Each of the six roles described above promotes a positive emotional environment within a team. As with task roles, you may feel more comfortable playing one role than another. However, excellent team players are ready and willing to use all the skills associated with the six social roles whenever needed. Always encourage others to participate, support them when they do, facilitate the communication of feelings, consciously observe the dynamics of your group, contribute to stress relief, and assist in mediating conflicts.

SIX HARMFUL GROUP MEMBER ROLES

Successful teams have members who fulfill their task roles and their social roles by skillfully using the six task skills and the six social skills that we described above. Unfortunately, in many groups this is not the case. All too often group members engage in counterproductive behaviours that result in poor group performance and strained relationships. These counterproductive actions are harmful because they prevent a group from functioning effectively. A number of harmful group member roles have been identified. Let's take a look at six that occur fairly frequently.[2]

1. The Free Rider

Free Riders don't contribute to the group's effort but expect to benefit from the group's work. They take a "free ride" on the work of others in the group. In school, for example, Free Riders will not do their share of the group project, but they will expect to get the same grade as the others on the project team. This is unfair, of

Free Rider
member who does not contribute to the group's effort but expects to benefit from the group's work

---

2   As noted in footnote 1, Benne and Sheats identified 8 dysfunctional roles. I discuss 6 harmful roles, using popular labels for each.

course, and often leads to hard feelings, which affect the team's cohesiveness. If Free Riders succeed, other members will be less likely to work hard on the group's next project. Consequently, group productivity declines. Effective group members carry their fair share of the load and avoid free riding. Free Riders may try to take a free ride on the work of others because of laziness, lack of commitment, overwork in other areas of life, or personal problems.

Healthy teams reduce the chances of free riding by establishing rules of conduct for the group, by stating clearly the penalties for violating those rules, and by enforcing the rules within the team. These expectations and penalties are often included in the team's written record, although they don't have to be. The key to preventing free riding lies in thorough and early discussion of the subject among all members of the group. In Chapter 3 we will talk about the importance of group rules for all aspects of group life.

2. The Dominator

Dominator
member who takes on excessive amounts of work to satifsy personal needs, denying other members the opportunity to make their own contributions

Dominators are at the opposite end of the contribution scale from the Free Rider. They take on excessive amounts of work, denying other members the opportunity to make their own contributions. Often Dominators assume authority and make decisions independently. They may behave in this way out of a need to control others or to prove themselves in the group. Unfortunately, they offend others, who feel they are not respected for what they can and want to do on the team. In contrast to other members, Free Riders are happy to have a Dominator in the group.

Effective teams confront offenders when they begin to engage in any of the six dysfunctional behaviours. This isn't always easy, but it is a skill that members need to develop to ensure that groups become real teams in the course of their lives. In Chapter 6 we'll learn about constructive confrontation and its use in managing group conflict. In addition, we'll see in Chapters 3 and 4 that groups that establish rules and goals that promote equality among their members dramatically reduce the chances of Dominators taking over.

3. The Rescuer

Rescuer
member who does an excessive amount of work, offers solutions prematurely, and makes decisions independently in order to save the group from failure

Rescuers are similar to Dominators in that they do an excessive amount of work, offer solutions prematurely, and make decisions independently. They do this particularly when the group is experiencing difficulties. They want to rescue the group from perceived disaster. The Rescuer is different from the Dominator in that the Rescuer is genuinely interested in the group. The Rescuer wants the team to be successful and tries to rescue the team out of concern for it. In other words, the Rescuer's motivation is not self-interest but group interest. Rescuers may, however, believe that they are more competent than others and that it is up to them to save the team. Again, such behaviour can damage team cohesiveness and, ultimately, be counterproductive.

Rescuers, like Dominators, must be confronted. While they have the group's best interests at heart, their actions are not consistent with healthy group dynamics. The energy of the Rescuer needs to be directed toward cooperative solutions to problems that the group faces. If the group is experiencing difficulties, everyone on the team needs to be involved in solving the problems. The group can't leave it to just one person to save the day. Once again, effective teams reduce or eliminate the need for Rescuers by ensuring that group norms (rules) foster accountability, cooperation, and mutual respect.

4. The Distracter

Distracters take the group away from its task using a variety of techniques. For example, the Distracter may talk excessively, especially on irrelevant topics (the talker), or he may use humour to distract, incessantly cracking jokes (the clown). While an appropriate use of humour can be beneficial in helping to relieve stress in a group, it can also be harmful when used excessively and for other purposes. The Distracter is often trying to satisfy personal needs, especially the need for attention, and, in doing so, diminishes the group's effectiveness.

Distracter
member who takes the group away from its task using a variety of techniques

Healthy groups confront Distracters to ensure that the group gets its work done efficiently. Time is important to almost everyone and few of us waste our own time. Distracters, however, waste everyone's time. The Distracter is simply unfair to others, assuming that his actions are more important than the group's work. As with other problem behaviours, the solution lies in group members discussing their expectations, agreeing on what behaviours are acceptable, and insisting on adherence to established norms. In order for a team to succeed, the Distracter has to give up his penchant for attention just as others have to give up things that they would like to do. Group success almost always requires some individual self-sacrifice.

5. The Cynic

Cynics don't trust others, individually or in groups. They believe, for example, that the group's plans won't work, that some members of the group will not carry their weight, or that group work in general is a waste of time. For the Cynic, nothing holds promise of success. Full of pessimism, Cynics regularly project their negativity onto new experiences, including those of the group. This negativity can affect other members and lead to the general view that the group's efforts are not worth it. Cynicism is detrimental, both to a team's task accomplishment and to its social development.

Cynic
member who is pessimistic and does not trust others, individually or in groups

Because the Cynic's pessimism often derives from unhappy life experiences that have left a deep and dark imprint on her personality, it may be particularly difficult to alter the Cynic's behaviour. With other dysfunctional behaviours, one can confront, establish rules and penalties, and attempt to alter behaviour through rewards and punishments. With the Cynic, these strategies may be less effective. Nevertheless, they should be employed with the hope of positive change. In addition, group members should counter the negativity of the Cynic with optimistic attitudes and actions. Just as pessimism can be infectious, so can optimism. It is the positive attitudes of the members of your team that will help to counterbalance the negativity of the Cynic.

6. The Aggressor

Aggressors intimidate other group members, make negative judgments about them, and seek unhealthy confrontation. In some cases, the Aggressor may have a real or imagined grievance against other members of the group and behave aggressively as a result. In other instances, the anger he feels for people outside the group may be directed toward group members. Aggressors run the range from the more subtle passive-aggressive type to the less subtle active-aggressive type. Regardless of the degree of aggression and the reason for it, the intimidation experienced by group members will reduce productivity and overall cohesion. Members may bond in a common defence against the Aggressor, but such cohesiveness is based on an unhealthy social situation that needs to be corrected.

The Aggressor is probably the most difficult person to deal with in group life. Fortunately, the overt aggressor is a fairly rare problem. If one appears in your group, he may have to be removed. Very few of us will tolerate his presence. If he doesn't leave, we very likely will. The group will not be able to function. More common in groups is the presence of the passive-aggressive personality. With this type of aggression, constructive confrontation is in order. In Chapter 6, we will examine strategies, such as confrontation, that will help you to deal with members who try to intimidate others. It's unfortunate, but the reality is that there are difficult people in small groups just as there are such people in virtually all other areas of our lives. Fortunately, there are some helpful strategies available for dealing with difficult people.

We have now described six harmful roles that some people play within small groups. The roles of the Free Rider, the Dominator, the Rescuer, the Distracter, the Cynic, and the Aggressor are, obviously, roles that team players avoid. In contrast, effective team members use the six task skills and the six social skills described earlier to contribute to the success of their groups. Team players avoid the harmful roles and cooperate with others to eliminate the dysfunctional behaviours associated with those roles. Eliminating dysfunctional behaviour is one of the most challenging aspects of working with people in groups. Since group work is essential in our world, we need to learn how to function effectively within groups. This chapter and the remaining chapters of this book are designed to help you do just that.

Harming Team Performance

The Role	The Action
Free Rider	Contributes little but wants team benefits
Dominator	Takes over to satisfy personal needs
Rescuer	Takes over to save the team from perceived disaster
Distracter	Does things that get the team off-track
Cynic	Makes negative comments that discourage others
Aggressor	Acts aggressively towards teammates

CHAPTER SUMMARY

We started our study of interpersonal and group dynamics by noting the importance of goals and roles within society. In order to achieve its goals, we said, society expects its members to fulfill their respective roles. We also saw that small groups succeed at achieving their task goals and social goals when members fulfill their respective roles. Within both societies and small groups, people can fulfill their roles effectively or not. We noted that there are both helpful and harmful roles within society and within small groups.

Next, we described the six helpful roles that contribute to the achievement of a group's task goals. These roles are those of the Idea Sharer, the Idea Seeker, the Comprehension Checker, the Progress Summarizer, the Direction Suggester, and the Group Motivator. With respect to the achievement of social goals, we described the roles of the Participation Encourager, the Participant Supporter, the Communication Facilitator, the Process Observer, the Stress Reliever, and the Conflict Mediator. We emphasized the fact that excellent team players are ready to use all the skills associated with these roles, as circumstances require.

Finally, we described six harmful roles that can cause groups to be less productive and less cohesive. The roles of the Free Rider, the Dominator, the Rescuer, the Distracter, the Cynic, and the Aggressor are roles to be avoided. In each case, we offered some preliminary thoughts on how group members can deal with these dysfunctional behaviours when they occur.

KEY TERMS

Aggressor   Participation Encourager
Communication Facilitator   Process Observer
Comprehension Checker   Progress Summarizer
Conflict Mediator   Rescuer
Cynic   role
Direction Suggester   social goal
Distracter   social roles
Dominator   social skills
Free Rider   Stress Reliever
Group Motivator   task goal
Idea Seeker   task roles
Idea Sharer   task skills
Participant Supporter

MASTERING THE MATERIAL

Now that you have read this chapter, use the following guides to ensure that you have mastered the material.

1. What is the difference between an actor "playing" a role and you "living" or "fulfilling" a role?

2. Define *goal* and *role*.

3. Name and define the two basic goals of every group.

   a. The name of the first basic goal is _____.
      Definition:

   b. The name of the second basic goal is _____.
      Definition:

4. The six roles that help a group get the job done are called _____ roles, and the six roles that help a group build good relationships are called _____ roles.

5. Name and describe the six helpful task roles.

a.

b.

c.

d.

e.

f.

6. Name and describe the six helpful social roles.

a.

b.

c.

d.

e.

f.

7. Name and describe the six harmful roles.

a.

b.

c.

d.

e.

f.

PRACTISING YOUR GROUP SKILLS

PURPOSE OF THIS SECTION

The purpose of "Practising Your Group Skills" and the ultimate purpose of this book is to help you become a more effective participant in the groups to which you belong. This section is designed to provide opportunities for you and your fellow students to practise your group skills in a structured environment.

TEAM RESPONSIBILITIES

A description of the team responsibilities for each of five different teams—the Executive Team, the Lesson Review Team, the Teaching Team, the Energizer Team, and the Evaluation Team—can be found in Appendix B, pages 177–180. Your professor may have chosen to use from one to five of these teams to conduct the teaching and learning activities of the class. Units 2 and 3 of the Teacher's Guide provide your professor with additional information on the responsibilities of these teams.

INDIVIDUAL ROLE RESPONSIBILITIES

A description of four individual role responsibilities—those of Leader, Recorder, Reporter, and Participant-Analyst—can be found in Appendix B, pages 180–182. Your professor may have chosen to use from one to four of these roles within teams to give individuals experience leading, recording, reporting, and analyzing. Units 2 and 3 of the Teacher's Guide provide your professor with additional information on these individual role responsibilities.

SPECIFIC TEAM ASSIGNMENTS

Specific team assignments for this chapter appear immediately below. Specific team assignments for each of the subsequent chapters can be found in "Practising Your Group Skills" in each chapter.

CHAPTER 1 TEAM ASSIGNMENTS

THE EXECUTIVE TEAM

- *Your Ultimate Goal*: to provide leadership to your classmates for your class session on Chapter 1.
- *Your Interim Goals*: to facilitate the class session by (1) ensuring a good classroom setup, (2) welcoming the class, (3) introducing the lesson topic, (4) coordinating activities, and (5) bringing the session to a close.
- *Instructions*: Ensure that the classroom is set up to accommodate the class activities. Post an agenda for the session. Welcome people to class and announce the topic, "Member Roles: Participating Effectively in Your Group," in a creative and interesting way. Remind the class that the topic includes an examination of task roles, social roles, and harmful roles. Introduce and thank all speakers when appropriate. Coordinate the day's activities and bring closure at the end of the class. If necessary, return the classroom to its original configuration.

THE LESSON REVIEW TEAM

- *Your Ultimate Goal*: to review (1) the professor's lesson or presentation from the previous class, or (2) good and bad experiences that classmates have had on teams in the past.
- *Your Interim Goals*: to (1) describe, explain, and summarize the key ideas presented by the professor in the previous week's lecture, or (2) solicit and discuss a variety of good and bad experiences that classmates have had on teams in the past.
- *Instructions*: Since this is the first chapter of this book, there may be nothing to review from last class. However, if your professor did an introductory lecture in the last class session, the team can review the material from that presentation. Alternatively, the team can lead a brief discussion of the past experiences that classmates have had on teams. The

discussion might focus, for example, on the best and the worst team experiences that class members have had. Either way, you must achieve the lesson review goals above.

THE TEACHING TEAM

- *Your Ultimate Goal*: to understand and demonstrate basic member participation skills in a small group setting.

- *Your Interim Goals*: to describe, explain, and demonstrate (1) the six task roles, (2) the six social roles, and (3) the six harmful roles.

- *Instructions*: As the Teaching Team, you have the freedom to choose how you will teach your lesson. You can be as creative as you wish, but you must achieve the lesson objectives. Your experiential exercise is called "Effective Participation" and you'll find it described fully in Appendix C, pages 186–188. Make sure that you refer to it when you teach and explain the task, social, and harmful roles. If time allows, you can also use exercises from the "Mastering the Material" sections of Chapter 1 to teach your lesson.

THE ENERGIZER TEAM

- *Your Ultimate Goal*: to motivate your classmates by conducting an energizer activity.

- *Your Interim Goals*: to facilitate the energizing of your classmates by (1) planning an energizer activity and (2) implementing the plan at an appropriate time in the class session.

- *Instructions*: Your team doesn't have a specific, assigned activity to conduct. Rather, the team should remember its energizing purpose and conduct an activity that will provide a break in the class learning routine. Popular games like Simon Says, Heads Up Seven Up, and Murder Wink usually work well. So do various mixers and ice breakers. (Your professor's Teacher's Guide identifies a number of sources of energizer exercises.) Whatever you decide on, you must be prepared to give clear instructions, conduct the exercise effectively, and achieve the energizer goals above. When you lead the energizer, you are leading and directing the entire class. Plan well and execute professionally, even if the exercise is a "kid's game." Encourage everyone to get involved.

THE EVALUATION TEAM

As a member of the Evaluation Team, you need to review the information in Chapter 10, pages 145–148, before you do anything else. There you will find helpful information on how to conduct your evaluation session. The most important thing to remember is that you are not to judge other people. Your role is to help the class make its own assessment of which practices worked well today and which didn't.

- *Your Ultimate Goal*: to assess group (or class) participation in today's class session.

- *Your Interim Goals*: to (1) assess group (or class) members' use of the six task roles, the six social roles, and the six harmful roles in today's class session and (2) identify practices in need of improvement.

- *Instructions*: Create an evaluation instrument based on the selected focus behaviours identified in the evaluation goals above. See Chapter 10, pages 146–147, for information on creating evaluation instruments. Figure 10.1 provides an example. Solicit feedback from the class using the evaluation instrument. Use the feedback to discuss the class session with the purpose of identifying improvements that can be made to individual, group, and class performance in future class sessions. Conclude by noting the specific actions that need to be repeated or avoided to make improvements.

REFERENCES AND RECOMMENDED READINGS

Bormann, E.G. (1990). *Small group communication: Theory and practice* (3rd ed., chaps. 7 & 8). New York: Harper & Row.

Fiedler, F.E. (1967). *A theory of leadership effectiveness.* New York: McGraw-Hill.

Johnson, D.W. (1991). *Human relations and your career.* Englewood Cliffs, NJ: Prentice Hall.

Johnson, D.W., & Johnson, F.P. (2003). *Joining together: Group theory and group skills.* Boston: Allyn and Bacon.

Mouton, J.S., & Blake, R.R. (1984) *Synergogy: A new strategy for education, training, and development.* San Francisco: Jossey-Bass.

USEFUL URLS

About.com Human Resources. http://humanresources.about.com.

Free Management Library. www.managementhelp.org.

MindTools. www.mindtools.com.

Pfeiffer Publishing. http://ca.pfeiffer.com/WileyCDA/Section/index.html.

Team Technology. www.teamtechnology.co.uk.

Your Meeting Resource Center. www.effectivemeetings.com.

Leader Roles: Leading Effectively in Your Group

2

If your actions inspire others to dream more, learn more, do more, and become more, you are a leader.
—John Quincy Adams, former US President

INTRODUCTION

Some of you reading this chapter may want to be leaders in your profession at some time in the future. Perhaps you have enjoyed leadership responsibilities and successes in the past at school, at work, or in community activities. If you were successful in your leadership roles, you may be especially keen to take on leadership in your future career. In contrast, other readers may see leadership in a different way. Perhaps you'd rather let other people do the leading while you concentrate on being a good follower. Not everyone wants to be a leader, and some people actually fear leadership.

Whether you're in the first group and like the idea of being a leader, or you're in the second and don't enjoy leading, an understanding of leadership is very important. Whether you direct others in the workplace or take direction, knowledge of leaders and leadership can help you become an excellent team player.

This chapter provides information about leadership to both future leaders and future followers. First, we'll describe three areas of leader responsibility, three styles of leadership, and the importance of adjusting leadership style to the maturity of the group being lead. Then, after examining the use of power by leaders, we'll conclude by highlighting the characteristics of an effective leader.

THREE AREAS OF LEADER RESPONSIBILITY

From the largest organizations to the smallest work teams, leaders are responsible for three important areas of a group's life. The first is to look forward and *provide direction* for the future by setting goals for the group. The second is to accurately note what the group has done in the past by *keeping records* of the team's activity. The third is to *report progress* that the team is making to both group members and outsiders.

1. Providing Direction

The major responsibility of some leaders is to *provide direction* for the group. For example, both the CEO of a major corporation and the chair of your student work group have the primary responsibility of giving direction to their respective groups. As we'll see, successful leaders collaborate with teammates to give their teams direction by establishing appropriate goals. They are the people in the organization—large or small—charged with the responsibility of ensuring that members know where the group is headed. In Chapter 4 we'll study in some detail the best practices for setting team goals and objectives.

2. Keeping Records

Other leaders are charged with the responsibility of *keeping records* of group decisions, accomplishments, and goals. In your college, for instance, the registrar keeps accurate records of student achievement. These official records are critically important for the students who will use them to secure employment in the future. They are also important to the college, because accurate records are critical to the good reputation of the college. On your student-project team, a good recorder will keep an accurate record of your team's decisions and actions. That record can, among other things, defuse many arguments about assignments because it notes what was decided and who is responsible for implementing the decisions.

3. Reporting Progress

Still other group members are responsible for ensuring that accurate reports of group accomplishments are made available to the group and to outside parties. These leaders bear primary responsibility for accurately *reporting progress*. In policing, for example, a designated spokesperson reports to the public on progress that police are making in their search for a missing person. The police service doesn't permit just any officer to make such reports. Only official police reporters are authorized to do so. Many student work teams designate one of their members to report to a professor, for example, on the team's progress. That person demonstrates leadership through reporting the group's progress accurately.

Leader Responsibilities

The Role	The Responsibility
Team leader (chair)	Providing overall direction to team efforts
Team recorder (secretary)	Keeping accurate records of team decisions
Team reporter	Giving progress reports from subgroups

You can consult Appendix A, page 167, for a brief description of Team Leader, Team Recorder, and Team Reporter responsibilities within the context of business meetings. In addition, Appendix B, pages 180–182, describes the roles of Leader, Recorder, and Reporter in greater detail as applied within the author's Experiential Model for teaching and learning group skills.

THREE STYLES OF LEADERSHIP

No doubt you have observed many different leaders in the past. In all likelihood, they had different leadership styles. You probably have encountered the autocratic leader, the democratic leader, and the laissez-faire leader, though you may not have been familiar with those labels. Let's look at each one now.

1. The Autocratic Leader

Some leaders see leadership as a matter of telling others what to do, a matter of bossing others around. Such leaders are very directive and like to make most, if not all, decisions. They look to group members to carry out their directives or orders, and their style of leadership is like that of a dictator or autocrat. The **autocratic leader** is a take-charge person who tells others what to do and sees that they do it.[1]

Autocratic leadership is often criticized for its less-than-democratic approach to group life. Many people find this style offensive and an insult to group members who are treated like children or slaves who have no minds of their own. Consequently, they react with feelings of anger and alienation. It's no wonder that autocratically led groups tend to experience a lot of hostility.

There are many situations, however, in which autocratic leadership is the most effective form of leadership and, in fact, may be absolutely necessary. With little children, for example, one may have to be autocratic in order to protect them from danger. With adults too, leaders may have to be autocratic in emergency situations where someone needs to take charge. In many emergencies, a take-charge autocrat has become a true hero.

autocratic leader
a take-charge leader who tells others what to do and sees that they do it

2. The Democratic Leader

For many situations, the democratic leader is the most effective leader. The **democratic leader** involves all members of the group in discussing the issues and making decisions. The CEO who takes a democratic approach in a meeting with senior managers—for example, the heads of design, production, and marketing—creates an atmosphere in which participation is encouraged. The various points of view of the managers are likely to surface in a constructive way.

Because the democratic leader places trust in members of the group, members feel that they can influence the group's action. They feel that their views count and that they are valued. Also, they are much more likely to commit to implementing decisions because they have been part of the decision-making process. Members of democratically run groups tend to experience far less hostility than do members of autocratically run groups.

A drawback of the democratic style is that discussion and consensus building take time. Members may become frustrated if there is insufficient time to reach a decision, or if trivial matters are constantly brought forward by the democratic leader. Democratic leaders have high regard for the contributions of all group members.

democratic leader
a leader who involves all members of a group in the discussion of issues and decision making

---

1   Lewin, Lippitt, and White (1939) were among the first to describe the autocratic, democratic, and laissez-faire leadership styles that appear commonly today in the literature on group dynamics.

Leadership Styles

Types	Approaches
Autocratic leaders	Decide what to do and tell others to do it
Democratic leaders	Work with others to decide and implement decisions
Laissez-faire leaders	Trust others to decide and implement decisions

This high regard is the result of the leader's emphasis on the social dimension of the group's life. Equally, though, the democratic leader values task completion.

3. The Laissez-Faire Leader

laissez-faire leader
a leader who leaves a mature group alone to accomplish its goals

The French expression "laissez-faire" means "to leave alone." The **laissez-faire leader** is the person who consciously leaves the members of a team alone to do their work because the members are mature, responsible, knowledgeable, and skilled. Knowing that the group consists of very responsible and self-motivated individuals, a laissez-faire leader deliberately sits back and lets the group direct itself. This can be a wise strategy because it recognizes and respects the competence of group members.

If a leader takes an autocratic approach with a group of very knowledgeable and highly skilled people, members are likely to become frustrated and hostile. In contrast, the supervisor who recognizes the expertise of her staff and allows them to do their work without interference is likely to get the job done and enhance the morale of her workers. Leadership requires a clear understanding of both the expertise of group members and the circumstances that the group is in. At times, the laissez-faire style of leadership is the most effective style.

LEADERSHIP STYLE AND GROUP MATURITY

We noted earlier that different styles of leadership are appropriate in different situations.[2] There is a place for autocratic leadership, a place for democratic leadership, and a place for laissez-faire leadership. One of the keys to successful leadership is knowing when to adopt a particular style and when not to. To help you understand this important aspect of leadership, we need to examine the concept of group maturity. The most appropriate style of leadership to use in any given case depends on the level of maturity of the members of your group.

group maturity
includes a group's achievement orientation, level of responsibility, and collective expertise

To begin, note carefully that the concept of **group maturity** includes three essential elements: a group's commitment to achievement, its level of responsibility, and its degree of expertise. "Commitment to achievement" refers to the group's dedication to achieving its goals. "Level of responsibility" refers to the degree to which members assume personal responsibility for reaching those goals, and "expertise" refers to the combined knowledge and skills that the group possesses. Successful leaders use these elements to assess their group's maturity and choose the most appropriate leadership style accordingly.

---

2   One of the best-known approaches to situational leadership is that of Hersey and Blanchard (1977). The description of different leadership styles for different maturity levels (different situations) presented here is based on their important work.

Has Your Group Grown Up Yet?

Your group is considered *mature* if it (1) is dedicated to accomplishing its goals, (2) accepts responsibility for accomplishing its goals, and (3) possesses the knowledge and skills necessary to accomplish its goals.

When a group consists of members who have a low desire to achieve, are not very responsible, and are not very knowledgeable, the group has a *low level* of maturity. In contrast, a group whose members are highly achievement-oriented, very responsible, and very knowledgeable has a *high level* of maturity. A group whose members have a moderate degree of self-direction, responsibility, and expertise has a *moderate level* of maturity.

Autocratic leadership is most effective with a group that has a low level of maturity. For example, when a group has little initiative, lacks responsibility, and is inexperienced with the job to be done, the leader needs to take a directive approach to help the group succeed.

In contrast, when faced with a group that is keen to achieve, takes responsibility seriously, and has knowledgeable and skilled members, the leader needs to respect the talent of the group. In such situations, the laissez-faire style is likely to be the most effective.

When a group has a moderate level of maturity, the democratic style is the best choice. The democratic leader can, for example, nurture a team's sense of responsibility, promote its interest in achievement, and develop its knowledge and skills. Recognizing the individual talents within a moderately mature group, the democratic leader works to maximize the benefits of those talents through a true team effort.

One of the key characteristics of successful leaders is their knowledge of both people and situations. They know the most appropriate leadership style to use in a particular situation and they are flexible enough to adjust their leadership accordingly. As a leader, you need to know when to be autocratic, when to be democratic, and when to be laissez-faire. And you need to be flexible. Before we examine further traits of successful leaders, let's say a few words about leadership and power.

LEADERSHIP AND POWER

Power is the ability to influence a situation in a desired direction. Notice that power, as defined here, is neither good nor bad in itself. It is neutral. However, it can be a force for good—a positive force for getting the job done and building a team. In this section of the chapter, we will focus on the positive and necessary aspects of power in groups, recognizing that power can be abused on occasion. Let's now examine five different forms of power that exist within most groups.[3]

power
the ability to influence a situation in desired directions

1. Legitimate Power

Some people are hired to be leaders, others are promoted to leadership positions, and still others are elected. We call all such individuals **designated leaders** because

designated leader
a leader selected to fill an official position within a group

---

3   French and Raven (1981, p. 317) have examined the basis of power in small groups and provided an excellent review of the subject.

they have been selected to occupy clearly defined, official positions within an organization or group. They are the official leaders of a group and they occupy special roles that are vital to the success of the group. The power associated with the official positions of designated leaders is called **legitimate power**.

The Prime Minister of Canada, for example, has certain powers that come with the office. For example, he can appoint the Governor General, Justices of the Supreme Court, and heads of Crown corporations. No other Canadian has the power to do these things. He has legitimate power. Whenever a person occupies a designated leadership role, that person has a certain amount of power by virtue of holding the office.

In small groups, team leaders usually have the power to call meetings, propose agendas, and speak to outsiders on behalf of the group. A recorder, too, will have certain powers associated with shaping and keeping the official records of the group. Other designated leaders will also have special powers associated with their positions in the group. The reason for this form of power within groups is that individuals need these special powers to carry out the responsibilities of their designated positions. You need legitimate power to fulfill a designated leadership role effectively.

Legitimate power almost always includes the two forms of power that we will examine next—reward power and coercive power. Even though these two forms of power are closely associated with legitimate power, we'll treat them below as separate powers in order to identify their respective characteristics more clearly.

2. Reward Power

Reward power is the power to give benefits to members who display appropriate or exemplary behaviour within a group. We can see reward power at work in many groups in society, including family groups. Parents, for example, may increase a child's allowance because the child has done an exceptional job of doing household chores. They reward the child for work well done.

In student-project groups, rewards are rarely of the monetary variety. Rather, teachers dispense praise, grades, and bonus marks to reward student efforts. Coaches have a different way of rewarding athletic performance. They promote players to leadership roles that increase their status within the group. On sports teams, for example, certain players are rewarded with the captain's "C" or the assistant captain's "A."

3. Coercive Power

Coercive power is the power to punish inappropriate behaviour. To coerce someone is to force the person to do what you want, and the threat of punishment is one form of coercive power. Corporate managers, for example, may punish employees who violate the company's code of ethics. They may reprimand, suspend, or dismiss the offender. Families "ground" errant children, sports teams "bench" players, and teachers "dispatch" students to the principal's office. Each of these practices illustrates the use of coercive power, which might just as well be called "punishment power."

4. Charismatic Power

Charismatic power is a power that results from an individual's personal qualities. We could call this type of power "personality power," because it derives from a person's ability to charm and persuade others. Charismatic power is often associated with **emergent leaders**, people who rise from ordinary membership ranks to provide temporary and unofficial leadership. Their winning personalities make them unofficial leaders for a limited period of time.

The word "charisma" comes from Greek and means "gifts." A charismatic individual, we might say, has a gifted personality. Students, for example, who are intelligent, well spoken, thoughtful, and fair often emerge as unofficial leaders within work groups because of their charisma. They become unofficial leaders because they are gifted.

Charismatic power can be combined with legitimate power, and often is. Former Canadian Prime Minister Pierre Elliott Trudeau is a good example of a leader who had both charismatic power and legitimate power. The most popular leaders are those who possess both. That doesn't mean, of course, that a person has to be charismatic to be a good leader. It just means that charisma can be an added advantage.

charismatic power
power resulting from personal qualities

emergent leader
a leader who assumes a temporary, unofficial leadership role because of his or her special talents

5. Expert Power

Another form of power is also associated with *emergent leadership*. **Expert power** is power that results from having special knowledge and skills that a group needs in a particular situation. When an individual knows something or possesses a skill that is needed by a group, that individual has power. In this case, the power comes not from a designated office (legitimate power) or from the individual's personal charm (charismatic power), but from his or her expertise (expert power).

The seasoned detective, for example, who has first-hand experience in criminal investigation, is likely to exercise expert power regardless of his rank. His knowledge and skill are forms of expert power that are extremely valuable to his policing agency. However, a person's expertise doesn't necessarily translate into power within the group.

Members gain expert power only when their expertise is needed by the group in order to accomplish its purposes. At the annual police–firefighter tug-of-war contest, the seasoned detective may be useless to the team. Knowledge and skill in investigative procedure mean nothing in a test of strength.

In this section, we have noted five forms of power common in both large organizations and small groups. Legitimate power, reward power, and coercive power are more closely associated with designated leadership, while charismatic power and expert power are more commonly associated with emergent leadership. We have pointed out, however, that these forms of power are not mutually exclusive.

A good leader can use all these forms of power, and the best leaders usually do. When you assume positions of leadership within your small groups, your knowledge of these five forms of power and the appropriate use of them will contribute to your success as a leader. We'll now move on to examine certain characteristics that are typical of the best leaders.

expert power
power resulting from particular knowledge or skill

CHARACTERISTICS OF AN EFFECTIVE LEADER

Our review of leadership in this chapter is intended to examine leadership in ways that will help you as you provide leadership in small groups both in school and in the workplace. It is not intended, however, to provide all the detail necessary for senior leadership within a large organization. That, of course, requires not only knowledge of the basic concepts studied in this chapter, but also much more specific knowledge of the responsibilities associated with that kind of senior position.

Regardless of whom they lead and what their level of leadership, leaders share certain key traits. Many studies have investigated the qualities associated with successful leadership, and the list of desirable characteristics is quite long. Rather than attempt to identify all the traits that have been studied by researchers,[4] we'll limit ourselves to five key characteristics of effective leaders. If you develop these five characteristics in your own life, you will possess the essential traits of successful leadership for both the present and the future.

1. Knowledge

Successful leaders are *knowledgeable*. Most important, they have a good understanding of group dynamics. They know how people in groups tend to interact, and they also know the essentials of working effectively with people in groups.

They also have a clear understanding of the two group goals that we noted in Chapter 1—the task goal and the social goal. Moreover, they understand the six member roles that facilitate the achievement of task goals, and the importance of the six roles that contribute to the achievement of social goals.

Effective leaders also understand the fundamentals of good leadership discussed in this chapter. In addition, their knowledge extends to the various topics that you will study in the remainder of this book—namely, the importance of group norms, goals, communication, conflict resolution, cohesion, critical discussion, problem solving, decision making, and performance evaluation. With a thorough understanding of interpersonal and group dynamics, you'll have the knowledge to succeed as a leader now and in the future.

2. Communication

Successful leaders are excellent *communicators*, skilled at *speaking, writing, listening,* and *giving feedback*. Effective leaders regularly use these important communication skills, and they encourage their teammates to do the same.

In Chapter 5, we'll examine several rules for sending messages effectively, listening actively, and providing constructive feedback. In Chapter 6, we'll study assertive communication and the resolution of conflict. These communication skills are critical for maximizing the benefits in all human relationships. Like all successful leaders, you need excellent communication skills.

---

4   Stogdill (1981, pp. 63–68), Shaw (1981, pp. 324–325), and Kenney and Zaccuro (1984, pp. 678–685) are only a few of many researchers who have examined the characteristics of effective leaders. The list of traits associated with leadership is very long. For the purpose of this book, the list has been reduced to five key characteristics.

3. Task Orientation

Have you ever worked for a "slave driver"? While the image underlying this question comes from a sad world—the world of slave ownership—it describes perfectly those leaders who pursue the completion of tasks with no concern for the feelings of people. Perhaps it was a boss, a teacher, or a coach who, in your experience, seemed fixated on tasks and oblivious to people.

Effective leaders are clearly *task-oriented*, but they don't emphasize task completion at the expense of relationships among group members. When groups meet, they usually have work to do, tasks to complete. Effective leaders know what that work is, and they ensure that it is done as efficiently as possible. But good leaders balance this concern for task completion with sensitivity to the social needs of group members. Your success as a leader will come in large part from your ability to strike a balance between the social needs of people and the need to be productive.

4. Social Orientation

You may have met leaders who pay little or no attention to the job that has to be done. These leaders often enjoy socializing and may do a good job of cultivating team spirit. If, however, they always socialize and the group doesn't complete its tasks, such leaders will fall out of favour with members.

Moreover, in the rough-and-ready world of competitive business, they are not likely to be around for very long if productivity suffers. The boss will fire them. In the world of groups outside the workplace, they may last longer, but they are likely to incur the disfavour of group members who get frustrated when tasks go uncompleted and valuable time is wasted. Effective leaders refrain from going to this extreme.

Effective leaders, then, are *people-oriented*. They do not, however, focus on social goals to the exclusion of task goals. Good leaders are empathic and sensitive to the feelings of group members, and they constantly monitor the emotional climate of the group. They balance this social concern, however, with a healthy regard for the work that needs to be accomplished. To succeed as a leader, you will need to balance concern for people (the social goal) with a concern for getting the job done (the task goal).

5. Flexibility

Earlier in this chapter, we distinguished among three different styles of leadership—autocratic, democratic, and laissez-faire. We noted that each type has its place depending on the circumstances of a given situation. We pointed out that autocratic leadership is effective when a group is immature. Democratic leadership, we said, was effective when a group is moderately mature. When faced with a mature group, we noted that laissez-faire leadership is often most effective.

Effective leaders are *flexible* with respect to leadership style. They understand when a laissez-faire approach is appropriate and adopt that approach. They also know when an autocratic approach is appropriate and change their leadership style accordingly. When circumstances require a democratic approach, the good leader shifts to that mode of leadership.

This flexibility allows the good leader to adjust to changing circumstances, while less effective leaders remain locked into their preferred style or fail to recognize and adjust to new realities. As a present and future leader, you will need to have the flexibility to demonstrate leadership in different ways depending on the situations that you face.

CHAPTER SUMMARY

We began this chapter by examining three different areas of leadership responsibility. Those areas included providing direction, keeping records, and reporting progress. We then went on to describe autocratic, democratic, and laissez-faire approaches to leadership and drew attention to the situations in which each is most effective. The key, we said, was group maturity, a concept that includes the degree of member commitment to achievement, the degree of responsibility the group assumes, and the degree of expertise within the group. Next, after examining the relationship between leadership and power—specifically, legitimate power, reward power, coercive power, expert power, and charismatic power—we proceeded to describe five qualities that are typical of successful leaders. Effective leaders, we noted, understand group dynamics, communicate clearly, ensure that tasks are completed, empathize with members, and adjust to new circumstances. They are knowledgeable, skilled at communication, task-oriented, people-oriented, and flexible.

KEY TERMS

autocratic leader	expert power
charismatic power	group maturity
coercive power	laissez-faire leader
democratic leader	legitimate power
designated leader	power
emergent leader	reward power

MASTERING THE MATERIAL

Now that you have read this chapter, use the following guides to ensure that you have mastered the material.

1. Name three areas of leader responsibility and give an example of each.

2. Describe the leadership style of an autocratic leader.

3. Describe the leadership style of a democratic leader.

4. Describe the leadership style of a laissez-faire leader.

5. Identify the three essential elements of group maturity.

6. Regarding group maturity, when should a leader be autocratic?

7. Regarding group maturity, when should a leader be laissez-faire?

8. Regarding group maturity, when should a leader be democratic?

9. Define *power*.

10. Define *designated leader*.

11. Define *emergent leader*.

12. What is legitimate power?

13. What is reward power?

14. What is coercive power?

15. What is charismatic power?

16. What is expert power?

17. Name and describe the five characteristics of an effective leader described in this chapter.
    a.
    b.
    c.
    d.
    e.

PRACTISING YOUR GROUP SKILLS

PURPOSE OF THIS SECTION

The purpose of "Practising Your Group Skills" and the ultimate purpose of this book is to help you become a more effective participant in the groups to which you belong. This section is designed to provide opportunities for you and your fellow students to practise your group skills in a structured environment.

TEAM RESPONSIBILITIES

A description of the team responsibilities for each of five different teams—the Executive Team, the Lesson Review Team, the Teaching Team, the Energizer Team, and the Evaluation Team—can be found in Appendix B, pages 177–180. Your professor may have chosen to use from one to five of these teams to conduct the teaching and learning activities of your class. Units 2 and 3 of the Teacher's Guide provide your professor with additional information on the responsibilities of these teams.

INDIVIDUAL ROLE RESPONSIBILITIES

A description of four individual role responsibilities—those of Leader, Recorder, Reporter, and Participant-Analyst—can be found in Appendix B, pages 180–182. Your professor may have chosen to use from one to four of these roles within teams to give individuals experience leading, recording, reporting, and analyzing. Units 2 and 3 of the Teacher's Guide provide your professor with additional information on these individual role responsibilities.

SPECIFIC TEAM ASSIGNMENTS

Specific team assignments for this chapter appear immediately below. Specific team assignments for each of the subsequent chapters can be found in "Practising Your Group Skills" in each chapter.

CHAPTER 2 TEAM ASSIGNMENTS

THE EXECUTIVE TEAM

- *Your Ultimate Goal*: to provide leadership to your classmates for your class session on Chapter 2.
- *Your Interim Goals*: to facilitate the class session by (1) ensuring a good classroom setup, (2) welcoming the class, (3) introducing the lesson topic, (4) coordinating activities, and (5) bringing the session to a close.
- *Instructions*: Ensure that the classroom is set up to accommodate today's class activities. Post an agenda for the session. Welcome people to class and announce the topic, "Leader Roles: Leading Effectively in Your Group," in a creative and interesting way. Remember that the topic includes autocratic, democratic, and laissez-faire styles of leadership. Introduce and thank all speakers when appropriate. Coordinate the day's activities and bring closure at the end of the class. If necessary, return the classroom to its original configuration.

THE LESSON REVIEW TEAM

- *Your Ultimate Goal*: to review Chapter 1, "Member Roles: Participating Effectively in Your Group."
- *Your Interim Goals*: to provide a review of (1) the experiential exercise, (2) the six helpful task roles, (3) the six helpful social roles, and (4) the six harmful roles.
- *Instructions*: As the Lesson Review Team, you have the freedom to choose how you will do the review. You can be as creative as you wish, but you must achieve the lesson review goals above. Remember that your time is limited, so don't try to re-teach last chapter's lesson.

THE TEACHING TEAM

- *Your Ultimate Goal*: to understand and demonstrate leadership skills in a small group setting.

- *Your Interim Goals*: to describe, explain, and demonstrate (1) three leadership styles and the situations in which they are effective and (2) five characteristics of an effective leader.

- *Instructions*: As the Teaching Team, you have the freedom to choose how you will teach your lesson. You can be as creative as you wish, but you must achieve the lesson goals above. Your experiential exercise is called "Leadership Styles," and you'll find it described fully in Appendix C, pages 188–189. Make sure that you refer to it when you teach and explain the autocratic, democratic, and laissez-fair leadership styles. Also, include it in the part of your lesson where you describe and explain the five characteristics of an effective leader. If time allows, you can also use exercises from the "Mastering the Material" sections of Chapter 1 to teach your lesson.

THE ENERGIZER TEAM

- *Your Ultimate Goal*: to motivate your classmates by conducting an energizer activity.

- *Your Interim Goals*: to facilitate the energizing of your classmates by (1) planning an energizer activity and (2) implementing the plan at an appropriate time in the class session.

- *Instructions*: Your team doesn't have a specific, assigned activity to conduct. Rather, the team should remember its energizing purpose and achieve the energizer goals above by conducting an activity that will provide a break in the class learning routine. Popular games like Simon Says, Heads Up Seven Up, and Murder Wink usually work well. So do various mixers and ice breakers. (Your professor's Teacher's Guide identifies a number of sources of energizer exercises.) Whatever you decide on, you must be prepared to give clear instructions and conduct the exercise effectively. When you lead the energizer, you are leading and directing the entire class. Plan well and execute professionally, even if the exercise is a "kid's game." Encourage everyone to get involved.

THE EVALUATION TEAM

As a member of the Evaluation Team, you need to review the information in Chapter 10, pages 145–148, before you do anything else. There you will find helpful information on how to conduct your evaluation session. The most important thing to remember is that you are not to judge other people. Your role is to help the class make its own assessment of which practices worked well today and which didn't.

- *Your Ultimate Goal*: to assess leadership skills within the group (or class) in today's class session.

- *Your Interim Goals*: to (1) assess group (or class) member use of autocratic, democratic, and laissez-faire leadership practices and (2) identify practices in need of improvement.

- *Instructions*: Create an evaluation instrument based on the selected focus behaviours identified in the evaluation goals above. See Chapter 10, pages 146–147, for information on creating evaluation instruments. Figure 10.1 provides an example. Solicit feedback from the class using the evaluation instrument. Use the feedback to discuss the class session with the purpose of identifying improvements that can be made to individual, group, and class performance in future class sessions. Conclude by noting the specific actions that need to be repeated or avoided to make improvements.

REFERENCES AND RECOMMENDED READINGS

Fiedler, F.E. (1964). A contingency model of leader effectiveness. In L. Berkowitz (Ed.), *Advances in experimental social psychology* (Vol. 1, pp. 149–150). New York: Academic Press.

French, J., & Raven, B. (1981). The basis of social power. In D. Cartwright & A. Zander (Eds.), *Group dynamics: Research and theory*. New York: McGraw-Hill.

Hersey, P., & Blanchard, K. (1982). *Management of organizational behavior: Utilizing human resources* (4th ed.) Englewood Cliffs, NJ: Prentice Hall.

Kenny, D., & Zaccuro, J. (1984). An estimate of variance due to traits in leadership. *Journal of Applied Psychology, 68,* 678–685.

Kottler, J.A. (1994). *Advanced group leadership*. Pacific Grove, CA: Brooks/Cole.

Portnoy, R.A. (1986). *Leadership!* Englewood Cliffs, NJ: Prentice Hall.

Shaw, M. (1981). *Group dynamics* (3rd ed., pp. 324–325). New York: McGraw-Hill.

Stogdill, R. (1981). *Handbook of leadership: A survey of theory and research* (pp. 63–82). New York: McGraw-Hill.

USEFUL URLS

About.com Human Resources. http://humanresources.about.com.

Free Management Library. www.managementhelp.org.

MindTools. www.mindtools.com.

Pfeiffer Publishing. http://ca.pfeiffer.com/WileyCDA/Section/index.html.

Team Technology. www.teamtechnology.co.uk.

Your Meeting Resource Center. www.effectivemeetings.com.

Norms: Establishing Effective Rules in Your Group

3

If you don't like their rules, whose would you choose?
–Charles M. Schulz, cartoonist

INTRODUCTION

In this chapter, our purpose is to examine the rules that contribute to the success of small groups. Both large groups and small groups alike need rules to guide and control the actions of group members. Another word for "rule" is "norm"—the word that we've chosen for the title of Chapter 3. A **norm**, as used in this chapter and throughout this book, is simply a written or unwritten rule of a group.

All groups of people who want to get along in a civilized fashion develop norms for their members. We need rules of conduct in order to work together for common purposes. The most important *societal norms* are expressed in the form of laws. Societies value the order and stability that laws protect, and they cannot abide the disorder and instability that lawbreaking creates.

Just as societies have rules, so do the various organizations within a society. The most important *organizational norms* take the form of policies and procedures. For example, employees who flagrantly defy the rules of their organization are likely to find themselves unemployed. Organizations require rules of conduct to accomplish their goals. The rules of the organization tell everyone within the organization how they must behave to succeed.

Norms are also an important part of family life. *Family norms*—the "rules of the house"—may differ among families, but all families have their rules. Families, like societies and organizations, require a degree of order if people are to live together in harmony under the same roof. The rules are intended to provide the order. When people break the rules of a society, an organization, or a family, they can expect to be punished, and we call these punishments **sanctions**.

In Chapter 2, we discussed coercive power, a form of power that is often built into the norms of a group. For example, designated leaders in positions of authority need rules and the power of sanctions to carry out their responsibilities. An em-

norm
a written or unwritten rule of a group

sanctions
the punishments incurred if one breaks the rules of a society, an organization, or a family

ployer, for instance, has to be able to fire an employee if the employee violates a serious rule of the company.

To function harmoniously, both societies and small groups need effective rules. In this chapter, we'll focus on norms within small groups. We'll first examine the social context in which small-group norms exist, and then we'll explain where rules come from. In addition, we'll review the basic principles of ethical conduct, and the ways in which your group should develop its own rules to ensure your group's success. Let's start with the social context in which rules originate.

SOCIETIES, CULTURES, AND SUBCULTURES

To understand the social context in which rules are created, we need to understand several related concepts—namely, the concepts of *society*, *culture*, and *subculture*. We'll examine each in turn.

society
a large, identifiable community of individuals who fulfill a variety of differing and interdependent roles

A **society** is a large, identifiable community of individuals who fulfill a variety of different and interdependent roles. Canada, Spain, and Japan are three examples. **Culture** is the word we use to describe the distinctive way of life of people within a society. Thus, we speak of Canadian culture, Spanish culture, and Japanese culture.

culture
the way of life of people in a given society or group

Moreover, where there are two or more identifiable cultures within a society, we speak of **subcultures**, smaller cultures within larger ones. For example, Canada has two dominant cultures, English and French, and a host of smaller ones. We speak of the Aboriginal, Chinese, and Italian subcultures that exist within Canada's dominant cultures, and we speak of Canadian society as a cultural mosaic.

subculture
a smaller culture within a larger culture

In addition to the cultures and subcultures of large societies, we also talk about the culture of small groups such as student work groups in college or ongoing employee work groups in the workplace. These are, of course, our main concern throughout this book.

When we try to understand the culture of any group, large or small, we focus on several important aspects of its way of life. We focus on the *language* it uses, the *knowledge* it possesses, the *technology* it uses, and *the arts and entertainment* that it prefers. When we want to understand a group's rules and why the group creates them, we focus on three additional aspects of culture: *values*, *principles*, and *norms*.

WHY GROUPS HAVE RULES

Why do all groups establish rules to govern the behaviour of their members? To answer that question, let's start with a simple example: the highway traffic laws of our society. Because we *value* our lives and our health, we use the *principle* of safety as a standard when making the *rules* that govern driver behaviour on our roads. For one thing, we know that excessive speed is clearly one cause of injuries and deaths on our roadways. Consequently, we use the principle of safety to establish speed laws that we trust drivers will obey, thus making our roads safer.

We create these rules of the road because life and good health are important to us. In short, safety on our roads is the *goal*. It is our *values* and *principles* that together lead us to establish the *norms* that will, we hope, let us achieve that goal.

1. Values

Values refer to whatever is of importance or worth to an individual or a group. As a member of a small group, you need to ask yourself what you value personally and what others in your group value. You will likely discover that you share some values and don't share others. Of course, you also have to ask about the values of those who have created your group. Today, it may be your college professor. After graduation, it may be your boss in the workplace.

Values are reflections of our feelings. They are a very important part of our affective or emotional makeup. To use the language of poetry, values are "things of the heart." Because we feel so strongly about highway safety, to return to our recent example, we develop rules that are designed to keep us safe on our roadways. Laws of the road are just one example of rules that have been generated by our values. What is important to your group? What do you and your teammates value? If you discuss these questions with your teammates and try to answer them, your basic ideas about your group will become evident.

values
whatever is of importance or worth to an individual or a group

2. Principles

In any area of life, we refer to our basic ideas as principles. There are, for example, principles of mathematics, physics, hygiene, road safety, and virtually every other area of our lives. When we drive on the roads, to continue our example, we are supposed to keep within the speed limit, wear seat belts, and stop at stop signs. These specific rules of the road are all based on the principle of safety. Because we value our well-being, we adhere to the principle of safety when we develop our traffic laws.

Principles are basic ideas that serve as standards to evaluate or judge a course of action. If a proposed traffic law, for example, violates the principle of safety, it should not be passed. It doesn't meet the standard. Principles of any kind are a part of our cognitive or thinking side. If, as we said above, values are things of the heart, then principles are "things of the head." Values and principles are much like two sides of the same coin, the emotional side and the intellectual side. Together, they generate the rules of conduct within all groups, large or small.

principles
the standards by which a group evaluates a course of action

A group that values fairness and individual responsibility, for example, will use the principles of equality and individual accountability to establish rules that require individual members to carry their own weight and to do their fair share of the group's work. Guided by these principles, the group will prohibit free riding and establish penalties for those who try to take a free ride. In this example, the group feels that fairness and responsibility are important (values), and it uses the basic ideas of equality and accountability (principles) to create rules (norms) that forbid free riding.

> *Rules are not necessarily sacred, principles are.*
> —Franklin D. Roosevelt, former US President

3. Norms

All group norms are generated by the values and principles held by the group's members or by the values and principles of a higher authority. If a group values human life, for example, it establishes laws against murder. If it values private property, it establishes laws against theft. Values, principles, and norms are intimately connected within all societies, cultures, and subcultures, including small-group subcultures. Let's now look more closely at the basic ethical values and principles that generate the norms of conduct for all civil societies and groups. When your group considers the rules that it wants to live by, it must consider the following principles.

THE BASIC PRINCIPLES OF ETHICAL CONDUCT

Any group that wants its members to cooperate in a civilized way must establish rules of conduct based on ethical principles. Adherence to these principles is essential for harmony and cooperation within the group. These principles are the same ones used to develop the laws of society. In Canada, these principles inform our *Charter of Rights and Freedoms*. The five principles described below are the minimum required to allow people to work cooperatively within a civilized community. They are essential for establishing societal laws and group rules.

1. Goodness

goodness
the ethical principle of doing good to others and not harming them

The first basic principle of ethics is **goodness**, the principle that says that you are to do good to others in your group and to refrain from harming them. The basic rule that is derived from this principle says, "Do good and don't harm." In your work group, then, this primary rule directs you to treat others well. Small groups, like societies, value the welfare of their members.

2. Equality

equality
the ethical principle of treating all members of a group equally

The second ethical principle, **equality**, says that you are to treat others in your group as equals. This principle, expressed as a norm, says, "Treat others as equals and don't discriminate against them." Both in society and in small groups we value mutual respect, and it is the equality principle that promotes mutual respect among group members. Equality is the principle that protects individual rights in both large societies and small groups.

3. Fairness

fairness
giving people what they have earned (merit), giving people equal shares (equity), or meeting a person's special needs (need)

Fairness, also called the *justice* principle, is the third of the basic ethical principles. Sometimes being just or fair means giving people what they have earned (merit), while at other times it means giving everyone involved an equal share of something (equity). At still other times, it means meeting the special requirements of a group member (need).

The principle of justice, stated as a rule, says, "Treat others fairly." We all value fairness and nobody wants to be treated unfairly in a group. Consequently, healthy teams develop rules that promote the fair treatment of all members. Both large societies and small groups need rules that ensure that we are treated fairly by others and that we treat them fairly in return.

4. Truth

truth
the ethical principle of honesty and integrity

The ethical principle called **truth** says that you are to have personal integrity by being truthful and trustworthy. Expressed as a rule, this principle says, "Be truthful, be honest, and have integrity." Nothing destroys interpersonal relationships faster than lying and cheating. This fact is obviously true of relationships in small groups. Because we value honesty and integrity in others, we do well to have rules that promote truthfulness. In society at large, for example, there are laws against libel and slander. Small groups, too, need to encourage honesty among members.

5. Freedom

Finally, the ethical principle of **freedom** says that you should respect the choices of others and they should respect yours, whether you agree with one another or not. This principle calls for mutual respect. As a rule, this principle says, "Respect the choices of others; don't force others." As adults, we value making our own choices. Rarely do we enjoy being told what to do. The freedom principle generates group rules that protect an individual's right to make personal decisions.

freedom
the ethical principle of respecting group members' choices

In civil societies, individuals are generally free to make personal choices provided that their choices don't harm others, discriminate against others, treat others unfairly, or deceive others. In healthy work groups, the same principles apply. These five principles of ethical conduct will be critically important to your group when it discusses and develops its code of conduct.

Principles in Practice

The following familiar oaths and Charter excerpts illustrate the five basic principles of ethical conduct in practice:

Goodness
I will prescribe regimens for the *good* of my patients according to my ability and my judgment and *never do harm* to anyone.—Hippocratic oath

Equality
Every individual is *equal* before and under the law and has the right to the equal protection and equal benefit of the law without discrimination and, in particular, without discrimination based on race, national or ethnic origin, colour, religion, sex, age, or mental or physical disability.—*Canadian Charter of Rights and Freedoms*, s. 15(1)

Fairness
Any person charged with an offence has the right to be presumed innocent until proven guilty according to law in a *fair* and public hearing by an independent and impartial tribunal.—*Canadian Charter of Rights and Freedoms*, s. 11(d)

Truth
Do you solemnly swear to tell the *truth*, the whole truth, and nothing but the truth?—Courtroom oath

Freedom
Everyone has the following fundamental *freedoms*: (a) freedom of conscience and religion; (b) freedom of thought, belief, opinion and expression, including freedom of the press and other media of communication; (c) freedom of peaceful assembly; and (d) freedom of association.—*Canadian Charter of Rights and Freedoms*, s. 2

EMPATHY: THE ETHICAL OR MORAL FEELING

Whenever we act according to the basic ethical principles, we do so only because we can identify with the feelings of others. In other words, we have the capacity to empathize with them. **Empathy** means "feeling what another feels" or "feeling with another person." The psychopath lacks empathy and, consequently, does hurtful things to others. Those who have empathy can and do act ethically because they can put themselves into the emotional shoes of others. To paraphrase an ancient source: "They do unto others as they would have done to them." Consequently, empathy has been called the ethical or moral feeling.

empathy
feeling what another person feels

IMPOSED NORMS AND DEVELOPED NORMS

Norms are either imposed upon a group by a higher authority or the group itself generates its own rules. We'll discuss both imposed and developed norms below, but we'll devote more time to developed norms, the rules that you and your teammates agree among yourselves to abide by.

1. Imposed Norms

An **imposed norm** is a rule established by an authority outside the group. Governments, for example, impose norms upon people within their jurisdiction. The *Criminal Code* applies to all people within Canada, including students working in groups in a college course. Assault is an offence under that code, whether it occurs on the streets or in a classroom. Institutions, like your college, also impose norms on those within their jurisdiction. Smoking, for example, is forbidden in college buildings. In addition, individual authorities, like teachers, also impose rules of conduct and academic standards for their particular courses.

imposed norm
a rule established by an authority outside the group

In each of these cases—governments, institutions, and teachers—norms are imposed upon the individual and the group by some authority beyond the group. We all live our lives in a social context that includes many imposed norms. Frequently, though, people in groups have the opportunity to develop their own rules within the context of the imposed norms that we have just noted.

2. Developed Norms

A **developed norm** is a rule created by the members of a group to govern conduct within their group. Members of a group may, for example, develop rules to prevent or minimize free riding within the group. As we'll see, members of small groups need to develop their own rules or sets of expectations in order to function at an optimal level. The norms that work groups develop are usually norms derived from the basic ethical principles of goodness, equality, fairness, truth, and freedom. These principles are, as emphasized previously, the same ones that underlie the laws of society. They are the fundamental principles of civilized life.

developed norm
a rule established by a group to govern behaviour within the group

DEVELOPING NORMS WITHIN YOUR GROUP

You will have many opportunities in both your personal and professional life to contribute to the development of group norms. There are four important points to remember when developing the rules of your group. The "four Cs" for developing effective rules within your group are consistency, critical discussion, consensus, and commitment. Let's look at each one in turn.

1. Consistency

To be **consistent** means to be in agreement with. The developed norms of your group, for example, must be *consistent* with imposed norms. That is to say, the rules of your small group must agree with the laws of society and the rules of any other organizations within which your group exists. If a college forbids smoking on campus, for instance, a student work group within that college mustn't allow smoking. It mustn't establish rules or practices that contradict those of the institution.

consistency
agreement with

Criminals and other deviants don't accept this premise. They knowingly break the laws of society for their personal gain. However, since most of us are not criminals, we will want to ensure that the rules that we develop within our groups will benefit our groups while remaining consistent with imposed societal and institutional norms. As your group develops its rules, make sure that your rules are consistent with those of your broader social context.

2. Critical Discussion

When developing group norms, everyone in your group should participate in the discussion, which should be conducted in an open, critical, and constructive manner. Critical discussion is a healthy exchange of differing views on a given issue. If all members of your group participate in the discussion, then all points of view can be considered. In Chapter 8, we will study the process of *critical discussion* in detail.

For the moment, we can describe it as a win–win approach in which participants criticize ideas but support persons. It's the opposite of win–lose approaches in which one person tries to beat or defeat another, as is the case in a formal debate. Rather, critical discussion involves the presentation of different and sometimes opposing ideas so that group members can identify the best ideas on which to base their decisions.

Critical discussion is the opposite of *groupthink*, an ineffective and uncritical approach to thinking and deciding that we will examine in Chapter 8. In groupthink, members do not challenge one another's ideas, and poor decisions often result. When a group uses critical discussion, everyone has a better chance of ending up a winner because the group is much more likely to make informed decisions. When your group develops its norms, you should insist upon a critical discussion of the proposed rules.

3. Consensus

Group norms should be established by *consensus* whenever possible. **Consensus** means unanimous agreement. In other words, everyone in the group agrees on the decision. Note that consensus is not the same as majority vote. When a decision is made by majority vote, it usually takes only 51 percent to decide an issue. If 51 percent of a group, for example, are in favour of establishing a particular rule, that

consensus
unanimous agreement within a group

leaves 49 percent opposed. In circumstances like this, it can be very difficult to get the losers to abide by the decision.

When establishing the rules of conduct for members, groups will want everyone to be in agreement if at all possible. Consensus achieves that. Majority vote does so only rarely. We will look at both consensus and majority vote in detail when we study decision making in Chapter 9. As your group members share their expectations of one another, strive to get consensus on the norms that you will want everyone to live by.

4. Commitment

commitment
a willingness to stick with things over the long term

If you use the three Cs above—consistency, critical discussion, and consensus—when developing norms within your group, you will get maximum commitment to abiding by the rules. The fourth C is **commitment**—in this case, a dedication to living by the rules of your group. Your group will be committed to keeping the rules for three reasons:

1. Your group's norms will not contradict those of a higher authority and your members will, consequently, be free of challenges from outside your group.

2. The use of critical discussion will ensure that all points of view are considered. All group members can have their say.

3. Getting consensus means getting unanimous agreement about the rules. With consensus, everyone on your team will be a winner and there will be no losers. By being consistent, discussing critically, and seeking consensus you will maximize commitment to the rules that you develop. Compliance with the norms should then follow easily.

NORMS: ENSURING YOUR GROUP'S SUCCESS

If you want your group to succeed, to become an effective team, then you have to develop norms in several key areas of your group's life. To achieve both your task goals and your social goals, ensure that your group has clearly stated expectations for its members in each of these key areas. Remember, as we proceed in this section, that expectations are just another type of rule or norm. In each of the areas below, your group should develop rules that require members to deal with matters in the most effective way possible. Your teammates should expect certain things of one another in each of the following areas.

1. Accountability

accountability
the obligation one has to explain or justify one's actions to others

Your team should expect that all its members are accountable for their actions within the group and on behalf of the group. Individual team members must fulfill their respective roles responsibly. *Individual accountability* is very important in this regard. **Accountability** is the obligation that one has to explain or justify one's actions to others. If your group establishes norms that require individuals to be accountable for their respective role responsibilities, then dysfunctional behaviours will be minimized.

2. Cooperation

Your team should establish rules that require your members to cooperate in order to achieve their goals. Establish *cooperative* goal structures whenever possible. When setting task goals and social goals, a group can pit one member against another by establishing *competitive* goal structures. It is also possible to establish *individualistic* goal structures. Individualistic structures encourage individuals to work independently on different aspects of the group's task. In contrast, the goals of the group can be *cooperatively* structured so that members have to work together to achieve the group's goals. Cooperative goal structures promote group cohesion and are superior to competitive and individualistic goal structures in most instances. Chapter 4 examines goals and goal setting in greater detail.

3. Communication

Your team should establish norms for your group that require two-way communication among members. *Two-way communication* involves sending messages, receiving messages, and giving feedback. It consists of active speaking and listening that engages members in ongoing dialogue that fosters healthy working relationships. In contrast, one-way communication is a monologue that is frequently detrimental to group life. We will examine several rules for effective communication in Chapter 5. For the moment, let's just say that successful groups expect their members to communicate effectively when critically discussing issues, making decisions, solving problems, and managing interpersonal conflict.

4. Confrontation

Your group should develop rules that require conflicts to be resolved through constructive *confrontation*. **Confrontation** is the act of facing up to and dealing directly with a problem or difficult situation. Conflict between individuals in a group occurs frequently and strikes at the cohesiveness of the team. It should not be avoided. Rather, it should be confronted and dealt with skillfully. Successful teams require their members to practise assertive confrontation when dealing with interpersonal conflict. You and your teammates need to ensure that disputes, when they arise, are dealt with openly and effectively. We'll explore the conflict resolution process in Chapter 6.

confrontation
the act of facing up to and dealing directly with a problem or difficult situation

5. Support

Members of successful teams expect *support* from their teammates, and they get it. You and your teammates need to create a supportive climate in which all members are free to give their very best. While the achievement of task goals is critical, equally important is the achievement of social goals, especially group cohesion. The norms of your group should promote teambuilding, the development of a supportive climate in which group members can excel in their roles and meet their responsibilities. When group members respect and support one another, team productivity and cohesion will result. Cohesion is the subject of Chapter 7, and in that chapter we'll provide details on how your group can build itself into a team.

6. Evaluation

Make sure that your team creates norms that require frequent *evaluation* of its performance. The members of your group should regularly assess your group's achievements. For a group to improve, it must measure its performance in an objective way. The task goals and social goals that the group has established are critical for performance evaluation. By determining whether its goals are being met, a group can rate its performance. Good performance will motivate the team to do more of the same. Poor performance will motivate it to change in ways that will achieve its objectives. Effective groups evaluate their performance on an ongoing basis. In Chapter 10 we'll examine the details of this important group activity.

7. Discussion

As we saw earlier in this chapter, when developing its rules, your team should include norms that require ongoing critical and constructive *discussion* of issues. Your group should routinely engage in critical discussion whenever there are decisions to be made and problems to be solved. Critical discussion involves exploring ideas with the hope of coming to the best decisions. When you challenge the ideas of another person in your group, avoid attacking the person. Critical discussion involves criticizing ideas, not people. You and your fellow members can learn to criticize ideas while remaining supportive of the person who presented them. Critical discussion is examined in Chapter 8.

8. Decisions

Because your group will make *decisions* on a regular basis, you should have norms that require members to know and use the best decision-making strategies possible. Effective decision-making strategies are crucial when deciding issues. Consensus, as we noted earlier in this chapter, is the ideal way for groups to decide an issue. It requires full participation of members and results in maximum support for the decision arrived at. However, because consensus is not always possible, it is important for teams to use other decision-making strategies as appropriate. Majority vote can be a legitimate method under certain circumstances, and there are several other ways of making group decisions that are also appropriate in different situations. Effective groups will require their members to understand and use the best decision-making method for each circumstance. In Chapter 9, we'll study several methods by which groups can arrive at decisions.

9. Solutions

The rules of your group should include the requirement to seek *solutions* to problems in a systematic way. Modern science has proved extremely successful in understanding human problems and finding solutions to them. The field of health care provides us with many excellent examples, from immunization to heart transplants. So, too, other areas of science have enjoyed great successes. These successes can be attributed to the scientific method. The problem-solving process, described in Chapter 9, is based on that powerful method. Your group should employ the problem-solving process whenever it works at solving problems.

CHAPTER SUMMARY

At the beginning of this chapter we reviewed the closely related concepts of society and culture and also explained what a subculture is. We also defined the word "norm" and explained why groups set rules for their members. Next we said that the values and principles that group members share lead to the creation of rules. We then examined the five principles of ethical conduct, the principles that underlie the norms of all civilized societies and groups. The principles are goodness, equality, fairness, truth, and freedom. Next, we pointed out that rules can be either imposed upon a group or developed by the group itself. Turning to the development of norms within small groups, we presented the four Cs—consistency, critical discussion, consensus, and commitment. Finally, we underscored the importance of developing norms or expectation statements for each of several key areas of group life. Specifically, we said that groups should have rules to ensure individual accountability, member cooperation, two-way communication, constructive confrontation, team building, frequent performance assessment, critical discussion, and the use of the best decision-making strategies and problem-solving methods.
accountability

KEY TERMS

accountability	freedom
commitment	goodness
confrontation	imposed norm
consensus	norm
consistent	principles
culture	sanctions
developed norm	society
empathy	subculture
equality	truth
fairness	values

MASTERING THE MATERIAL

Now that you have read this chapter, use the following guides to ensure that you
have mastered the material.

1. Define *norm.*

2. The most important rules of a society are called _____.

3. The most important rules of an organization are part of the organization's
   *policies* and _*procedures*_

4. Define *sanctions.*
   punishment for breaking rules

5. Define *society, culture,* and *subculture.*
   Society - Lrg identifiable comm. see text.

6. What are values?

7. What are principles?

8. What are the five basic principles of ethical conduct?
   a. *Goodness*
   b. *Equality*
   c. *Fairness*
   d. *Truth*
   e. *Freedom*

9. Define *empathy.*
   Feeling what another person feels.

10. Distinguish between imposed norms and developed norms.
    laws   *ones you creaP*
                    (family)
                    (group)

criticise ideas, NOT people

11. When developing group norms, what are the four Cs? Explain each one briefly.

   a. *consistency - with all norms imposed. (cant smoke inside, cant make a norm to smoke)*

   b. *Critical discussion - constructive criticism*

   c. *consensus*

   d. *Commitment*

12. Identify and explain the nine key areas of group life that require norms.

   Area #1:

   Area #2:

   Area #3:

   Area #4:

   Area #5:

   Area #6:

   Area #7:

   Area #8:

   Area #9:

PRACTISING YOUR GROUP SKILLS

PURPOSE OF THIS SECTION

The purpose of "Practising Your Group Skills" and the ultimate purpose of this book is to help you become a more effective participant in the groups to which you belong. This section is designed to provide opportunities for you and your fellow students to practise your group skills in a structured environment.

TEAM RESPONSIBILITIES

A description of the team responsibilities for each of five different teams—the Executive Team, the Lesson Review Team, the Teaching Team, the Energizer Team, and the Evaluation Team—can be found in Appendix B, pages 177–180. Your professor may have chosen to use from one to five of these teams to conduct the teaching and learning activities of the class. Units 2 and 3 of the Teacher's Guide provide your professor with additional information on the responsibilities of these teams.

INDIVIDUAL ROLE RESPONSIBILITIES

A description of four individual role responsibilities—those of Leader, Recorder, Reporter, and Participant-Analyst—can be found in Appendix B, pages 180–182. Your professor may have chosen to use from one to four of these roles within teams to give individuals experience leading, recording, reporting, and analyzing. Units 2 and 3 of the Teacher's Guide provide your professor with additional information on these individual role responsibilities.

SPECIFIC TEAM ASSIGNMENTS

Specific team assignments for this chapter appear immediately below. Specific team assignments for each of the subsequent chapters can be found in "Practising Your Group Skills" in each chapter.

CHAPTER 3 TEAM ASSIGNMENTS

THE EXECUTIVE TEAM

- *Your Ultimate Goal*: to provide leadership to your classmates for your class session on Chapter 3.
- *Your Interim Goals*: to facilitate the class session by (1) ensuring a good classroom setup, (2) welcoming the class (3) introducing the lesson topic, (4) coordinating activities, and (5) bringing the session to a close.
- *Instructions*: Ensure that the classroom is set up to accommodate today's class activities. Post an agenda for the session. Welcome people to class and announce the topic, "Norms: Establishing Effective Rules in Your Group," in a creative and interesting way. Remind the class that norms are rules and that groups need norms to function effectively. Introduce and thank all speakers when appropriate. Coordinate the day's activities and bring closure at the end of the class. If necessary, return the classroom to its original configuration.

THE LESSON REVIEW TEAM

- *Your Ultimate Goal*: to review Chapter 2, "Leader Roles: Leading Effectively in Your Group."

- *Your Interim Goals*: to provide a review of (1) the experiential exercise, (2) the three leadership styles, and (3) the five characteristics of an effective leader.

- *Instructions*: As the Lesson Review Team, you have the freedom to choose how you will do the review. You can be as creative as you wish, but you must achieve the lesson review goals above. Remember that your time is very limited, so don't try to re-teach last chapter's lesson.

THE TEACHING TEAM

- *Your Ultimate Goal*: to understand and demonstrate the role of group norms in a small group setting.

- *Your Interim Goals*: to describe, explain, and demonstrate the four Cs for developing effective group norms.

- *Instructions*: As the Teaching Team, you have the freedom to choose how you will teach your lesson. You can be as creative as you wish, but you must achieve the lesson goals above. Your experiential exercise is called "Mutual Expectations" and you'll find it described fully in Appendix C, pages 189–191. Make sure that you refer to it when you teach and explain the components of culture, especially values, principles, and norms. The exercise should also be included in the part of your lesson when you describe and explain the four Cs for developing effective group norms. If time allows, you can also use exercises from "Mastering the Material" to teach your lesson.

THE ENERGIZER TEAM

- *Your Ultimate Goal*: to motivate your classmates by conducting an energizer activity.

- *Your Interim Goals*: to facilitate the energizing of your classmates by (1) planning an energizer activity and (2) implementing the plan at an appropriate time in the class session.

- *Instructions*: Your team doesn't have a specific, assigned activity to conduct. Rather, the team should remember its energizing purpose and conduct an activity that will provide a break in the class learning routine. Popular games like Simon Says, Heads Up Seven Up, and Murder Wink usually work well. So do various mixers and ice breakers. (Your professor's Teacher's Guide identifies a number of sources of energizer exercises.) Whatever you decide on, you must be prepared to give clear instructions and conduct the exercise effectively. When you lead the energizer, you are leading and directing the entire class. Plan well and execute professionally, even if the exercise is a "kid's game." Encourage everyone to get involved.

THE EVALUATION TEAM

As a member of the Evaluation Team, you need to review the information in Chapter 10, pages 145–148, before you do anything else. There you will find helpful information on how to conduct your evaluation session. The most important thing to remember is that you are not to judge other people. Your role is to help the class make its own assessment of which practices worked well today and which didn't.

- *Your Ultimate Goal*: to assess group (or class) conduct in today's class session.

- *Your Interim Goals*: to (1) assess group (or class) member compliance with school, classroom, and individual team rules and (2) identify practices in need of improvement.

- *Instructions*: Create an evaluation instrument based on the selected focus behaviours identified in the evaluation goals above. See Chapter 10, pages 146–147, for information on creating evaluation instruments. Figure 10.1 provides an example. Solicit feedback from the class using the evaluation instrument. Use the feedback to discuss the class session with the purpose of identifying improvements that can be made to individual, group, and class performance in future class sessions. Conclude by noting the specific actions that need to be repeated or avoided to make improvements.

REFERENCES AND RECOMMENDED READINGS

Bjorkquist, B.D. (2002). *The principles of ethical reasoning: Ethics and policing in a civil society.* Toronto: Prentice Hall.

Clarke, R.R., & Mouton, J.S. (1981). *Productivity: The human side.* New York: AMACOM.

Drews, E.M., & Lipson, L. (1971). *Values and humanity.* New York: St. Martin's Press.

Facione, P.A., Scherer, D., & Attig, T. (1978). *Values and society.* Englewood Cliffs, NJ: Prentice Hall.

Gilligan, C. (1982). *In a different voice: Psychological theory and moral development.* Cambridge, MA: Harvard University Press.

Gilligan, C., Ward, J., Taylor, J., & Barbige, B. (1988). *Mapping the moral domain.* Cambridge, MA: Harvard University Press.

Hurka, T. (1999). *Principles: Short essays on ethics.* Toronto: Harcourt Brace.

Johnson, D.W. (1970). *The social psychology of education.* New York: Holt, Rinehart, & Winston.

Mappes, T.A., & Zembaty, J.S. (1992). *Social ethics.* New York: McGraw-Hill.

USEFUL URLS

About.com Human Resources. http://humanresources.about.com.

Free Management Library. www.managementhelp.org.

MindTools. www.mindtools.com.

Pfeiffer Publishing. http://ca.pfeiffer.com/WileyCDA/Section/index.html.

Team Technology. www.teamtechnology.co.uk.

Your Meeting Resource Center. www.effectivemeetings.com.

Goals: Setting Clear Targets for Your Group

4

I don't care how much power, brilliance, or energy you have, if you don't harness it and focus it on a specific target and hold it there, you're never going to accomplish as much as your ability warrants.

—Zig Ziglar, sales expert

INTRODUCTION

No doubt you have set many personal goals for yourself over the years, and you can be sure that you are not alone in doing so. People routinely set goals for themselves in many areas of their lives. For example, they set goals for their health, their leisure, their education, and their careers. One person wants to lose 20 pounds, another wants to ski Whistler, another wants to save enough money to return to school, while another seeks work in the high-tech world of mobile phones.

When individuals set personal goals, the process is fairly simple because only one person decides what goals to pursue. However, when small groups set goals, the process is much more complex. Discussion among members has to take place and decisions have to be made by several people, all of whom may have slightly different views of what the team should devote its time and energy to accomplishing. Consider the complexity of goal setting in a large institution like a college.

A college's goals are usually set by its senior administrators who have to ensure that the goals are clear and that the organization can achieve them in a systematic, calculated way. For example, if the goal is to increase the average passing grade of next year's graduates by 5 percent, the president, working with faculty and staff from various departments in the organization, will establish the target and the practices necessary to hit the target. The practices, in our example, might include increasing professional development for teachers, hiring new faculty, and reducing class size. All of these actions would be consciously undertaken to achieve the institutional goal of raising graduate grades.

CHAPTER GOALS

After completing this chapter, you should be able to:

- Define *goal*.
- Define *ultimate goal* and give examples.
- Define *interim goal* and give examples.
- Identify four questions that clearly stated goals answer.
- Identify five problems related to unclear goals.
- Explain the role of critical discussion in goal setting.
- Explain the importance of setting goals by consensus.
- Identify and describe five considerations to make when setting goals.
- Identify and describe five benefits of clear goals.

To achieve this goal, the senior administrative officers must know how to set clear goals for the future. It is also essential that faculty and staff in the organization understand the process. A solid understanding of goal setting throughout the college is important because the practices designed to achieve the goals will be implemented throughout the organization. Moreover, since education is a team effort, members in all areas of the school will contribute more readily to success if they understand the importance of goal setting and the best ways to go about it.

In this chapter we'll explain what a goal is, discuss the importance of setting specific goals, and describe how your team should develop its goals. We'll also identify important considerations to keep in mind whenever you set goals. Finally, we'll describe the benefits that clear goals bring to a team. Let's start now with the word "goal" itself.

WHAT IS A GOAL?

The dictionary tells us that a goal is an objective, end, aim, purpose, or target. We can, for example, refer to Jose's goal of graduating from college as Jose's objective, or his end, or his aim, or his purpose, or his target. Regardless of the word we choose, his goal refers to what he wants for his future.

goal
a desired state of future affairs; also called objective, end, aim, purpose, or target

A **goal**, then, is a desired state of future affairs. It is how a person or group wants the world to be in the future. In Jose's case, he wants the future world to be one that includes him as a college graduate. Sometimes we use the image of a target, like a bull's eye, to designate a goal. Using that image, Jose's target is college graduation. If he succeeds, he will have hit the bull's eye.

If Jose is a first-year student in a three-year program, he will have to set and achieve many interim goals before achieving his ultimate goal of graduating. These interim goals include all the educational goals that Jose sets and accomplishes before his graduation. We might say, then, that successful completion of years one, two, and three are interim goals that need to be reached before he can achieve his ultimate goal of graduation.

ultimate goal
the final goal in a series of related goals; also called end goal

interim goal
a goal that must be achieved in order to reach an ultimate goal

Achieving one's interim goals, in this example, is only a means to achieving the ultimate end. In summary, an **ultimate goal** is the final goal in a series of related goals, and an **interim goal** is any goal that has to be achieved in order to reach an ultimate goal. "Ultimate" means "occurring at the end of a process," and "interim" means "occurring between events in a process."

Throughout this book, when you and your teammates consult the *Team Assignments* in each chapter, you will see that we first identify your team's ultimate goal and then its interim goals. For example, here's how the *Executive Team* assignment appears in this chapter, page 60:

- "*Your Ultimate Goal*: to provide leadership to your classmates for your class session on Chapter 4."

- "*Your Interim Goals*: to facilitate the class session by (1) ensuring a good classroom setup, (2) welcoming the class, (3) introducing the lesson topic, (4) coordinating activities, and (5) bringing the session to a close."

Having defined the terms "goal," "interim goal," and "ultimate goal," let's now look at the importance of setting goals that are very specific. Poor goals are fuzzy. Effective goals are not.

MAKING YOUR GOALS SPECIFIC

Being unclear about your goals is one of the biggest mistakes your small group can make. When goals are fuzzy, confusion and misunderstanding will prevail. In contrast, **specific goals**—goals that are clearly defined or specified—reduce confusion and improve understanding of your team's purpose. Therefore, it's critically important for you and your team to set goals that are very specific, very precise, and very clear. Although the following example uses an individual, it clearly illustrates the point about setting goals that are specific.

specific goal
a goal that is clearly defined or specified

One of a student's goals might be the following: "To successfully complete the first year of the registered practical nursing program at the end of the current school year by attending all classes, dedicating a minimum of three hours to homework per day, and achieving an 'A' average in all subjects." Notice that this goal is very specific and gives a lot of direction to the student.

With this goal, we know precisely *what* the target is—namely, to complete year one with an "A" average. We also know precisely *when* the goal will be achieved—namely, by the end of the current academic year. We know, further, precisely *how* the goal will be achieved—namely, by dedicated study and regular class attendance. We also know, although it isn't stated, precisely *who* is responsible for the achievement of the goal—namely, the student. This goal is specific because it includes the "who," "what," "when," and "how" of hitting the target.

When we set our goals, then, we need to identify precisely *what* the goal is, *when* we will know that it has been reached, *how* it will be achieved, and *who* is responsible for its achievement. Consider the following example, where a very fuzzy goal statement is made very specific. Here's the fuzzy goal: "Our group will raise money to give to charity." This goal sounds worthy enough, but it is very general and offers little direction.

Arriving at one goal is the starting point to another.

—John Dewey,
psychologist and educational reformer

Stated much more precisely, the goal might be: "Under the leadership of Bradley Brown, by May 1 of this year our group will raise $10,000 for the Red Cross through weekly car washes." In this specific goal, we can see who has the lead responsibility, what amount of money has been targeted, when the target is to be reached, and how the money is to be raised.

Several problems are likely to arise if your group fails to set clear and specific goals.

- First, if members aren't clear on your group's goals, your group will lack *direction*.

- Second, your group is likely to lack *motivation* because success in hitting your stated targets will not be easily determined.

- Third, your *communication* is likely to suffer because members will be uncertain about your group's focus or purpose.

- Fourth, this uncertainty is likely to generate unnecessary *conflict*.

- Finally, your group will lack the standards necessary for effective *evaluation* of its performance.

In the last section of this chapter we will examine the benefits that come to groups when they set clear and specific goals. Before discussing those benefits, let's look at a process for developing well-crafted goals within your group.

HOW TO DEVELOP TEAM GOALS

As we saw in Chapter 3, effective groups use critical discussion and consensus to develop their norms or rules. The same process should be used when setting team goals. Your group should first use critical discussion to exchange and explore ideas. Then it should establish its ultimate and interim goals by consensus.

Critical discussion, you'll recall, is a process that encourages not only an exchange and critique of ideas but also support of those who offer their ideas. *Consensus* is unanimous agreement, and it fosters maximum commitment from members to the decisions of the group. Successful teams establish their goals by engaging in critical discussion and making decisions by consensus. We'll study both processes in detail later, critical discussion in Chapter 8 and consensus in Chapter 9.

For the present, though, consider your group as it sets about to establish its goals using critical discussion. One member, for example, adopts a particular point of view (Option A) and argues for it, offering as many good reasons in support of it as possible. Other members then offer critiques of that position and suggest alternatives (Options B, C, D, etc.). They, too, provide reasons for their positions. All of this is done in a mutually supportive manner. The point is not to criticize people but to examine ideas.

When your group has considered all reasonable points of view, it should then set its goals by consensus—that is, by unanimous agreement among the members of the group. When all your members have offered their points of view and everyone has agreed to a particular goal, your team's commitment to achieving that goal should be very high. Also, the conceptual conflict that you have engaged in should produce very clear goals.

IMPORTANT CONSIDERATIONS
WHEN SETTING GOALS

You need to take five things into consideration when setting your team goals. First, you need to consider both your team's task goals and its social goals. Second, you need to consider the needs of your group as a whole and those of the individual members of your team. Third, you need to promote cooperation among group members. Fourth, you need to develop goals that are realistic. Fifth, in addition to being realistic, your goals must be specific and measurable. Let's now take a look at each consideration in turn.

1. Include Both Task and Social Goals

First, your team goals should reflect the fact that your group has two goals to achieve: its task goal and its social goal. In Chapter 1, you will recall, we studied both. Successful groups get their work done, regardless of what that work may involve. They set clear goals for task completion and they achieve them. In addition, effective groups set goals to promote team spirit. They consciously build themselves into teams. They develop a sense of cohesion, a sense of togetherness among their members. Successful teams set clear goals for both social development and task achievement.

2. Address Both Individual and Group Needs

Second, your team should set goals that take into account both individual needs and group needs. Your group, like all groups, includes individuals with personal needs such as family, work, and school commitments and obligations. If individual needs are not addressed when setting goals, your group may suffer. This is not to suggest, however, that your group can cater to each individual's every wish.

When joining a group, we usually have to give up some of our personal goals in order to help the group reach its goals. This is the compromise of group life. Effective goals, however, will be set up with both individual and group interests in mind. Your team should strive to establish goals that meet group needs while accommodating, as much as possible, the needs of individual members.

3. Build in Cooperation

Third, your group should build member cooperation into its goals. **Cooperatively structured goals**, you will recall from Chapter 3, require that members work together to achieve them. They require positive interaction and interdependence among members; thus, they build cohesion. Sports teams, for example, require that members cooperate and work closely together to achieve the team's goals. They build cooperation into their goals. Everyone must work together to win.

cooperatively structured goal
a goal that is achieved only by cooperative efforts

In contrast, **competitively structured goals** pit one member against another. This approach tends to create a win–lose atmosphere that can be very detrimental to team spirit. For example, a car dealership might build competition into its monthly sales goal in order to increase sales. It might offer a bonus to individual sales personnel for each car sold. In this example, one sales person might earn more money each month by taking sales from another. The prospect of a personal bonus is an incentive to compete with others on the sales team, and a competitive, win–lose environment is the result.

competitively structured goal
a goal that is achieved only when people compete with one another

It is also possible to create **individualistically structured goals**. With individualistic structures, you will remember from Chapter 3, individual members work independently to reach goals. The auto factory provides a good example of individualistic structures where, for example, the company sets goals in which the windshield installer neither cooperates with nor competes with the fuel-tank installer. Each works independently of the other, as the company achieves its production goals.

individualistically structured goal
a goal that is achieved only when people work independently

While each type of goal structure has legitimate uses, only cooperative goal structures promote interdependence and cohesion among members. When setting its goals, your team should build in cooperation.

4. Set Realistic Goals

Fourth, your team should set realistic goals for itself. **Realistic goals** are ones that a group can achieve given its expertise. Research shows that groups that set realistic

realistic goal
a goal that a group can achieve given its expertise

goals are more likely to achieve their goals than those that don't. If your group is overly enthusiastic and sets goals that are beyond its capacity to achieve, members will be frustrated and morale will likely decline. In contrast, if your group sets goals that are achievable with little effort, it will likely become stagnant.

For example, the high jumper who has repeatedly jumped 1.5 metres with maximum effort will, no doubt, be frustrated if the bar is set at 2.0 metres. The same jumper will be bored with the bar at 1.0 metre. A realistic goal for our jumper might be 1.6 metres. The best course of action is to set realistic goals that provide sufficient challenge to your members to motivate them to achieve those goals. The successful achievement of realistic goals will be a rewarding motivator for future achievements.

5. State Team Goals in Specific, Measurable Terms

Fifth, your team should express its goals in clearly measurable terms. We made this point earlier in this chapter when we emphasized that goal statements must include answers to the "who," "what," "when," and "how" questions. By specifying *what* is to be done, *when* it is to be done by, *how* it is to be done, and *who* is responsible for getting it done, you state your goals in specific, measurable terms. In other words, you can measure your team's success in achieving its goals. For this reason, specific goals are also called **measurable goals**.

measurable goal
a goal that is clearly defined or specified; a specific goal

THE BENEFITS OF EFFECTIVE GOALS

If your team sets clearly measurable goals, it can expect to gain five benefits that will contribute to the success of your team. Let's look at each benefit in turn.[1]

Obstacles are those frightful things you see when you take your eyes off your goal.
—Henry Ford,
founder of the Ford Motor Company

1. Direction

First, clear goals will give your group direction for its activities by providing a guide for planning and coordinating group efforts. If the goals of your group are unclear or non-existent, then your group will tend to flounder and waste its time. When this happens, members will become frustrated and lose interest. In contrast, when goals are clear, they become the targets toward which group energy can be directed. Your members will understand why the group exists, and they will know where it is heading. Instead of feeling that they are wasting time and energy, your members will feel productive. Their efforts will be rewarded as each goal is achieved.

2. Motivation

Second, clear goals will increase the motivation of the members of your group. The old expression "Nothing succeeds like success" expresses this point well. When your group members see that meaningful goals have been met, they will experience a sense of accomplishment. This sense of achievement is a powerful motivator.

---

1   Four of the five benefits presented here are based on Johnson and Johnson's work (1997, p. 78). I have added the benefit of communication.

Groups that succeed in achieving their interim goals are motivated toward the achievement of their ultimate goals. Clear goals stated in measurable terms will benefit your team by motivating members to higher levels of achievement.

3. Communication

Third, clear goals will improve communication among the members of your group. When goals are clearly stated in measurable terms, then your group has a focus for its communication. When members seek ideas and share ideas, for example, the team's goals determine what information is or is not relevant.

Similarly, when your team meets to make decisions, if proposed actions (goals) are specific and clearly stated, discussion is likely to remain focused and decision making will be easier. Members will know exactly what they're deciding to do. If your team sets clear and measurable goals, members will find it easier to communicate with one another as you conduct your business.

4. Conflict Resolution

Fourth, clear goals will facilitate conflict resolution among the members of your group. Often, conflicts arise because different members have different perceptions of what the group is supposed to be doing. If the group's goals are clear, however, the group has a way of bringing disputing members back to previously agreed-upon goals. If the group's goals have not been identified clearly, it is difficult or impossible to employ them in conflict resolution. Your team will experience benefits in the area of conflict resolution if it sets clear goals for itself. Fewer conflicts are likely to arise, and those that do arise will be easier to handle.

5. Performance Evaluation

Fifth, clear goals will benefit your group by providing standards for performance evaluation. When an archer shoots an arrow at a clear target, it is easy to see whether the target has been hit or missed. If the archer sees that her shot has gone up and to the right of the bull's eye, she can adjust her next shot downward and to the left. She can adjust her performance in the

> *If you aim at nothing, you'll hit it every time.*
> —Anonymous

direction of success. Similarly, when your group has well-defined targets, your members can measure their performance by reference to the team's goals and adjust their performance in the direction of success. If your group has fallen short of the target, it can establish new strategies to get a bull's eye next time.

CHAPTER SUMMARY

In the introduction to this chapter, we defined a goal as a desired state of future affairs. After noting the difference between ultimate goals and interim goals, we proceeded to distinguish between goals that are quite general or fuzzy and goals that are very specific and clear. A goal is specific and clear when it includes information about what is to be done, when it is to be done, how it is to be done, and who has responsibility for getting it done. Next, we emphasized the importance of setting group goals by critically discussing them and reaching consensus about them. Then, we went on to describe five key things to consider when setting team goals. We said that team goals should direct both task and social dimensions of a group, include both individual and team needs, foster cooperation among members, be realistic, and both specific and measurable. We concluded our examination of goal setting by summarizing the benefits that accrue to teams that have clear goals. These benefits include direction for the team, motivation for members, improved communication, more effective conflict resolution, and standards for assessing team performance.

KEY TERMS

competitively structured goal	measurable goal
cooperatively structured goal	realistic goal
goal	specific goal
individualistically structured goal	ultimate goal
interim goal	

MASTERING THE MATERIAL

Now that you have read this chapter, use the following guides to ensure that you have mastered the material.

1. Define *goal*.

2. Define *ultimate goal* and give examples.

3. Define *interim goal* and give examples.

4. What four questions does a clear and specific goal answer?
   a. who
   b. what
   c. when
   d. how

5. Identify five problems associated with unclear, imprecise goals.

   a.

   b.

   c.

   d.

   e.

6. When developing its goals, a team should use _____ and

   _____.

7. Make the following goal specific: "To improve health care in our
   community."

8. Identify and explain the five things to consider when you set group goals.

   a.

   b.

   c.

   d.

   e.

9. Identify and explain the five benefits of clear and specific goals.

   a.

   b.

   c.

   d.

   e.

PRACTISING YOUR GROUP SKILLS

PURPOSE OF THIS SECTION

The purpose of "Practising Your Group Skills" and the ultimate purpose of this book is to help you become a more effective participant in the groups to which you belong. This section is designed to provide opportunities for you and your fellow students to practise your group skills in a structured environment.

TEAM RESPONSIBILITIES

A description of the team responsibilities for each of five different teams—the Executive Team, the Lesson Review Team, the Teaching Team, the Energizer Team, and the Evaluation Team—can be found in Appendix B, pages 177–180. Your professor may have chosen to use from one to five of these teams to conduct the teaching and learning activities of the class. Units 2 and 3 of the Teacher's Guide provide your professor with additional information on the responsibilities of these teams.

INDIVIDUAL ROLE RESPONSIBILITIES

A description of four individual role responsibilities—those of Leader, Recorder, Reporter, and Participant-Analyst—can be found in Appendix B, pages 180–182. Your professor may have chosen to use from one to four of these roles within teams to give individuals experience leading, recording, reporting, and analyzing. Units 2 and 3 of the Teacher's Guide provide your professor with additional information on these individual role responsibilities.

SPECIFIC TEAM ASSIGNMENTS

Specific team assignments for this chapter appear immediately below. Specific team assignments for each of the subsequent chapters can be found in "Practising Your Group Skills" in each chapter.

CHAPTER 4 TEAM ASSIGNMENTS

THE EXECUTIVE TEAM

- *Your Ultimate Goal*: to provide leadership to your classmates for your class session on Chapter 4.

- *Your Interim Goals*: to facilitate the class session by (1) ensuring a good classroom setup, (2) welcoming the class, (3) introducing the lesson topic, (4) coordinating activities, and (5) bringing the session to a close.

- *Instructions*: Ensure that the classroom is set up to accommodate today's class activities. Post an agenda for the session. Welcome people to class and announce the topic, "Goals: Setting Clear Targets for Your Group," in a creative and interesting way. Remind the class that goals and objectives are essential if groups are to function effectively. Introduce and thank all speakers when appropriate. Coordinate the day's activities and bring closure at the end of the class. If necessary, return the classroom to its original configuration.

THE LESSON REVIEW TEAM

- *Your Ultimate Goal*: to review Chapter 3, "Norms: Establishing Effective Rules for Your Group."

- *Your Interim Goals*: to provide a review of (1) the experiential exercise, (2) values, principles, and norms, and (3) the "four Cs" for developing group rules.

- *Instructions*: As the Lesson Review Team, you have the freedom to choose how you will do the review. You can be as creative as you wish, but you must achieve the lesson review goals above. Remember that your time is very limited, so don't try to re-teach last chapter's lesson.

THE TEACHING TEAM

- *Your Ultimate Goal*: to understand and demonstrate the role of goals in a small group setting.

- *Your Interim Goals*: to describe, explain, and demonstrate (1) the difference between ultimate goals and interim goals, (2) the correct way to write an effective goal, and (3) the five benefits of clear, specific, and measurable goals.

- *Instructions*: As the Teaching Team, you have the freedom to choose how you will teach your lesson. You can be as creative as you wish, but you must achieve the lesson goals above. Your experiential exercise is called "Writing Clear Goals" and you'll find it described fully in Appendix C, pages 191–192. Make sure that you refer to it when you teach and explain your lesson goals. The exercise should also be included in the part of your lesson when you describe and explain the benefits of group goals. If time allows, you can also use exercises from "Mastering the Material" to teach your lesson.

THE ENERGIZER TEAM

- *Your Ultimate Goal*: to motivate your classmates by conducting an energizer activity.

- *Your Interim Goals*: to facilitate the energizing of your classmates by (1) planning an energizer activity and (2) implementing the plan at an appropriate time in the class session.

- *Instructions*: Your team doesn't have a specific, assigned activity to conduct. Rather, the team should remember its energizing purpose and conduct an activity that will provide a break in the class learning routine. Popular games like Simon Says, Heads Up Seven Up, and Murder Wink usually work well. So do various mixers and ice breakers. (Your professor's Teacher's Guide identifies a number of sources of energizer exercises.) Whatever you decide on, you must be prepared to give clear instructions and conduct the exercise effectively. When you lead the energizer, you are leading and directing the entire class. Plan well and execute professionally, even if the exercise is a "kid's game." Encourage everyone to get involved.

THE EVALUATION TEAM

As a member of the Evaluation Team, you need to review the information in Chapter 10, pages 145–148, before you do anything else. There you will find helpful information on how to conduct your evaluation session. The most important thing to remember is that you are not to judge other people. Your role is to help the class make its own assessment of which practices worked well today and which didn't.

- *Your Ultimate Goal*: to assess group (or class) members' goal-setting practices.

- *Your Interim Goals*: to (1) assess the degree to which the class, both as individuals and in groups, consciously set goals and objectives and achieved them and (2) to identify practices in need of improvement.

- *Instructions*: Create an evaluation instrument based on the selected focus behaviours identified in the goals above. See Chapter 10, pages 146–147, for information on creating evaluation instruments. Figure 10.1 provides an example. Solicit feedback from the class using the evaluation instrument. Use the feedback to discuss the class session with the purpose of identifying improvements that can be made to individual, group, and class performance in future class sessions. Conclude by noting the specific actions that need to be repeated or avoided to make improvements.

REFERENCES AND RECOMMENDED READINGS

Engleberg, I.N., & Wynn, D.R. (1997). *Working in groups: Communication principles and strategies*. New York: Houghton Mifflin.

Frey, L.R., & Barge, K.J. (Eds.). (1997). *Managing group life: Communicating in decision-making groups*. New York: Houghton Mifflin.

Harris, T.E., & Sherblom, J.C. (1999). *Small group and team communication*. Needham Heights, MA: Allyn & Bacon.

Johnson, D.W., & Johnson, F.P. (1997). *Joining together: Group theory and group skills* (6th ed.). Needham Heights, MA: Allyn & Bacon.

Robbins, S.P., & Hunsaker, P.L. (1996). *Training in interpersonal skills*. Upper Saddle River, NJ: Prentice Hall.

Wilson, G.L. (1999). *Groups in context: Leadership and participation in small groups* (5th ed.). Boston: McGraw-Hill.

USEFUL URLS

About.com Human Resources. http://humanresources.about.com.

Free Management Library. www.managementhelp.org.

Goal Setting Guide. www.goal-setting-guide.com.

MindTools. www.mindtools.com.

Pfeiffer Publishing. http://ca.pfeiffer.com/WileyCDA/Section/index.html.

Team Technology. www.teamtechnology.co.uk.

Your Meeting Resource Center. www.effectivemeetings.com.

Dialogue: Speaking and Listening Effectively in Your Group

5

The words with which you choose to say something are just as important as the decision to speak.

—Anonymous

INTRODUCTION

When problems arise in relationships, we frequently blame them on a failure to communicate. Marriage partners in a troubled relationship, for example, are urged to improve their communication. Parents who become increasingly alienated from their teenaged children are advised to communicate more effectively with them. And frequently when an organization fails, the failure is attributed to communication breakdown. Clearly, we see communication as the answer to many of life's problems. Not surprisingly, good communication is essential for successful teamwork.

In this chapter we'll examine the process of dialogue, focusing our attention on the skills required to speak and listen effectively in a face-to-face discussion with others. Teams of students in college classrooms and teams of workers in business and industry need to know how to discuss issues in order to succeed in school and in the workplace.

Later in the chapter we'll present rules for effective dialogue—that is, rules for speaking, listening, and giving feedback to others. Take careful note that the rules for speaking and listening differ from the rules for writing and reading. The skills and rules described in this chapter, then, do not necessarily apply to writing skills or reading skills, but they definitely apply to **dialogue**, a face-to-face conversation between two or more people.

We'll begin our study of the dialogue process by examining a descriptive model that identifies important aspects of the process. Once we've discussed these elements, we'll provide several rules that will, if followed, ensure that your spoken communication, your listening skills, and your ability to provide feedback to others are excellent. Just as marriage partners, parents and their children, and people in the workplace need to discuss their issues constructively in order to solve problems,

CHAPTER GOALS

After completing this chapter, you should be able to:

- Describe a model of the dialogue process.
- Explain the difference between an encoder and a decoder.
- Define *message*, and identify the two dimensions of a message.
- Distinguish between verbal and non-verbal communication.
- Identify and describe three different types of noise.
- Describe the characteristics of a two-way message.
- Explain what a feedback message is.
- State and explain six rules for speaking effectively.
- State and explain three rules for listening effectively.
- State and explain three rules for giving feedback effectively.

dialogue
a face-to-face conversation between two or more people

so, too, do the members of your team. Constructive dialogue gives you a chance to resolve differences and enhance your interpersonal relationships.

A MODEL OF THE DIALOGUE PROCESS

Before we look at specific rules for effective dialogue, we'll examine a model of the communication process itself. A **model** is a simplified description of a process that is expressed in a diagram (see Figure 5.1). The model presented in this chapter is called an explanatory model because it attempts to explain all the elements of the dialogue process, both the positive features and the negative ones.

As we begin to examine our model, take note that **communication** occurs when there is a successful exchange of information or feelings between members of a group. In other words, communication succeeds only when the receiver of a message understands it in the way that the sender intended.

To assist with understanding the dialogue process, imagine a small work team of six people gathered together in the meeting room of a manufacturing plant in a major city. They have been given the task of recommending a course of action to their boss, the head of the manufacturing department. The boss is not present but the team begins to discuss its assignment. The exchange of ideas and feelings among the six people in the meeting room is a very complex process. To simplify things, we'll focus on just two members of the group as they begin the dialogue.

Our model of the dialogue process includes a message *sender*, the *message* itself, a *receiver* of the message, and a *feedback* message (Figure 5.1). Imagine, now, the two people on the work team above as they begin to converse. First of all, someone has to start the process. This happens when one person is motivated to send a message to another person.

SENDER AND RECEIVER

The dialogue process starts when the **sender** first has an idea or a feeling (or both) that she wants to communicate to another person, the **receiver** of the message (see Figure 5.1, phase 1). The sender must then put her thoughts and feelings into words and say those words to the receiver. Putting the message into words is called **encoding**, and the sender is called the **encoder**. If the receiver interprets the sender's message correctly, then communication has taken place. Interpreting a message is called **decoding**, and the receiver can be called the **decoder**.

THE MESSAGE

The **message** is *what* the sender communicates to the receiver. Messages are generally of two kinds. They are about the sender's *ideas* or about the sender's *feelings* or both. Because human beings are thinking beings, we frequently communicate our ideas, thoughts, and opinions to one another. We refer to our thinking or intellectual side as our **cognitive dimension**. We are, however, much more than thinkers. We also have feelings and we experience moods. We refer to these feelings and moods as our **affective dimension**. Successful communicators learn to express both thoughts and feelings clearly so that others easily understand their messages.

---

model
a simplified description of a process, often expressed as a diagram

communication
the successful exchange of information and feelings between people in a group

sender
the person who begins the communication process by expressing thoughts and feelings in words

receiver
the person in the communication process who interprets the sender's words

encoding
expressing a message in spoken or written words

encoder
sender who encodes a message

decoding
interpreting a spoken or written message accurately

decoder
receiver who interprets a message

message
the thoughts and feelings communicated by a sender, whether verbally or non-verbally

cognitive dimension
our thinking or intellectual side

affective dimension
our feelings and moods

Figure 5.1   A Model of the Dialogue Process

Communication includes a sender, a receiver, a message, and a feedback message. Noise (physical, physiological, or psychological) can interfere with communication at a number of points in the process.

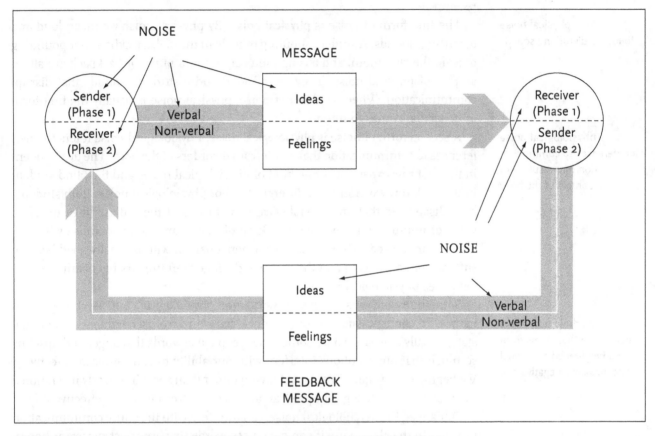

VERBAL AND NON-VERBAL COMMUNICATION

What we communicate is the message. *How* we communicate that message is by using words or actions or both—that is, we send our messages both verbally and non-verbally.

When we send our message in words, we are using **verbal communication**. "Verbal" means "in words" and includes both written and spoken words. When we convey a message through actions, like a hand-wave or a thumbs-up, we are using **non-verbal communication**. "Non-verbal" means "without words." Non-verbal communication includes gestures, eye contact, and body posture.

In recent years, much has been written on the subject of non-verbal communication, and these studies have helped us understand the importance of non-verbal messages in the communication process. When words and actions are used in combination to complement one another, then the messages they convey become stronger.

verbal communication
a message expressed in words (speech or writing)

non-verbal communication
a message expressed by gestures, eye contact, or body posture, but not words

NOISE

In our model of the dialogue process, anything that interferes with the communication of a message from a sender to a receiver is called **noise**.[1] Noise, we need to

noise
any physical, physiological, or psychological interference that impedes communication

---

1   Wilson (1999, p. 14) provides an excellent review of the varieties of noise that can affect communication in groups. This summation is based on his categories.

note, takes three distinctly different forms. The three types of noise are physical noise, physiological noise, and psychological noise. Consider, for example, a typical classroom in which the teacher is the message sender and students are the receivers.

physical noise
loud and disturbing sounds

The first form of noise is **physical noise**. By physical noise we mean loud and disturbing sounds. A student shouting outside in the hall, a jackhammer pounding outside the classroom, and a cellphone ringing in a purse or backpack are all examples of physical noise. They are all loud and disturbing sounds that disrupt communication. When we think of noise, physical noise is usually the first form of noise that comes to mind.

physiological noise
interferences to communication that result from disorders of the body

A second form of noise is **physiological noise**. Physiological noise refers to interferences to communication that result from disorders of the body. The deaf student in the first row experiences one kind of physiological noise, and the blind student in the back row experiences a different kind of physiological noise. Both students have disabilities that are physiological in nature, and these disabilities interfere with communication. Note that this kind of noise can also affect those who normally hear and see well. For example, when a person with normally good hearing suffers from a bad cold and the associated congestion impairs his hearing, he experiences physiological noise.

psychological noise
interference that stems from a heightened emotional state, usually a negative one

Sometimes noise is neither physical nor physiological, but psychological in nature. **Psychological noise** is interference that stems from a heightened emotional state, usually a negative one. Sometimes people use words that anger and upset us so much that our emotions interfere with our ability to communicate effectively. We begin, for example, ranting and raving rather than speaking clearly in a rational manner. Our psychological upset can also keep us from listening effectively.

Our anger, the psychological noise, can interfere with the entire communication process. In the classroom, if someone uses words that are racist, sexist, or homophobic, both students and teacher are likely to experience psychological noise. Emotions can run high for very good reason, and, when they do, they usually create psychological noise. Any emotional experience that interferes with communication is a form of noise.

TWO-WAY COMMUNICATION

Our model of the dialogue process indicates that communication is a two-way process in which a message goes from a sender to a receiver and back again. Two-way communication is the ideal way to communicate in a small group. Sometimes, however, two-way communication is replaced by one-way communication. In **one-way communication**, the sender sends the message and the receiver receives it, without any feedback occurring. This shift is often, but not always, a sign that there are problems within the group.

one-way communication
the sender sends the message and the receiver receives it, without any feedback occurring

If, for example, someone in your group doesn't listen to others in the group, then two-way communication doesn't occur. If the situation persists, the group will suffer. Unhealthy one-way communication also occurs when one or two members dominate the group's discussions. If, for instance, a member of your group is vocal and convinced that his ideas are the only good ones in the group, then one-way communication will occur, especially if other members tend to be passive.

Two-way communication occurs when the receiver of a message becomes the sender of a return message and the original sender becomes the new receiver. The return message is called a **feedback message**, and it is a normal part of healthy two-way communication. Take note that feedback messages include all the things that the original message did. There's a sender, a receiver, messages, and possibly noise.

Two-way communication is the ideal for small groups and should be both encouraged and expected. Good communication is essential for success in many areas of life, including our life in small groups. Let's look now at some important rules for successful two-way communication. We'll look at rules for speaking effectively, listening effectively, and giving feedback effectively.

We began our look at the model of the dialogue process by inviting you to imagine a team of workers gathered together face to face to develop a recommendation for their boss. All the elements that we identified above in the dialogue process will be at play as all six members of the work team discuss their assigned task. To ensure that their discussion is productive, they would do well to observe some basic communication rules—that is, rules for speaking, rules for listening, and rules for giving feedback.

two-way communication
when the receiver of a message becomes the sender of a return message and the original sender becomes the new receiver

feedback message
a return message sent by a receiver to the original sender

SPEAKING EFFECTIVELY IN A DIALOGUE

There are six rules to follow when speaking to other members of your group.[2] If you follow these rules in your discussions, you will help to ensure that the communication in your group is both two-way and effective.

> *Don't speak unless you can improve on the silence.*
> — Spanish proverb

Rule #1: Use First-Person Pronouns in Your Messages

In grammar, the words "I," "me," "my," and "mine" are called first-person pronouns. We use these words to refer to ourselves without continually repeating our names. If you use these pronouns, you can indicate clearly to others what you are thinking or feeling. By using first-person pronouns you take responsibility for your thoughts and feelings and communicate that fact clearly to others. They will know what you think and feel.

POOR: "*Some people* get angry when *they* are continually interrupted."

BETTER: "*I* feel angry when *I* am continually interrupted."

POOR: "Our team has decided to support the college fund raiser."

BETTER: "*I* have decided to support the college fund raiser and so has my team."

Rule #2: Convey Your Frame of Reference, and Know the Receiver's Frame of Reference

The expression **frame of reference** refers to the social and psychological context from which a person is speaking or listening. In any conversation there are at least two frames of reference, the sender's and the receiver's. In common language, this second rule might be: "Tell the other person where you're coming from, and find

frame of reference
the context from which a person speaks or listens

---

2   Johnson and Johnson (1997, p. 144) present eight guidelines for sending messages effectively. Five are included in this section, plus Rule #3 on communicating ideas.

out where he's coming from." When speaking in a conversation, you should let your listener know your frame of reference. Likewise, when listening in a conversation, you should understand the speaker's frame of reference. Understanding the context in which you're communicating contributes to improved communication.

> POOR: "I don't want to study with you today." [Providing no context]
>
> BETTER: "I've had a really rough day, so I'm not up to studying with you." [Providing a context]
>
> POOR: "Let's go for a coffee. I'm sure you've got time." [Assuming a context]
>
> BETTER: "How's your day going? Do you have time for a coffee?" [Seeking the context]

Rule #3: Present Your Ideas Clearly and Concisely

Messages, you will recall, may convey our ideas, our feelings, or both. This rule addresses the communication of our ideas, thoughts, and opinions. It is about our cognitive messages and tells us to convey them clearly and concisely. While the rule itself is straightforward, keeping it is often difficult. Following this rule requires the skillful use of words and correct use of sentence structure.

> POOR: "John, eh, you know, like asked his dad, like if he could, you know, make the use of his dad's wheels, eh, so like his dad says, 'ya man,' so like, that's cool, eh?"
>
> BETTER: "Isn't it great that John's dad loaned him the car?"
>
> POOR: "Like it was so boss, like him, eh, like his new wardrobe, eh, like it was, like, so him. Like, you know what I mean?"
>
> BETTER: "He looked really good in his new suit, didn't he?"

Rule #4: Describe Your Feelings; Don't Express Them

The previous rule gave guidance on the communication of *ideas*. Rule #4 addresses the communication of *feelings*. We can communicate our feelings in two ways: We can express them, and we can describe them. The word "express," as used here, means "letting your emotions pour or burst out." If you're angry, you may yell and shout. If you're sad, you may weep. If you're happy, you may laugh or giggle. Often, we can express our feelings and no harm is done, particularly when the feelings are happy ones. Sometimes, however, the expression of emotion can be disastrous. Anger, in particular, can cause problems if expressed rather than described.

Powerful emotions, like anger, can be communicated most effectively through description. When you describe your angry feelings, you let the other person know what you are experiencing emotionally, but you avoid the negative repercussions of an emotional outburst. There are two helpful ways to describe your emotions, by naming them and by comparing them to something.

- One way to describe your feelings is to *name* them. Just as we need a good vocabulary for communicating ideas, so we need a good vocabulary for describing our feelings. Words like "angry," "upset," "disappointed," "happy," and "delighted" are only a few examples of feeling words that should be a part of our vocabulary.

- A second way to describe feelings is to use *comparisons*. Grammatically, we have two forms of comparison—similes and metaphors. Both make comparisons between two things. A *simile* uses the words "like" or "as," to make a direct comparison. A *metaphor* is an indirect comparison that does not use the words "like" or "as." Both similes and metaphors can be used to describe our emotions.

POOR: "@**&@**, I don't give a #%**@ whether I ever see you again!!! You *%##@* me off with your *&%%##@* attitude." [Expressing anger]

BETTER: "When you talk to me that way, I get really angry." [Describing anger by naming]

BETTER: "When you talk to me that way, I feel like a pit bull in a leg trap." [Describing anger by simile]

BETTER: "When you talk to me that way, my blood starts to boil." [Describing anger by metaphor]

Rule #5: Describe the Behaviour; Don't Judge the Person

When people do things that we disagree with, a natural reaction is to make a judgment about the person. For example, if a person in your group has been late for several meetings in a row and has also left early each time, you may assume that she doesn't care about the group. Your assumptions, in this case, amount to judgments about the character of the other person. In effect, you are attributing a flaw or weakness to that person's character as you question her motives.

Making personal judgments can be detrimental to the group. They are not a very helpful communication practice as they are often inappropriate and inaccurate. Rather than making judgments, you should restrict your comments to a description of the other person's behaviour. Sticking with the facts and avoiding judgments about others allows them to tell you what's happening in their lives. There may be perfectly good reasons for their behaviour. Here are two possible approaches to the person who arrives late and leaves early.

POOR: "You're always late and you always leave early. It's obvious that you're not committed to our group. Or is it that you're just plain lazy?" [Judging the person]

BETTER: "You've arrived late and left early several times recently. Have we scheduled our meetings at a bad time?" [Describing behaviour]

Rule #6: Request Feedback, and Don't Ignore It

Requesting feedback from others is an excellent communication practice. First of all, it allows you to see whether the other person has understood your message. If the receiver has understood your message, you can let him know that he has. If he hasn't, you can clarify it. Second, requesting feedback gives you an opportunity to understand what the other person feels about what you have said. Finally, feedback can give you a chance to adjust your views or your behaviour in light of the views of others. Sometimes, but not always, that may be an important thing to do.

POOR: "I think that we should buy the Apple computer. It's got everything we need. My mind's made up." [Taking a position but not requesting feedback]

BETTER: "I think that we should buy the Apple computer. It's got everything we need. What do you think? Have I missed anything here?" [Taking a position but requesting feedback]

Asking for feedback but then ignoring the feedback that you get is not very helpful. For one thing, you're not likely to get feedback in the future.

> *Wisdom is the reward you get for a lifetime of listening when you would have preferred to talk.*
>
> —Doug Larson, newspaper columnist

POOR: "Well, I'm happy with the way I did that. If I had to do it again, I'd do exactly the same thing." [Ignoring feedback]

BETTER: "Well, I thought I had done a pretty good job. In light of what you've said, however, I can see an even better way to do it next time. Thank you." [Acting on feedback]

LISTENING EFFECTIVELY IN A DIALOGUE

The six rules we studied for sending messages are designed to help us do a better job of *speaking* more effectively. Now, we turn our attention to *listening* more effectively. **Active listening** is the name that we give to a three-fold process that includes the skills of expressing intention, listening with your whole person, and paraphrasing the messages of others. To be a good listener, you need to use all of these active listening skills. The rules that follow are designed to help you employ these skills in your communications with others. Here, then, are three important rules for listening effectively.

active listening
a three-fold process that includes the skills of expressing intention, listening with your whole person, and paraphrasing the messages of others

Rule #1: Communicate Your Intention to Listen

The first step in active listening is to let the speaker know that you want to hear his message and that you intend to listen. You can communicate your intention in two ways, by asking inviting questions and by using inviting statements.

- First, you can show your intention to listen by asking *inviting questions,* questions that encourage the speaker to elaborate on his views and feelings. Generally speaking, inviting questions cannot be answered with a single word, such as "yes" or "no." If, for example, I ask, "Would you please tell me all about yourself?" I am inviting you to disclose yourself to me in a way that encourages more than a one-word response.

- Second, you can express your intention to listen by using *inviting statements.* You might say, for instance, "I would love to hear your thoughts about the government. I'll bet they're very interesting." These statements invite the other person to share her thoughts with you in some detail. Our statements and our questions, when expressed sincerely, show others that we intend to listen and that we are genuinely interested in what they have to say.

Rule #2: Listen with Your Whole Person

Listening is often considered to be simply a matter of perking up one's ears. Active listening, however, involves much more than just your ears. To listen effectively, you need to listen with your whole person—your ears, your heart, your head, and your body.

Active listening starts with your feelings. In particular, it starts with empathy, the fellow feeling. *Empathy*, we noted in Chapter 3, is "feeling what another person feels" or "feeling with another person." It's a type of emotional connection that tends to engage our minds in the act of listening. Putting the point differently, an emotional connection leads to a cognitive connection. In effect, when we listen with our hearts, we also begin to listen with our heads.

Behavioural listening, or "listening with the body," is the natural result of both emotional (affective) and intellectual (cognitive) engagement with another person. For example, when a charismatic speaker has captured your attention (your heart and your head), you naturally lean forward to watch and listen; you are fully engaged. Good listeners listen with their whole persons.

behavioural listening
listening with one's whole person, the result of both emotional (affective) and intellectual (cognitive) engagement with another person

Rule #3: Paraphrase the Feelings and Ideas of the Sender

To **paraphrase** is to restate in different words what another person has said. This part of the communication process is extremely important, but it is often neglected in conversation. Paraphrasing is a key skill in providing feedback, and when you paraphrase the sender's message, you allow the sender to confirm that you have understood him correctly. If you have misunderstood, the sender can immediately clarify his message. We noted this important skill above in Rule #6 for sending messages effectively. Communication experts call this exchange between sender and receiver **negotiation**. They say that the two parties are *negotiating* for meaning; they are ensuring that they understand one another.

paraphrasing
the skill of accurately restating another's position in words different from the original

Since messages convey both ideas and feelings, active listeners paraphrase both aspects of the sender's message. When this occurs, both parties in the communication process "stay tuned" to each other at the level of emotions (affectively) and at the level of ideas (cognitively). The negotiation of meaning is made easier when both parties are attuned to each other. Active listening involves listening for both thoughts and feelings. It also requires paraphrasing both kinds of message, cognitive and affective.

negotiation
exchange between sender and receiver as they ensure that they understand one another

GIVING FEEDBACK EFFECTIVELY IN A DIALOGUE

In our model of communication (Figure 5.1), there are two phases in the process. In phase one, there is a sender and a receiver. In phase two, the original sender and receiver reverse roles. In two-way communication, we are always switching between the roles of sender and receiver. It should not be surprising, then, to find that the six rules for sending messages presented earlier in this chapter apply to the giving of feedback. In addition to those rules, however, there are three additional rules that are specific to giving feedback.[3]

---

3   Johnson (1993, pp. 38–39) presents eight rules. Four of those form the basis of this summary.

Rule #1: Don't Force Feedback on Others

Successful groups create supportive climates in which members can give and receive feedback freely and comfortably. Not all groups develop supportive climates, however, so it is important to note that you shouldn't force feedback on others. Rather, you and the other members of your group should work on creating and maintaining an environment in which feedback occurs naturally without threat or fear, so that everyone can benefit from it. We'll explain how to build a supportive climate in your group in Chapter 7.

Note, now, that there are two exceptions to rule #1. Two situations require that feedback be given, whether people welcome the feedback or not.

- First, in a performance review, your supervisor will give you feedback whether you want it or not. This is a necessary part of supervising others.

- Second, in the management of group conflict, it may be necessary to give feedback to a member even when the person does not want it. Constructive confrontation is an essential part of conflict resolution.

Rule #2: Target Specifics, Not Generalities

Good feedback zeroes in on specifics. Because the information is focused, it is more useful to the original sender. When you provide feedback to others, identify specific things that may be helpful to the other person, things that they can identify and change. For example, rather than saying that someone's overhead presentation wasn't helpful, tell them exactly what made the presentation weak. Perhaps there was too much information on each slide or the font was too small or the colour was washed out when projected on the screen. If you give constructive feedback on specifics, the other person can benefit more readily from your feedback.

> POOR: "Sometimes when you speak to the group you tend to pause quite a lot and that interrupts your flow of thought." [Feedback too general]
>
> BETTER: "I noticed that you said 'uh' and 'you know' several times during the course of your remarks, and each time I was distracted from your topic." [Feedback very specific]

The information in the second statement is more useful because the speaker learns precisely what aspects of his speech need work.

Rule #3: Offer Options, Not Advice

Many of us love to tell others what to do. It may be that we get some kind of ego boost from this or it may reflect a need, on our part, to control others, or both. In our conversations with others, all too often we give advice. If advice is specifically requested, it may be appropriate to offer some. However, unsolicited advice can inhibit communication.

When advice is not specifically asked for, you should focus on describing the other person's options as you see them. By highlighting the options, you can help others to see their situation more clearly. You avoid telling them what to do, but you help them identify their choices. In the process, you will help them to make better choices for themselves. In effect, offering options is a way of showing respect to others.

POOR: "I think you're crazy if you don't buy the Civic. There's no other choice." [Unsolicited advice]

BETTER: "For that money, you can get a Civic, a Jetta, or a Focus. Have you done a comparison?" [Offering options]

CHAPTER SUMMARY

After emphasizing the importance of good communication for both our professional lives and personal lives, we presented a descriptive model of the dialogue process. The model included the basic ideas of a sender, a receiver, and a message. The message, we noted, can be about ideas or feelings or both, and it can be delivered both verbally and non-verbally. Next, we examined noise, pointing out three forms of noise—physical, physiological, and psychological—that interfere with the dialogue process. Then we described the nature of two-way communication and underscored the importance of feedback messages. Next, keying in on the sender, we presented six rules for speaking effectively in a dialogue. These rules emphasized the importance of using "I" messages, providing frames of reference, conveying ideas clearly, describing feelings, avoiding judgments, and asking for feedback. Turning to the receiver, we reviewed three rules for active listening. These rules emphasized the importance of communicating intention, listening with your whole person, and paraphrasing the messages of others. Finally, focusing on feedback, we presented three rules for giving constructive feedback. These rules direct us to refrain from forcing feedback on others, to provide specific feedback to others, and to avoid giving unsolicited advice to others.

KEY TERMS

active listening

affective dimension

behavioural listening

cognitive dimension

communication

decoder

decoding

dialogue

encoder

encoding

feedback message

frame of reference

message

model

negotiation

noise

non-verbal communication

one-way communication

paraphrase

physical noise

physiological noise

psychological noise

receiver

sender

two-way communication

verbal communication

MASTERING THE MATERIAL

Now that you have read this chapter, use the following guides to ensure that you have mastered the material.

1. Identify the four main parts of the dialogue model presented in the text.

    a.

    b.

    c.

    d.

2. Putting a message into words is called _____.

3. Interpreting a message is called _____.

4. Message senders are sometimes called _____ because they put their thoughts and feelings into words.

5. Message receivers are sometimes called _____ because they interpret the sender's message.

6. What two types of message content do people usually send to one another?

    a.

    b.

7. We call the thinking side of our nature the _____ dimension.

8. We call the feeling side of our nature the _____ dimension.

9. The word "verbal" means _____ and includes both _____ words and _____ words.

10. Define *noise*.

11. Identify and explain three different kinds of noise.

    a.

    b.

    c.

12. Give examples of both one-way and two-way communication.

    a.

    b.

13. What is a feedback message?

14. From memory, list the six rules for speaking effectively in a dialogue.

   Rule #1:

   Rule #2:

   Rule #3:

   Rule #4:

   Rule #5:

   Rule #6:

15. From memory, list the three rules for listening effectively in a dialogue.

   Rule #1:

   Rule #2:

   Rule #3:

16. From memory, list the three rules for giving feedback effectively in a dialogue.

   Rule #1:

   Rule #2:

   Rule #3:

PRACTISING YOUR GROUP SKILLS

PURPOSE OF THIS SECTION

The purpose of "Practising Your Group Skills" and the ultimate purpose of this book is to help you become a more effective participant in the groups to which you belong. This section is designed to provide opportunities for you and your fellow students to practise your group skills in a structured environment.

TEAM RESPONSIBILITIES

A description of the team responsibilities for each of five different teams—the Executive Team, the Lesson Review Team, the Teaching Team, the Energizer Team, and the Evaluation Team—can be found in Appendix B, pages 177–180. Your professor may have chosen to use from one to five of these teams to conduct the teaching and learning activities of your class. Units 2 and 3 of the Teacher's Guide provide your professor with additional information on the responsibilities of these teams.

INDIVIDUAL ROLE RESPONSIBILITIES

A description of four individual role responsibilities—those of Leader, Recorder, Reporter, and Participant-Analyst—can be found in Appendix B, pages 180–182. Your professor may have chosen to use from one to four of these roles within teams to give individuals experience leading, recording, reporting, and analyzing. Units 2 and 3 of the Teacher's Guide provide your teacher with additional information on these individual role responsibilities.

SPECIFIC TEAM ASSIGNMENTS

Specific team assignments for this chapter appear immediately below. Specific team assignments for each of the subsequent chapters can be found in "Practising Your Group Skills" in each chapter.

CHAPTER 5 TEAM ASSIGNMENTS

THE EXECUTIVE TEAM

- *Your Ultimate Goal*: to provide leadership to your classmates for your class session on Chapter 5.
- *Your Interim Goals*: to facilitate the class session by (1) ensuring a good classroom setup, (2) welcoming the class, (3) introducing the lesson topic, (4) coordinating activities, and (5) bringing the session to a close.
- *Instructions*: Ensure that the classroom is set up to accommodate today's class activities. Post an agenda for the session. Welcome people to class and announce the topic, "Dialogue: Speaking and Listening Effectively in Your Group," in a creative and interesting way. Remind the class that the topic includes rules for speaking effectively, listening effectively, and giving feedback effectively. Introduce and thank all speakers when appropriate. Coordinate the day's activities and bring closure at the end of the class. If necessary, return the classroom to its original configuration.

THE LESSON REVIEW TEAM

- *Your Ultimate Goal*: to review Chapter 4, "Goals: Setting Clear Targets for Your Group."

- *Your Interim Goals*: to provide a review of (1) the experiential exercise, (2) the difference between ultimate goals and interim goals, (3) the correct way to write an effective goal statement, and (4) the five benefits of effective goals.

- *Instructions*: As the Lesson Review Team, you have the freedom to choose how you will do the review. You can be as creative as you wish, but you must achieve the lesson review goals above. Remember that your time is very limited, so don't try to re-teach last chapter's lesson.

THE TEACHING TEAM

- *Your Ultimate Goal*: to understand and demonstrate effective dialogue skills in a group setting.

- *Your Interim Goals*: to describe, explain, and demonstrate (1) six rules for speaking effectively, (2) three rules for listening effectively, and (3) three rules for giving constructive feedback.

- *Instructions*: As the Teaching Team, you have the freedom to choose how you will teach your lesson. You can be as creative as you wish, but you must achieve the lesson goals above. Your experiential exercise is called "One-Way and Two-Way Communication" and you'll find it described fully in Appendix C, pages 192–194. Make sure that you refer to it when you teach and explain your lesson goals. The exercise should also be included in the part of your lesson when you describe and explain the benefits of group goals. If time allows, you can also use exercises from "Mastering the Material" to teach your lesson.

THE ENERGIZER TEAM

- *Your Ultimate Goal*: to motivate your classmates by conducting an energizer activity.

- *Your Interim Goals*: to facilitate the energizing of your classmates by (1) planning an energizer activity and (2) implementing the plan at an appropriate time in the class session.

- *Instructions*: Your team doesn't have a specific, assigned activity to conduct. Rather, the team should remember its energizing purpose and conduct an activity that will provide a break in the class learning routine. Popular games like Simon Says, Heads Up Seven Up, and Murder Wink usually work well. So do various mixers and ice breakers. (Your professor's Teacher's Guide identifies a number of sources of energizer exercises.) Whatever you decide on, you must be prepared to give clear instructions and conduct the exercise effectively. When you lead the energizer, you are leading and directing the entire class. Plan well and execute professionally, even if the exercise is a "kid's game." Encourage everyone to get involved.

THE EVALUATION TEAM

As a member of the Evaluation Team, you need to review the information in Chapter 10, pages 145–148, before doing anything else. There you will find helpful information on how to conduct your evaluation session. The most important thing to remember is that you are not to judge other people. Your role is to help the class make its own assessment of which practices worked well today and which didn't.

- *Your Ultimate Goal*: to assess group (or class) members' dialogue practices.
- *Your Interim Goals*: to (1) assess the speaking skills, the listening skills, and the feedback skills within the group (or class) and (2) identify practices in need of improvement.
- *Instructions*: Create an evaluation instrument based on the selected focus behaviours identified in the evaluation goals above. See Chapter 10, pages 146–147, for information on creating evaluation instruments. Figure 10.1 provides an example. Solicit feedback from the class using the evaluation instrument. Use the feedback to discuss the class session with the purpose of identifying improvements that can be made to individual, group, and class performance in future class sessions. Conclude by noting the specific actions that need to be repeated or avoided to make improvements.

REFERENCES AND RECOMMENDED READINGS

Burley-Allen, M. (1995). *Listening: The forgotten skill* (2nd ed.). New York: John Wiley & Sons.

Engleberg, I.N., & Wynn, D.R. (1997). *Working in groups: Communication principles and strategies*. New York: Houghton Mifflin.

Frey, L.R., & Barge, J.K. (Eds.). (1997). *Managing group life: Communicating in decision-making groups*. Boston: Houghton Mifflin.

Harris, T.E., & Sherblom, J.C. (1999). *Small group and team communication*. Needham Heights, MA: Allyn & Bacon.

Johnson, D.W. (1993). *Reaching out* (5th ed.). Needham Heights, MA: Allyn & Bacon.

Johnson, D.W., & Johnson, F.P. (1997). *Joining together: Group theory and group skills* (6th ed.). Needham Heights, MA: Allyn & Bacon.

Nichols, M.P. (1995). *The lost art of listening*. New York: Guilford.

Wolvin, A.D., & Coakley, C.G. (1996). *Listening* (5th ed.). Madison, WI: Brown & Benchmark.

USEFUL URLS

About.com Human Resources. http://humanresources.about.com.

EffectiveMeetings.com. www.effectivemeetings.com.

Free Management Library. www.managementhelp.org.

MindTools. www.mindtools.com.

Pfeiffer. www.pfeiffer.com.

Team Technology. www.teamtechnology.co.uk.

Conflict: Resolving Disputes in Your Group

If you have learned how to disagree without being disagreeable, then you have discovered the secret of getting along—whether it be in business, family relations, or life itself.
—Bernard Meltzer, radio show host

INTRODUCTION

It is not uncommon for disputes to arise between members of small groups. Group dynamics are complex, and it isn't surprising that the interests of one member will conflict with those of others from time to time. These interpersonal disagreements are to be expected, as they are a natural part of group life. However, when they occur, such disagreements must be managed constructively.

Ideally, when disagreements arise within your team, the members who are in conflict will resolve their differences constructively among themselves. However, if they can't or won't do so, other team members will have to intervene to mediate a resolution of the conflict. In other words, they will have to function as conflict mediators in order to assist in resolving the issues and strengthening relationships among group members. In Chapter 1 we noted the important role of the Conflict Mediator, one of the six helpful social roles.

The current chapter will say a good deal more about conflict and how to deal with it, both as a *disputant* and as a *mediator*. A **disputant** is a person who is in conflict with another person or persons, and a **mediator** is a person who intervenes between or among disputants in order to help them reach an agreement or reconciliation. Before discussing these matters, however, we'll examine a number of other important aspects of interpersonal conflict.

We'll begin by taking a look at a positive form of conflict that should be encouraged on your team, and then we'll examine four potentially destructive forms of conflict. These negative forms of conflict are the

disputant

a person who is in conflict with another person or persons

mediator

a person who intervenes between or among disputants in order to help them reach an agreement or reconciliation

ones that require individual group members to dispute constructively with one another, and, if necessary, to seek the assistance of a mediator to ensure that the conflict is resolved successfully.

After describing a number of different conflict styles that individuals typically adopt when they're in conflict situations, we'll focus on the ideal way to engage in a conflict and provide some rules that individual disputants should follow when they find themselves in conflict with others. Hopefully, any disputes that arise in your group can be managed effectively by following these rules.

However, when two or more disputants on your team are unable to resolve their differences on their own, mediation is in order. We'll conclude our look at conflict by describing both the mediation process and the role of a mediator in dispute resolution, and we'll include a number of practical suggestions for dealing with disputes within your group.

Let's start with a desirable form of conflict that you should encourage within your team.

A DESIRABLE FORM OF CONFLICT

Conceptual conflict is a type of conflict that is beneficial to groups, and it is absolutely necessary for your team to experience it regularly if your team is to excel. This form of conflict should be promoted and encouraged because it is the type of conflict that leads a group to the best ideas and the best solutions to its problems and challenges.

conceptual conflict

beneficial conflict that critiques ideas, not people

ideational conflict

a second name for conceptual conflict

constructive controversy

a third name for conceptual conflict

The adjective "conceptual" derives from the word "concept," which means "idea." **Conceptual conflict** is a disagreement or controversy about ideas, opinions, or points of view. It is often referred to as a conflict of ideas or battle of ideas. Because this type of conflict is about competing ideas, it is also called **ideational conflict**, the word "ideational" deriving from the word "ideas." Finally, we should note that this type of conflict is sometimes called **constructive controversy**.

When group members engage in conceptual conflict, they critically challenge one another's ideas and thinking. They are involved in a criticism of ideas, not an attack on people. For example, Monica can criticize Andy's ideas without criticizing Andy as a person. To argue that Andy's suggestion is weak is not to attack him personally. Monica can criticize her teammate's ideas while supporting him as a person, and that is the essence of conceptual conflict.

Effective decision making and problem solving depend on the critical analysis of ideas, and conceptual conflict is designed to identify a group's best ideas. The best ideas should lead to the best decisions and the best solutions. Successful teams create an atmosphere in which members feel comfortable not only challenging the ideas of others but also having their own ideas challenged by others in their group.

There is a danger associated with conceptual conflict. Unfortunately, many of us take the criticism of our ideas personally. We think that a criticism of our suggestions is an attack on us because we seem unable to differentiate our ideas from our personalities. When group members take criticism of their ideas as personal affronts, then conceptual conflict can degenerate quickly into personality conflict, a destructive form of conflict that we'll examine shortly.

One of the biggest challenges in group life is to receive criticism of your ideas without taking the criticism personally. It requires a certain maturity and confidence to detach yourself from your ideas. It also requires maturity to criticize the ideas of others constructively without making the criticism personal. We'll return to these important ideas in detail in our study of critical discussion in Chapter 8.

FOUR DANGEROUS FORMS OF CONFLICT

Conflict within small groups can be defined as an interpersonal dispute between or among group members. Such disputes or disagreements occur for a variety of reasons. In this section, we'll discuss four types of conflict that can, if not dealt with appropriately, seriously harm relationships among group members. If unresolved, these forms of conflict are detrimental to group life. Let's now look at four dangerous forms of conflict.

conflict
an interpersonal dispute between or among members of a group

1. Personality Conflict

Conflict that is rooted in the differing personality traits of group members is called **personality conflict**. Perhaps one member is very easy-going while another is a hard-driving Type A personality. Ted, for example, may want to relax and enjoy the social aspects of the group meeting. In contrast, Fatima feels strongly that the group is lazy and not as productive as it should be. Ted and Fatima may clash because of their differing personalities.

personality conflict
an interpersonal dispute arising from differing personal traits

Since this form of conflict stems from differing personality traits, it is particularly difficult to manage. How do you get people to change their personalities? And in a conflict, who should do the changing? Despite the fact that it's impossible to get a leopard to change its spots, it is still possible to manage the leopard's behaviour. While this analogy may be a weak one, it still makes a point. Personality conflicts, like other conflicts, need to be managed constructively for the sake of the group.

In the previous section of this chapter, we said that conceptual conflict can easily disintegrate into personality conflict. For example, if two members of a team are both immature and unable to take criticism of their ideas, the battle of ideas may quickly turn into a battle of personalities. Instead of debating ideas, people end up attacking one another in a personality conflict that can upset the entire team.

If personality differences lead to conflict that is not managed well, it is easy to see how this can negatively affect a team's performance. In contrast, effective conflict management within small groups can lead to more harmonious and effective group performance and make life on the job more enjoyable. Indeed, when conflicts are resolved fairly and effectively, relationships often become stronger. Much of your time is spent with others in groups and, as noted in Chapter 1, you need to be an effective Conflict Mediator on your team. This can be an extremely rewarding experience, both for you personally and for those you help.

2. Resource Conflict

When a group lacks resources to do its work and disagreements arise as a result, the dispute is called **resource conflict**. When resources are scarce, group members are often forced to compete with one another for the available resources. Suppose there are only three computers for a group of five people, and each person needs

resource conflict
an interpersonal dispute arising from unequal distribution of resources

one. It is easy to see how conflicts might arise in this situation. Resource conflict often occurs in large organizations, such as hospitals and similar institutions, when one part of the organization gets a "better deal" than another. Resource conflict can, however, occur in small groups as well.

In our example, even if members try to share the use of the existing computers, you can see how easily disputes might occur. Mary, for example, thinks that her assignment has higher priority than Claude's, and that she, therefore, deserves the only available computer. Claude sees the situation very differently. He thinks that he needs it first. If Mary gets access to the computer before him, Claude may well accuse Mary of hogging it. Or he may keep pressuring her to hurry up and finish. This kind of behaviour is typical of group members who have to compete for scarce resources.

The obvious solution in this example is for the organization to buy more computers. While institutions are often to blame for inadequate resources, the interpersonal disputes that result need resolution at the personal level. Mary and Claude have to work together. They can't stop working until the company supplies them with another computer, so they need to resolve their disputes and get on with their jobs in the best way possible, given the lack of resources. They need to resolve their disputes constructively through some form of compromise.

3. Power Conflict

Sometimes people engage in power struggles in an attempt to gain control of a group. Two people, for example, keenly want to be leader of the group. They want to have the greatest influence among its members and, consequently, they get into disputes with one another as to who should be in charge. They may also try to court other members to gain their support against the rival. A **power conflict** is a dispute over control of a group or part of a group. Power conflicts often arise within political parties and large organizations. However, power struggles can occur in every kind of group, including small groups. Someone has to provide leadership in a group, and members often disagree over who that person should be.

Organizations that elect their leaders often experience power conflicts. A trade union provides a good example. Union members frequently compete for positions of power within the association. Sometimes this simply reflects healthy competition in a democratic organization. At other times, it degenerates into unhealthy personal conflict. Psychologists may have theories to explain why people engage in power struggles, but those theories are not our immediate interest. Rather, we need to understand the practical steps that need to be taken to resolve power conflicts when they occur. Regardless of *why* power conflicts occur, we need to know *how* to deal with them.

power conflict
an interpersonal dispute arising from the desire to control a group

4. Status Conflict

Status conflict occurs when members of a group compete for recognition within the group. Status conflict is not the same as power conflict, although they do often occur together. If Jack, for example, wants to exercise control over others in his group, then he may engage in a power conflict to achieve his goal. In contrast, if he simply wants to be on the executive so that he's recognized by others—wants

status conflict
an interpersonal dispute arising from the desire to be recognized within a group

Figure 6.1   Conflict Styles

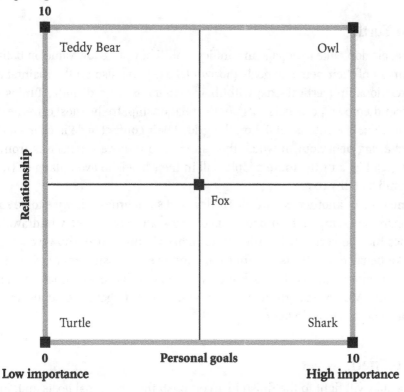

Source: Johnson and Johnson (1997, p. 284). Reprinted by permission.

to be seen as a "somebody"—then he may compete for status, without competing for power. Of course, Jack may be interested in both status and power. To distinguish between power conflict and status conflict, remember that the former is about control and the latter is about recognition

CONFLICT STYLES

Now that we have defined conflict and noted several different types of conflict, let's take a look at **conflict styles**, typical ways that people behave when they have disputes with others. Figure 6.1 represents a variety of conflict styles. The horizontal axis measures the degree to which individuals will fight for their personal goals. The extreme left (0) indicates little concern for one's own personal goals; the extreme right (10) indicates maximum concern for one's own goals. The vertical axis measures the degree to which the same individuals value their relationship with the person(s) with whom they are in the conflict.[1] The bottom of the vertical line (0) marks the point of little or no interest, while the top (10) marks maximum interest

conflict style
the manner in which a group member typically engages in disputes with others

---

1   The distinction between one's own goals and the importance of the relationship was introduced into conflict studies by Blake and Mouton (1964). Since then various authors have used these two dimensions to discuss conflict styles. Thomas and Kilmann (1974) use the terms "avoiding," "competing," "accommodating," "compromising," and "collaborating." My description follows Johnson and Johnson (1997, pp. 340–341). The animal designations, I believe, originate with them.

in the relationship. By using this grid, we can plot five distinctly different conflict styles with each style represented by a different animal.

1. The Turtle

Some people don't like to engage in conflict at all. They place low value on both the achievement of their personal goals (horizontal axis) and also on the maintenance of the relationship (vertical axis) with their disputants. In a dispute, **Turtles** care for neither their own personal goals nor the relationship. In the most extreme case, these individuals would be at 0,0 on the grid. Their conflict style is characterized by **withdrawing behaviour** in which they attempt to remove themselves from the conflict. Just like a turtle, these people pull in their heads to avoid danger. Turtles avoid conflict at any cost.

At one time or another, we are all Turtles, and sometimes it is wise to be so. To use an extreme example, if a mugger wielding a knife accosts you, withdrawal and avoidance may be perfectly in order. In ordinary circumstances, however, regular turtle-like behaviour reflects an unhealthy and overly passive approach to interpersonal relationships. Turtles lack the assertiveness that is essential for mature relationships. Moreover, a group of turtles is not likely to get much done and will never become an effective team.

2. The Shark

Some people will fight to the finish to accomplish their personal goals and, in the process, care little or nothing about their relationship with the other party. In a dispute, **Sharks** place high value on their own goals and care little for the relationship. In the extreme, these individuals would be at 10 on the horizontal axis and 0 on the vertical axis. They adopt a win–lose approach to conflict, and intend to be the winners. Like a shark moving in for the kill, these individuals apply force to come out on top. *Sharks* will engage in **forcing behaviour** in an attempt to win at all costs. Forcing behaviour is intimidating, threatening, or coercive behaviour.

We can all be Sharks at times, but some people regularly adopt this approach. They are ready at any time to eat up the opposition. Sharks are aggressive when it comes to conflict, and they can be very detrimental to a group. We first met the Shark when we studied harmful roles in Chapter 1. There, you will recall, we described the harmful effects of the Dominator and the Aggressor. A group full of sharks will try to destroy one another and they will never become a team. At times being a Shark may be necessary, but regular aggression causes serious problems.

3. The Teddy Bear

Some people will do anything to maintain a relationship, even give up their personal goals. They try to preserve the relationship at all costs, giving up their goals in order to preserve harmony. In a dispute, **Teddy Bears** place great value on the relationship and little value on their own goals. In the extreme case, these individuals will be at the 0,10 position on the grid. They try to smooth out the bumps or rough edges in their relationships. Teddy Bears are known for their **smoothing behaviour.**

Turtle
conflict style of one who withdraws or avoids conflict

withdrawing behaviour
avoiding conflict by removing oneself from a dispute

Shark
conflict style of one who forces others to do his will

forcing behaviour
using intimidating behaviour to get one's way in a dispute

Teddy Bear
conflict style of one who smoothes things over to maintain harmony

smoothing behaviour
attempting to "rub the rough edges off" a dispute

As with the other conflict styles, most of us will be Teddy Bears at one time or another. Sometimes, for example, more will be accomplished in a relationship if you "pour oil on troubled waters." That is, more will be gained by temporarily setting aside your personal goals for the sake of the relationship. For some people, however, smoothing is their typical approach to conflict. Such passive behaviour is not healthy, either for one's group or for oneself. A group of Teddy Bears may be reasonably good at superficial socializing, but they are not likely to develop mature relationships that result in team productivity.

4. The Fox

Some people are willing to compromise—that is, to give up something in order to get something in return. A compromise is an agreement that is reached when both sides make concessions. In a dispute, **Foxes** balance concern for achieving their goals with concern for the relationship. Because each gives up some personal goals, this approach could be described as a lose–lose approach. However, since both parties also gain something, it is equally appropriate to call this a win–win situation. In our presentation, we'll emphasize this more positive view. Compromise is essential if disputing parties are to deal reasonably with their conflicts. Foxes use **compromising behaviour** to resolve interpersonal conflicts.

Once again, most of us are Foxes at one time or another, taking the 5,5 position on the conflict grid. Some individuals, however, make this their typical style. Foxes are neither aggressive nor passive. In contrast to the Shark and the Teddy Bear, Foxes are rationally self-interested when in conflict with others. This means that they calculate their possible gains and losses, and then act in their own self-interest. A group full of foxes may become an effective team, but they will likely fall short in the area of team spirit and cohesion. Nevertheless, engaging in conflict like a Fox is generally good, but there is an even better way to deal with conflict.

Fox
conflict style of one who compromises to resolve differences

compromising behaviour
making concessions to resolve a dispute

5. The Owl

The ideal conflict style is one that takes a real win–win approach to conflict. In a dispute, **Owls** try to achieve their own goals, they try to help the other party achieve their goals, and they try to strengthen the relationship. This style requires **confronting behaviour** that leads to an ideal solution. To confront means to face up to and deal directly with a problem or situation. If disputants can confront each other and resolve their conflict by having both parties achieve their personal goals and by improving the relationship, then both parties have been very wise indeed. *Owls* wisely confront to achieve a true win–win solution. Owls take the 10,10 position on the grid.

Ideally, we should all be Owls all the time. In reality, however, such wise solutions occur too infrequently. Nevertheless, there is nothing to keep us from trying to resolve our interpersonal problems in this way. Owls are assertive rather than aggressive, recognizing both their own rights and the rights of others. In addition, they are altruistic, showing genuine concern for others, yet egoistic, seeking their own self-interest. A group of Owls will become a true team, practising constructive confrontation and collaboration. They will get the job done and have mutual respect for one another.

Owl
conflict style of one who confronts in order to achieve win–win solutions

confronting behaviour
facing up to and dealing reasonably with others in a dispute

Different situations require different approaches to conflict, and different individuals have different conflict styles. To be an effective group member, you need to understand withdrawing, forcing, smoothing, compromising, and confronting behaviours, and consciously choose the style most appropriate to the circumstances. Throughout, however, you should strive to be the wise, confronting owl.

ASSERTIVE COMMUNICATION

When you are in a conflict, your respect for the other person is critically important, as is the other person's respect for you. If there is mutual respect between you, then there is hope for resolving your differences. Mutual respect between disputing parties allows both individuals to *compromise* (the approach of the Fox) and to *confront* (the approach of the Owl) in order to overcome differences between them. In other words, mutual respect empowers both parties to resolve their conflict.

However, the respect you have for yourself is also an essential ingredient in conflict resolution. It is your self-respect that empowers you to prevent abuse from others or to end abuse from others. It is your self-respect that enables you to stand up for yourself and your rights when others ignore them or try to take them away. Unfortunately, those individuals who lack sufficient self-esteem and self-respect to defend themselves become the victims of others.

assertive communication
communication between and among disputing group members in which self-respect, together with respect for others, aids in conflict resolution

Assertive communication is communication that respects the rights of both parties in a dispute. These two forms of respect—respect for others and self-respect—are the keys to effective conflict resolution between disputing parties. They enable both parties to compromise, to confront, and to collaborate in the resolution of their disagreements. Respect for others and self-respect are at the heart of assertive communication, the kind of communication that is required to solve interpersonal disputes. Not all people, however, practice assertive communication.

passive person
one who lacks sufficient self-respect to defend his or her rights in a dispute and withdraws from conflict

Passive persons who have low self-esteem or no self-esteem are at one end of the communication spectrum. They don't stand up for their own rights in a conflict because they lack self-respect in conflict situations. They will not, for example, speak up for themselves to defend their interests. In this regard, they are Turtles.

aggressive person
one whose concern for personal rights outweighs concern for the rights of others

Aggressive persons, at the opposite end of the spectrum, take their own rights seriously but ignore the rights of others. They speak up for themselves but don't listen to or care about others. Aggressive persons are the Sharks of this world and they'll gladly eat the opposition.

assertive person
one whose self-interest is balanced by concern for others, who speaks up yet also listens

In contrast to both passive and aggressive persons, **assertive persons** respect their own rights as well as those of others. They speak up, but they also listen respectfully. Some people communicate passively, others communicate aggressively, and still others communicate assertively. Like the Owl and the Fox, you should communicate assertively with others.

RULES FOR DISPUTING CONSTRUCTIVELY WITH OTHERS IN YOUR GROUP

The respectful, assertive communication that we described in the previous section is the communication style of the confronting Owl, who represents the ideal approach to conflict resolution. The rules below are consistent with the Owl's approach.

If you follow these rules, you will bring the wisdom of the Owl to bear on the conflicts that you help to resolve. To some degree, the compromising Fox also practices assertive communication, but it is the Owl who sets the highest standard.

Rule #1: Be Assertive

Most conflict involves some degree of aggression. Hostile words, for example, are a form of aggression in which inner anger is outwardly expressed. It's quite natural for people in disputes to react emotionally with anger. Unfortunately, words spoken in anger tend to intensify the conflict rather than resolve it. Frequently, the parties in a conflict behave like Sharks. The key to resolving conflicts lies in more rational behaviour, the assertive behaviour of the Owl.

In any conflict, you should *know* your rights and the rights of the other party. In addition, you should *respect* your rights and those of the other person. If you communicate assertively and choose an appropriate time and place for confronting the other person, there is a good chance that the dispute can be resolved. Healthy conflict resolution is characterized by assertive communication. In conflict, then, you should be assertive, not aggressive and not passive.

> *Whenever you're in conflict with someone, there is one factor that can make the difference between damaging your relationship and deepening it. That factor is attitude.*
>
> —William James, psychologist

Rule #2: Use Your Best Speaking Skills

Conflict resolution is possible only when assertive communication is effective. In Chapter 5 we noted six rules for speaking effectively in a dialogue. These rules of effective communication need to be followed in the process of managing conflicts. In conflict, as in all situations, you should

- Use first-person pronouns in your messages.
- Convey your frame of reference.
- Present your ideas clearly and concisely.
- Describe your feelings, don't express them.
- Describe behaviours, don't judge the person.
- Request and pay attention to feedback.

Rule #3: Use Your Best Listening Skills

Active listening is also critical to the resolution of interpersonal conflicts. Chapter 5 presented three rules for listening effectively in a dialogue, and these rules should be followed as you try to resolve your differences with others. Remember, always

- Communicate your intention to listen.
- Listen with your whole person.
- Paraphrase the ideas and feelings of the sender.

In a heightened emotional state, it is easy to talk and not listen. Often, we don't want to hear what the other person has to say. The third rule for disputing constructively reminds you to use your best listening skills when communicating in a conflict situation.

Rule #4: Jointly Define the Conflict

Conflicts will never get resolved if the disputing parties don't agree on the nature of the problem. Conflict resolution is a special kind of problem solving, and the first step in solving any problem is to define it clearly, concisely, and accurately. "What, exactly, is our problem?" is the important question. The answer to that question must be clear and acceptable to both parties in a dispute.

In other words, you must jointly define the problem with your adversary. Together, you need to define the exact nature of your dispute. In addition to jointly defining your problem, you should define the problem as one which can be solved in a win–win way. Win–lose approaches should be avoided. In conflict, then, you should define the problem together with the person with whom you are in conflict.

Rule #5: Encourage Negotiation in Good Faith

The win–win approach can be strengthened if both parties indicate, sincerely and clearly, that they want to resolve the dispute. Expressed differently, you need to encourage negotiation in good faith. Negotiations will succeed only if there is mutual trust between the parties in dispute. It is essential, therefore, for you to build and maintain trust between you and your adversary. This can be done in part by expressing the intention to find a mutually acceptable solution.

In addition, good-faith bargaining will be encouraged if both you and your adversary understand the *benefits* to each of you of finding a solution, and the *costs* to each of you of not finding one. Notice, here, that the compromising Fox stands ready to accept certain costs in resolving the dispute. The Fox will lose a bit to win a bit. The Fox is willing to make concessions.

In contrast, the confronting Owl strives to have only benefits and no costs *for both parties*. This expectation—both of you will be winners and neither will be a loser—is why the Owl represents the ideal in conflict resolution. In your conflicts, encourage negotiation in good faith by expressing your intention to bargain sincerely and by identifying the costs and benefits of not resolving the dispute.

Rule #6: Confront in Order to Reach an Agreement

Being assertive, speaking and listening effectively, jointly defining the problem, and negotiating in good faith are all typical of both the Fox and the Owl. We noted earlier that while the Fox's position can be described as a lose–lose approach, it can also be viewed more positively as a win–win approach. The Fox compromises to resolve a dispute, winning some but also losing some.

The approach of the confronting Owl, however, places the emphasis more clearly on win–win solutions. Confrontation—communicating directly, honestly, and assertively—is the ideal, and it takes a great deal of maturity to engage in constructive confrontation. When you and the others in your group confront your interpersonal problems with the win–win hope of the Owl, your team will be in a position to handle virtually any problem that comes along. When conflict is seen as a problem to be solved, parties who respect one another can usually agree to a mutually beneficial solution. You should confront, then, to reach an agreement that benefits everyone concerned: you, your adversary, and the other members of your team.

MEDIATION

If all members in a group dispute issues constructively and function as conflict mediators, there is a high probability that disputes will be avoided, or, if they do arise, that they will be resolved by the group. However, while many groups and in-

Strategies and Techniques of Mediators

Mediators use a variety of strategies and techniques when helping parties solve problems. The following are some of the essential steps and skills that can be used in your own group when working to solve problems.

1. *Improve communication among group members* Mediators (a) encourage reluctant speakers to tell their story, (b) ask questions to learn more about the concerns raised by each speaker, and (c) demonstrate ("model") active or effective listening. Mediators are especially effective at summarizing the contribution of each member and then providing an opportunity for others to ask clarifying questions. It is important that everyone fully understand the problem from the perspective of each group member.

2. *Issue identification and agenda setting* After everyone has spoken, questioned, and listened, the mediator will summarize the group's issues (often on a flip chart) and suggest an order in which the issues can be tackled (the agenda). Having a plan about when and how each issue will be addressed is essential if the group is to be successful. Most mediators will propose that the group tackle the easiest issues first and then move on to the more difficult ones, after the group has experienced some success with the initial issues.

3. *Brainstorming and option generation* This is the most creative part of mediation, and it involves the mediator working with the group to identify as many ideas (options) as possible about how to solve the issues facing the group. Mediators are especially adept at facilitating these brainstorming sessions and suggesting options, either on an issue-by-issue basis or as one comprehensive solution.

4. *Winning agreement of all group members* The best solutions are those discovered and supported by the group. This may mean that the mediator will have to meet with some group members individually (a caucus) to better understand their concerns and then help them see either the advantages of an emerging solution or the disadvantage for the group if an agreement can't be reached. Either way, the mediator works with all parties to find a result that everyone "can live with."

For examples and information about more formal institutional mediation services, search for mediation at the following sites:

- Ministry of Attorney General, Government of British Columbia at **www.gov.bc.ca/ag**.
- Department of Justice, Government of Australia at **justice.vic.gov.au**.
- Durham College, School of Justice & Emergency Services at **jes.durhamcollege.ca**.

dividuals are capable of solving their own problems, other groups struggle and get bogged down. This may be because individual group members lack facilitation and problem-solving skills, because the group lacks an effective procedure for tackling its problems, or because the group has a history of suspicion and mistrust and the members simply cannot work together. In such cases, mediation—specifically, facilitated or problem-solving mediation—can be a very effective way for groups to solve problems together.[2]

mediation

the process in which a person (the mediator) intervenes between the disputants to help them reach an agreement or reconciliation

In its most basic form, **mediation** is the process in which a person (the mediator) intervenes between disputants to help them reach an agreement or reconciliation. In other words, it is the addition of an "outsider" whose sole function is to assist disputants in resolving their differences. The independent mediator may be a professional, or a peer or trusted friend of the parties in conflict. The use of a mediator is an increasingly popular way for groups to resolve especially difficult disputes, and is particularly useful for groups whose members have an ongoing relationship and where there is a need to resolve a conflict so that each member can continue to work as a part of the group.

Mediators help the disputing parties clarify the nature of their dispute, identify their individual interests in the dispute, and reach a win–win resolution of the dispute. They don't take sides, and they don't try to impose their own solution on the disputants. Rather, they are active listeners and good speakers who use their dialogue skills to help the disputing parties resolve their differences. The important thing is that the mediator be independent and work with *all* members of the group to reach a mutually satisfactory resolution of the issues. The mediator has no power to make a decision for the group. His or her sole role is to assist the members in reaching their own decision, preferably through a form of interest-based problem solving or negotiation.

If a mediator is invited to help parties resolve a dispute or make a decision, the disputants must first commit to observing certain guidelines. First, they must be willing to solve their problem and abide by the dialogue rules that the mediator puts in place. Second, they must agree to listen actively to the other person without interrupting. Third, they must agree to show respect for the other party throughout the proceedings. Through respectful dialogue, the parties and the mediator seek a solution that is acceptable to both parties. Once a settlement appears to be achieved, the mediator ensures that both parties have the same understanding of the settlement. Once an agreement is reached, it will be written down and signed by both parties in a more formal setting. In a less formal setting, a handshake will suffice.

---

2   The author is grateful to Paul Emond, professional mediator, for the valuable contribution that he has made to the chapter section on mediation and mediators.

CHAPTER SUMMARY

In this chapter we have examined conflicts of interest and their resolution. We defined conflict as an interpersonal dispute and then described conceptual conflict, a form of dispute that is necessary and beneficial within teams. Conceptual conflict involves a healthy critiquing of ideas that avoids criticizing people. It is essential for bringing out the best ideas in a group. Next we examined four common but dangerous forms of conflict that are problematic and need resolution—personality conflict, resource conflict, power conflict, and status conflict. Then, we identified five conflict styles that people typically employ in their disputes with others. These styles are represented by various animals: the Turtle, the Shark, the Teddy Bear, the Fox, and the Owl. Each places different emphasis, in a conflict, on the importance of achieving personal goals versus maintaining good relationships. We then proceeded to emphasize the importance of respect and assertive communication in the resolution of disputes. Next, we examined six rules for managing conflicts effectively. These rules emphasized the importance of being assertive, speaking effectively, listening actively, defining the problem mutually, encouraging trust in negotiations, and confronting constructively. We concluded with a brief description of the mediation process and the approach to mediation taken by professional dispute resolution services.

KEY TERMS

aggressive person	mediation
assertive communication	mediator
assertive person	Owl
compromising behaviour	passive person
conceptual conflict	personality conflict
conflict	power conflict
conflict style	resource conflict
confronting behaviour	Shark
constructive controversy	smoothing behaviour
disputant	status conflict
forcing behaviour	Teddy Bear
Fox	Turtle
ideational conflict	withdrawing behaviour

MASTERING THE MATERIAL

Now that you have read this chapter, use the following guides to ensure that you have mastered the material.

1. Identify the social role from Chapter 1 that is most relevant to this chapter.

2. Define *conflict*.

3. Define *disputant*.

4. Define *mediator*.

5. Explain *conceptual conflict* and its importance.

6. Conceptual conflict is also called _____ conflict and constructive _____.

7. Identify and describe four dangerous types of conflict that are potentially harmful to groups.

    a.

    b.

    c.

    d.

8. The five conflict styles are distinguished by the different values that they place on two aspects of group experience. Identify those aspects.

    a.

    b.

9. From memory, identify the five styles of conflict and the distinguishing behaviour associated with each style. Use the various animals to identify each style.

    a.

    b.

    c.

    d.

    e.

10. The two forms of respect that underlie assertive communication are _____ and _____.

11. Describe the behaviour of a passive person in a conflict.

12. Describe the behaviour of an aggressive person in a conflict.

13. Describe the behaviour of an assertive person in a conflict.

14. From memory, list the six rules for disputing constructively with others.

    a.

    b.

    c.

    d.

    e.

    f.

15. Define *mediation*.

16. Describe several key aspects of a mediator's role.

    a.

    b.

    c.

    d.

    e.

    f.

17. What important commitments are required of a disputant in mediation?

    a.

    b.

    c.

18. Identify four specific strategies and techniques used by mediators.

    a.

    b.

    c.

    d.

PRACTISING YOUR GROUP SKILLS

PURPOSE OF THIS SECTION

The purpose of "Practising Your Group Skills" and the ultimate purpose of this book is to help you become a more effective participant in the groups to which you belong. This section is designed to provide opportunities for you and your fellow students to practise your group skills in a structured environment.

TEAM RESPONSIBILITIES

A description of the team responsibilities for each of five different teams—the Executive Team, the Lesson Review Team, the Teaching Team, the Energizer Team, and the Evaluation Team—can be found in Appendix B, pages 177–180. Your professor may have chosen to use from one to five of these teams to conduct the teaching and learning activities of the class. Units 2 and 3 of the Teacher's Guide provide your professor with additional information on the responsibilities of these teams.

INDIVIDUAL ROLE RESPONSIBILITIES

A description of four individual role responsibilities—those of Leader, Recorder, Reporter, and Participant-Analyst—can be found in Appendix B, pages 180–182. Your professor may have chosen to use from one to four of these roles within teams to give individuals experience leading, recording, reporting, and analyzing. Units 2 and 3 of the Teacher's Guide provide your professor with additional information on these individual role responsibilities.

SPECIFIC TEAM ASSIGNMENTS

Specific team assignments for this chapter appear immediately below. Specific team assignments for each of the subsequent chapters can be found in "Practising Your Group Skills" in each chapter.

CHAPTER 6 TEAM ASSIGNMENTS

THE EXECUTIVE TEAM

- *Your Ultimate Goal*: to provide leadership to your classmates for your class session on Chapter 6.
- *Your Interim Goals*: to facilitate the class session by (1) ensuring a good classroom setup, (2) welcoming the class, (3) introducing the lesson topic, (4) coordinating activities, and (5) bringing the session to a close.
- *Instructions*: Ensure that the classroom is set up to accommodate today's class activities. Post an agenda for the session. Welcome people to class and announce the topic, "Conflict: Resolving Disputes in Your Group," in a creative and interesting way. Remind the class that conflict in groups is normal but must be handled effectively if groups are to become strong teams. Introduce and thank all speakers when appropriate. Coordinate the day's activities and bring closure at the end of the class. If necessary, return the classroom to its original configuration.

THE LESSON REVIEW TEAM

- *Your Ultimate Goal*: to review Chapter 5, "Dialogue: Speaking and Listening Effectively in Your Group."

- *Your Interim Goals*: to provide a review of (1) the experiential exercise, (2) six rules for speaking effectively, (3) three rules for active listening, and (4) three rules for giving constructive feedback.

- *Instructions*: As the Lesson Review Team, you have the freedom to choose how you will do the review. You can be as creative as you wish, but you must achieve the review objectives. Remember that your time is very limited, so don't try to re-teach last chapter's lesson.

THE TEACHING TEAM

- *Your Ultimate Goal*: to understand and demonstrate effective conflict resolution skills in a small group setting.

- *Your Interim Goals*: to describe, explain, and demonstrate (1) five different conflict styles and (2) six effective practices (rules) for managing conflict in small groups.

- *Instructions*: As the Teaching Team, you have the freedom to choose how you will teach your lesson. You can be as creative as you wish, but you must achieve the lesson goals above. Your experiential exercise is called "Conflict Styles" and you'll find it described fully in Appendix C, pages 194–195. Make sure that you refer to it when you teach and explain your lesson goals. The exercise should also be included in the part of your lesson when you describe and explain the five conflict styles and the six rules for managing conflict effectively. If time allows, you can also use exercises from "Mastering the Material" to teach your lesson.

THE ENERGIZER TEAM

- *Your Ultimate Goal*: to motivate your classmates by conducting an energizer activity.

- *Your Interim Goals*: to facilitate the energizing of your classmates by (1) planning an energizer activity and (2) implementing the plan at an appropriate time in the class session.

- *Instructions*: Your team doesn't have a specific, assigned activity to conduct. Rather, the team should remember its energizing purpose and conduct an activity that will provide a break in the class learning routine. Popular games like Simon Says, Heads Up Seven Up, and Murder Wink usually work well. So do various mixers and ice breakers. (Your professor's Teacher's Guide identifies a number of sources of energizer exercises.) Whatever you decide on, you must be prepared to give clear instructions and conduct the exercise effectively. When you lead the energizer, you are leading and directing the entire class. Plan well and execute professionally, even if the exercise is a "kid's game." Encourage everyone to get involved.

THE EVALUATION TEAM

As a member of the Evaluation Team, you need to review the information in Chapter 10, pages 145–148, before you do anything else. There you will find helpful information on how to conduct your evaluation session. The most important thing to remember is that you are not to judge other people. Your role is to help the class make its own assessment of which practices worked well today and which didn't.

- *Your Ultimate Goal*: to assess group (or class) members' conflict resolution skills.
- *Your Interim Goals*: to (1) assess the different conflict styles and conflict resolution skills within the group (or class) and (2) identify practices in need of improvement.
- *Instructions*: Create an evaluation instrument based on the selected focus behaviours identified in the evaluation goals above. See Chapter 10, pages 146–147, for information on creating evaluation instruments. Figure 10.1 provides an example. Solicit feedback from the class using the evaluation instrument. Use the feedback to discuss the class session with the purpose of identifying improvements that can be made to individual, group, and class performance in future class sessions. Conclude by noting the specific actions that need to be repeated or avoided to make improvements.

REFERENCES AND RECOMMENDED READINGS

Blake, R.R., & Mouton, J.S. (1985). *The managerial grid III*. Houston, TX: Gulf.

Deutsch, M. (1973). *The resolution of conflict*. New Haven, CT: Yale University Press.

Ellis, D.G., & Fisher, A.B. (1994). *Small group decision making* (4th ed.). New York: McGraw-Hill.

Filley, A.C. (1988). *Interpersonal conflict resolution* (2nd ed.). Glenview, IL: Scott, Foresman.

Johnson, D.W., & Johnson, R. (1997). *Creative conflict*. Edina, MN: Interaction Book Company.

Rubin, J., Pruitt, D., & Kim, S. (1994). *Social conflict*. New York: McGraw-Hill.

USEFUL URLS

About.com Human Resources. http://humanresources.about.com.

Free Management Library. www.managementhelp.org.

MindTools. www.mindtools.com.

Pfeiffer Publishing. http://ca.pfeiffer.com/WileyCDA/Section/index.html.

Team Technology. www.teamtechnology.co.uk.

Your Meeting Resource Center. www.effectivemeetings.com.

Cohesion: Building Your Group into a Unified Team

7

Coming together is a beginning. Keeping together is progress. Working together is success.
—Henry Ford, founder, Ford Motor Company

INTRODUCTION

Many jobs in today's work world require teamwork, and many schools preparing students for the workplace include group work in their program of studies. In hospitals, factories, offices, and schools, teams of workers get the jobs done. We see the same phenomenon in the design, manufacturing, and marketing of products for our modern consumer economy. Cooperative efforts between and among inter-dependent employees are a necessity in a marketplace that is extremely competitive and rapidly changing. The world in which we live and work is a world of groups and group dynamics.

In its most general sense, the word "group" refers to a number of people who are located close together. In this sense, several strangers waiting at a bus stop are a group, even though they don't know each other or have any relationship to one another apart from waiting for the bus.

In contrast, the word "team" implies that the members of a group collaborate to accomplish some common task, share a common sense of identity, and have some shared sense of unity. Moreover, when members participate in this experience with enthusiasm and commitment, we say that the team has "spirit."

It is highly likely that in both your educational career and in your future employment you will be put into groups with strangers and given tasks to do. When this happens, you can help to make the experience more enjoyable and more productive. This chapter is dedicated to helping you develop the skills and attitude necessary to build your group into a unified team that gets its work done with spirit.

In this chapter, we'll examine the typical stages of group development, the characteristics of a cohesive team, the nature and importance of trust, six rules for building a unified team, and three benefits of being a member of a team. We'll start with the stages that groups typically go through as they develop over time.

CHAPTER GOALS

After completing this chapter, you should be able to:

- Identify and describe five stages of group development.
- Define *cohesion*.
- Identify three characteristics of a cohesive team.
- Define *cooperation*, *unity*, and *identity*.
- Define *trust*.
- Identify three actions that are characteristic of trust.
- State and explain six rules for building a group into a cohesive team.
- Describe three benefits of team membership.

STAGES OF GROUP DEVELOPMENT

Social scientists have studied the stages that groups go through from the time they form to the time that they disband. Different researchers have described the process in different ways. One of the simplest and most useful summaries identifies five typical stages in the development of a group. Since groups are as diverse as their members, we shouldn't assume that this pattern is always the same. When you are a member of a newly formed group, however, chances are that you will experience the following stages as your group develops.[1]

1. Forming

forming stage
first stage of group development marked by uncertainty and anxiety

Stage 1 is the **forming stage**, and it is marked by great uncertainty within the group. Since the group has just formed, people don't know one another and they are often reluctant to say very much. They may not trust one another. It is a time for sizing up the other members of the group. Many members will be tentative and some will be downright anxious. More assertive members may take advantage of this situation and try to give direction to the group, but, for the most part, no one is very sure how things will develop.

2. Storming

storming stage
second stage of group development marked by conflict

After a period of time, the group is likely to enter the **storming stage**. Stage 2 gets its name from the fact that members tend to get angry and upset with one another as they begin to express themselves more readily and as differences of opinion begin to surface. It quickly becomes evident that different members have different expectations for the group. Emotions begin to storm. Feelings run high and disputes occur frequently. Often there is a jockeying for positions of leadership and influence as different members try to get others to do things their way. Usually an absence of clear norms contributes to the upset that members feel. This is often a challenging and upsetting time for group members. It is a time of emotional storms that result from both greater openness in the group and an absence of rules.

3. Norming

norming stage
third stage of group development marked by agreement on rules

Before long, members realize they aren't getting the job done, and that storming is both uncomfortable and unhealthy. Eventually, cooler heads prevail, and members begin to share their expectations for the group. In the **norming stage**, rules of conduct are established formally or informally, and the group begins to stabilize as members conduct themselves according to newly established norms. The norming stage is a time in which adherence to the rules creates a new atmosphere within the group, one in which members can begin to get down to work. This stage prepares the group for the next stage, the stage of productivity.

---

1   Stage theories in group studies are numerous. This section reflects the work of Tuckman (1965, pp. 384–389).

4. Performing

Stage 4, the **performing stage**, is characterized by productivity. The group gets down to work as cooperation replaces conflict, and members work together to achieve common goals. With the successful achievement of goals, the group often experiences a greater sense of cohesion and identity, and members accomplish both task goals and social goals more effectively as a team.

performing stage
the fourth stage of group development marked by productivity

5. Adjourning

Some groups have a long life span, while others do not. At some time, most groups disband. Stage 5 is the **adjourning stage**. The experience of team members at the end of a group's life depends very much on how the group performed. The members of ineffective groups that have struggled throughout with ongoing difficulties may greet adjournment with relief. Members of highly productive and cohesive teams may reach adjournment and experience sadness as well as accomplishment.

adjourning stage
the last stage of group development marked by dispersal

Bearing in mind that not all groups will necessarily go through these stages in the order presented, let's now proceed to examine the key characteristics of a group that has become a team.

THREE CHARACTERISTICS OF A COHESIVE TEAM

Cohesion is the act of uniting or sticking together. In chemistry we talk about molecular cohesion and in group studies we talk about group-member cohesion, teammates uniting or sticking together. Teams that are truly cohesive can be identified by three characteristics.

cohesion
the act of uniting or sticking together

The first characteristic of a cohesive team is a shared commitment to **cooperation**, a mutual effort to achieve common goals. Successful teams consist of individual members who willingly and enthusiastically collaborate to achieve common goals. When individuals cooperate, they freely combine their energy to get a job done, and their collaborative effort contributes to a sense of mutual accomplishment. It quite naturally generates good feelings among the collaborators. "Collaboration," of course, is another word for "cooperation."

cooperation
a mutual effort to achieve common goals; also called colloboration

The second characteristic of a cohesive team is a shared sense of **unity**, a sense of oneness or togetherness. Sometimes groups form and get the job done, but group members don't feel a sense of belonging. They complete their tasks but they don't feel or function like a unified team. On a cohesive team, members move beyond minimal commitment and cooperation to a real sense of unity. They stick together, they want to stick together, and they feel as if they truly are a unit.

unity
a shared sense of oneness or togetherness

The third characteristic of a cohesive team is a shared sense of **identity**, a shared sense of sameness. For example, we may identify with our family, our school, or our country. In some way, we feel the same as others in our group and we feel good about that. Members who identify with their group feel that they are members of a team. Team colours, uniforms, logos, pennants, and flags, are symbols of team identity. So, too, are the colours of street gangs and the insignias of motorcycle gangs.

identity
a shared sense of sameness

Let's now look at trust, an essential ingredient in building a team that cooperates, coheres, and shares a common identity.

TRUST

All healthy human relationships begin with trust, and without mutual trust no positive relationship with another person is possible. "Trust" is a common word in our vocabulary, but the details of its meaning are not always clear. We'll begin this section with a simple but important question, and we'll try to provide a clear answer to that question. Our question is: What is trust?

The best way to find out if you can trust somebody is to trust him.

—Ernest Hemingway, author

trust
the act of placing confidence in another person without full assurance that the confidence is well placed; entails mutual disclosure, sharing, and reliance

Trust is the act of placing confidence in another person without knowing whether your confidence is well placed or not. In other words, trust is an act of faith. We can call it an act of faith, because trusting another person comes with no guarantees. When you trust someone, you may be disappointed. If you are let down, you are likely to feel betrayed and may be unwilling to trust your betrayer again. However, if your faith is well placed, the relationship is strengthened, and you are more likely to trust again.

Trust always involves taking a risk. It means making yourself vulnerable to others who may let you down, humiliate you, manipulate you, exploit you, or judge you. Because of these potentially nasty outcomes, many people are reluctant to place their faith in others, particularly if they have been hurt in the past. When individuals join new groups, they are often inhibited from fully contributing because they don't know whether others in the group can be trusted or not. To find out, you have to take risks.

So far we've described trust as an act of faith and a risk-taking activity. We need to get more specific now by noting three particular actions that are associated with trust: *disclosure, sharing,* and *reliance*. Let's look at each of these actions in turn.

disclosure
trusting act in which one reveals one's thoughts and feelings to others

First, trust involves disclosure. **Disclosure** is the act of revealing or making something known. If you share a secret with someone, for example, you disclose some aspect of your personal life to that person. In your group life, you are not likely to reveal your deepest secrets. However, to help build the team you will have to regularly disclose your thoughts and feelings. Each time you do, you'll take a risk. We hope that others won't ridicule our views, but there's no guarantee that they won't.

sharing
trusting act in which one gives or lends resources to others

Second, trust involves sharing. **Sharing**, of course, means lending or giving your possessions or resources to others. You will, for example, lend your car to a good friend but not to a stranger. You trust the friend. You don't trust the stranger. True teamwork requires the regular sharing of resources. You may, for example, be asked to lend your study notes to a teammate in order for your team to complete a particular task. Will the notes be returned to you before the next test? If you trust that they will, you'll lend them. If you don't, you won't.

reliance
trusting act in which one places confidence in another or depends on another

Third, trust involves reliance. **Reliance** means placing confidence in another person and depending upon that person. For example, if you do a major school project with a classmate who promises to type, proofread, and submit the final draft by a certain date and time, you rely on her to do it. Notice once again, relying on your colleague comes with no guarantees. She may or may not be worthy of your trust. If she keeps her promise, she is trustworthy. If she fails to keep her promise for no good reason, then she is unworthy of the confidence that you placed in her. You can't rely on her.

HOW TO BUILD A GROUP INTO A COHESIVE TEAM

Effective teams foster a positive, supportive climate in which members can thrive, as the group accomplishes its various tasks and develops a sense of cohesion. In this section, you will find six rules for developing a positive group climate, a climate of trust.[2] If you and the other members of your group follow these rules, you will create and enjoy a supportive climate that fosters both increased productivity and an enhanced sense of cohesion. Your group will become a unified team.

> *Teamwork is the ability to work together toward a common vision and to direct individual accomplishment toward organizational objectives. It is the fuel that allows common people to attain uncommon results.*
>
> —Andrew Carnegie, entrepreneur and philanthropist

Rule #1: Be Empathic, Not Neutral

The emotional basis of all ethical behaviour is empathy. In Chapter 3, we defined *empathy* as feeling what another person feels. The person who goes to the aid of someone in trouble, for example, identifies emotionally with the person in distress. The psychopath, in contrast, has no empathy. He is emotionally neutral and, consequently, does terrible things to others without feeling anything. Thankfully, most people have some degree of empathy and, therefore, do not deliberately hurt people or treat them as though they were objects. Most people are not emotionally neutral. They are empathic and are able to identify with others.

This first rule for building a climate of trust encourages you and the others in your group to empathize with one another. It urges you to see things from the other person's point of view. It encourages you to get into the "emotional shoes" of your teammates so that you understand them better. Likewise, the absence of empathy will contribute to a negative climate that will prove detrimental to your group. If you want to help build your group into a supportive team by creating a climate of trust, be empathic, not neutral.

Rule #2: Relate to Others as Equals, Not Inferiors

Respect is the cognitive and behavioural equivalent of the emotion of empathy. In other words, while empathy is a matter of feelings, respect is a matter of attitude and behaviour. If you have the attitude that you are superior to others in your group, for example, then you are very likely to treat them as inferiors. Such an attitude and behaviour will, no doubt, provoke resentment and anger from others. People generally know when they are being treated as inferiors and they don't like it. All of this will contribute to a negative climate within your group.

In contrast, if you believe that others are your equals, you will treat them as such. Rule #2 reminds us to treat others in our group with respect. Based on the ethical principle of equality, it reminds us to relate to them as equals and not as inferiors. When we give respect, we usually get respect in return. Mutual respect among members of a group contributes enormously to the creation of a climate of trust and the building of a cohesive team.

---

2   The six rules presented in this section are based on the influential work of Gibb (1961, pp. 142–148), who examined behaviours that contribute to defensive and supportive climates within a group.

At this point, it is important to note carefully what is *not* being said in this rule. In a very real sense, people are not all equals. When it comes to public speaking, for example, one person on your team may be superior to everyone else. So, too, with many other skills we find a very real inequality among people.

Rule #2 does not mean to say that there are no differences among people with respect to knowledge and skill. And it doesn't mean that we shouldn't honour those who have superior skills and knowledge. What it is saying is that any superior knowledge and skill that a person possesses does not make that person *morally* superior to others. Our talents do not give us licence to treat others as inferiors. Despite any superior talents that you may have, you should relate to others as equals and not as inferiors.

As mentioned previously, mutual respect, grounded in equality, contributes to the development of a climate of trust. The principle of equality, you will recall, was discussed in Chapter 3 along with the other ethical principles of goodness, fairness, truth, and freedom.

Rule #3: Be Cooperative, Not Competitive

In Chapter 4, we discussed the importance of setting clear goals for your group. Among the things that we emphasized at that time was the importance of establishing cooperative goal structures and avoiding, for the most part, competitive and individualistic structures. Rule # 3 requires that you cooperate with others in your group rather than competing with them. It encourages you to be an Owl, not a Shark.

As we saw in our examination of conflict, if you and your teammates approach challenges as problems to be solved in a win–win fashion, then you will contribute to the creation of a supportive climate within your group. You will foster a climate of trust, not suspicion. In contrast, when people approach their problems in a win–lose manner, then individuals become suspicious of one another and mistrust develops.

Successful groups emphasize cooperation among members rather than competition. By identifying problems together, mutually developing a range of solutions, reaching consensus on a course of action, and cooperatively implementing the chosen solution, your team will be able to tackle virtually any challenge successfully. You will enjoy the benefits of working on a team in a supportive climate of trust.

Rule #4: Be Genuine, Not Manipulative

Sometimes individuals come to their groups with hidden agendas. Hidden agendas refer to things that members want to accomplish but in a secretive, dishonest, and manipulative manner. John, for example, says that he wants Petra to serve as leader, but he secretly wants Nadia to become chair. His speech and behaviour are designed to get the group to think one way, when, in fact, John wants things to go a very different way. He is trying to manipulate the group to achieve the objectives of his hidden agenda.

Members who have hidden agendas are dishonest. They lack integrity as they practise deception. Unfortunately, some people attempt to manipulate groups in order to achieve their personal ends. However, it is not uncommon for others to catch on to what's happening. Needless to say, they can get very angry with those who are trying to use them or dupe them.

Members who engage in manipulative behaviour undermine the trust that others have placed in them. Rule #4 is based on the principle that honesty and integrity build trust, while manipulative dishonesty destroys it. The rule urges you to be genuine and to refrain from dishonesty and manipulation. Truth telling and honesty, as first noted in Chapter 3, are essential to building trust in your group, just as they are essential to building trust in any relationship.

Rule #5: Be Open, Not Closed, to New Ideas

Groups can very easily become closed to new ideas, especially if they have been in existence for some time. "We've always done it this way" is a statement that is all too commonly heard in groups. It's a statement designed to shut down further discussion and new ideas. Whether motivated by laziness, the desire to control others, or the fear of new ideas, some group members are closed to new ways of thinking and new ways of doing things.

As a group member, you may hold strong views about some issue that your group has to deal with. In your meetings, however, it is important for you to hear all points of view. It is important to remain open to the ideas of others. Perhaps others have also given thought to the issue, and they may have some useful ideas to share. If you are closed to their ideas, they may well close their minds to your ideas. This creates a closed environment that can only work against the best interests of your group.

The members of effective groups remain open to new and better ideas, regardless of their origin. This is the approach of all great thinkers and problem solvers. A positive climate within a group allows for honest and open sharing of all ideas with a view to finding the best solution to the group's problems. If you want your group to develop a climate of trust, then be open, not closed, to new ideas.

Rule #6: Be Supportive, Not Judgmental

One of the most difficult things to do in a group is to criticize ideas that you feel are weak. Much of the difficulty seems to lie in the fact that many people take the criticism of their ideas very personally. They seem unable to separate themselves from their ideas. You find it difficult to criticize their ideas, then, because you fear that it's going to cause a blow up. You fear that they'll take it personally.

For example, if I present an idea and someone points out its weakness, I may take it personally and see the criticism as an attack on me. I will likely react defensively, thus contributing to a negative climate. When you criticize the ideas of others, you should make it clear that you support the person but are critical of the idea. You might say, for example, "Jamal, I'm not criticizing you personally, but I think that your suggestion won't work. Here's why." In words like these, you are expressing support for Jamal and avoiding personal judgments.

In cases where we feel that someone's behaviour is inappropriate, we should describe their *actions* without imputing a motive. We've made this same point before, both in our study of communication in Chapter 5 and in our study of conflict resolution in Chapter 6. We'll make the same point again in Chapter 8 where we look at critical discussion. A non-judgmental approach within your group will do much to create a supportive climate. People will feel free to offer their views without fear of personal attack. If you want to contribute to the creation of a climate of trust in your group, be supportive, not judgmental.

> *When a gifted team dedicates itself to unselfish trust and combines instinct with boldness and effort, it is ready to climb.*
>
> —Patanjali, yogi

If you are empathic, cooperative, honest, open, and non-judgmental, and respect others as equals, then you and the members of your group will be a powerful force for creating a climate of trust in which your group can become a team. When this occurs, your team is likely to achieve both its task goals and its social goals. It will be both productive and cohesive.

THREE BENEFITS OF TEAM MEMBERSHIP

While teams exist to get work done, they can create climates in which individual members derive benefits. In particular, they allow individual members to satisfy three very important social needs. These needs are *affiliation*, *influence*, and *respect*.[3]

1. Affiliation

affiliation
a sense of association or connection with others

Most people have a need to belong to a group or groups. We are born into a group, the family, and we continue to live and work in groups throughout our lives. The need to associate with others is called **affiliation**. Membership in a group—be it a sports team, a social club, or a street gang—is often a source of pride and, in many instances, contributes to our sense of identity. The group becomes, in effect, a real part of who we are.

If you and the members of your group create the kind of supportive climate that we have discussed in this chapter, you will establish a social environment in which individuals can satisfy, at least in part, their need for affiliation. Individuals will enjoy being a part of your team and they will take pride in your team and its accomplishments.

2. Influence

influence
the ability to affect circumstances and people

Influence is the ability to affect circumstances and people. It is a form of power. Most of us feel good when we are successful at favourably affecting events around us. In groups, we respond positively when we see that we have influence on group outcomes, that our input makes a difference. However, if one or two others make all the decisions and ignore our views, then we feel impotent and may get discouraged or resentful. Why belong to a group if you don't make a difference, if you don't really count?

If your team encourages everyone to contribute, takes everyone's views seriously, and allows all members to influence the actions of the team, then your members can satisfy their need to have influence. A supportive climate of trust empowers all members. Everyone will have the sense that they count, that they do have influ-

---

3   Schutz (1958) discussed group members' needs for inclusion, control, and affection. In this section, the focus is on the very similar concepts of affiliation, influence, and respect.

ence within the group. Members who have these kinds of feelings are members who will redouble their efforts on future tasks.

3. Respect

To **respect** someone means to hold that person in honour or esteem. One of the highest forms of respect that we can experience in life is to be honoured by our peers. When we are accepted as an equal within a group, we feel welcome. If, in contrast, we sense that others view us as inferiors and are disrespectful of us, then we will not want to associate with them. To respect others within your group is one of the best ways of involving them and gaining their commitment to the team.

And, for you to enjoy the respect of others is, naturally, a tremendous feeling. When others show you that they respect you and the contributions that you make to the team, then you are likely to increase your involvement and commitment. The person who works to ensure that all members of the team feel that they belong (affiliation), that they have a contribution to make (influence), and that they are equals on the team (respect) will be a person who, in turn, gains the respect of others.

respect
honour and esteem, particularly among peers

CHAPTER SUMMARY

In this chapter, we first described five stages of development that groups typically go through. Members experience uncertainty in the forming stage, they vent feelings in the storming stage, they adopt rules for themselves in the norming stage, they become productive in the performing stage, and they eventually separate in the adjourning stage. Next, we defined "cohesion" and identified three key characteristics of a cohesive team—namely, cooperation, unity, and identity. Then we examined trust, the basis for all healthy relationships and the fundamental ingredient in building a team. In addition, we noted that trust is necessary for disclosing our views to others, sharing our resources with them, and relying on them. Next, we provided six rules for developing and maintaining a climate of trust within a group. These rules emphasized the importance of empathy, equality, cooperation, integrity, openness, and support. Finally, we noted how successful teams benefit members by providing opportunities for satisfying the basic social needs of affiliation, influence, and respect.

KEY TERMS

adjourning stage	norming stage
affiliation	performing stage
cohesion	reliance
cooperation	respect
disclosure	sharing
forming stage	storming stage
identity	trust
influence	unity

MASTERING THE MATERIAL

Now that you have read this chapter, use the following guides to ensure that you have mastered the material.

1. Briefly describe the five stages of group development.

   Stage 1: Forming

   Stage 2: Storming

   Stage 3: Norming

   Stage 4: Performing

   Stage 5: Adjourning

2. Define *cohesion*.

3. Identify and explain three characteristics of a cohesive team.

   a.
   b.
   c.

4. What is trust?

5. Identify the three specific actions associated with trust.

   a.
   b.
   c.

6. From memory, list six rules for building a group into a cohesive team.

   Rule #1:

   Rule #2:

   Rule #3:

   Rule #4:

   Rule #5:

   Rule #6

7. Identify and explain three benefits of team membership.
   a.
   b.
   c.

PRACTISING YOUR GROUP SKILLS

PURPOSE OF THIS SECTION

The purpose of "Practising Your Group Skills" and the ultimate purpose of this book is to help you become a more effective participant in the groups to which you belong. This section is designed to provide opportunities for you and your fellow students to practise your group skills in a structured environment.

TEAM RESPONSIBILITIES

A description of the team responsibilities for each of five different teams—the Executive Team, the Lesson Review Team, the Teaching Team, the Energizer Team, and the Evaluation Team—can be found in Appendix B, pages 177–180. Your professor may have chosen to use from one to five of these teams to conduct the teaching and learning activities of your class. Units 2 and 3 of the Teacher's Guide provide your professor with additional information on the responsibilities of these teams.

INDIVIDUAL ROLE RESPONSIBILITIES

A description of four individual role responsibilities—those of Leader, Recorder, Reporter, and Participant-Analyst—can be found in Appendix B, pages 180–182. Your professor may have chosen to use from one to four of these roles within teams to give individuals experience leading, recording, reporting, and analyzing. Units 2 and 3 of the Teacher's Guide provide your professor with additional information on these individual role responsibilities.

SPECIFIC TEAM ASSIGNMENTS

Specific team assignments for this chapter appear immediately below. Specific team assignments for each of the subsequent chapters can be found in "Practising Your Group Skills" in each chapter.

CHAPTER 7 TEAM ASSIGNMENTS

THE EXECUTIVE TEAM

- *Your Ultimate Goal*: to provide leadership to your classmates for your class session on Chapter 7.
- *Your Interim Goals*: to facilitate the class session by (1) ensuring a good classroom setup, (2) welcoming the class, (3) introducing the lesson topic, (4) coordinating activities, and (5) bringing the session to a close.
- *Instructions*: Ensure that the classroom is set up to accommodate today's class activities. Post an agenda for the session. Welcome people to class and announce the topic, "Cohesion: Building Your Group into a Unified Team," in a creative and interesting way. Remind the class that cohesion is a group's sense of togetherness or oneness, and that the topic includes instructions on how to create a climate of trust within groups. Introduce and thank all speakers when appropriate. Coordinate the day's activities and bring closure at the end of the class. If necessary, return the classroom to its original configuration.

THE LESSON REVIEW TEAM

- *Your Ultimate Goal*: to review Chapter 6, "Conflict: Resolving Disputes in Your Group."
- *Your Interim Goals*: to provide a review of (1) the experiential exercise, (2) the five different conflict styles, and (3) the six effective practices (rules) that help to resolve conflicts in small groups.
- *Instructions*: As the Lesson Review Team, you have the freedom to choose how you will do the review. You can be as creative as you wish, but you must achieve the review objectives. Remember that your time is very limited, so don't try to re-teach last chapter's lesson.

THE TEACHING TEAM

- *Your Ultimate Goal*: to understand and demonstrate effective team-building skills in a small group setting.

- *Your Interim Goals*: to describe, explain, and demonstrate (1) cohesion, unity, and identity; (2) six rules for building a cohesive team; and (3) the importance of affiliation, influence, and respect.

- *Instructions*: As the Teaching Team, you have the freedom to choose how you will teach your lesson. You can be as creative as you wish, but you must achieve the lesson goals above. Your experiential exercise is called "Cohesion and Cooperation" and you'll find it described fully in Appendix C, pages 195–196. Make sure that you refer to it when you teach and explain the lesson goals and objectives. The exercise should also be included in your lesson when you describe and explain the five conflict styles and the six rules for managing conflict effectively. If time allows, you can also use exercises from "Mastering the Material" to teach your lesson.

THE ENERGIZER TEAM

- *Your Ultimate Goal*: to motivate your classmates by conducting an energizer activity.

- *Your Interim Goals*: to facilitate the energizing of your classmates by (1) planning an energizer activity and (2) implementing the plan at an appropriate time in the class session.

- *Instructions*: Your team doesn't have a specific, assigned activity to conduct. Rather, the team should remember its energizing purpose and conduct an activity that will provide a break in the class learning routine. Popular games like Simon Says, Heads Up Seven Up, and Murder Wink usually work well. So do various mixers and ice breakers. (Your professor's Teacher's Guide identifies a number of sources of energizer exercises.) Whatever you decide on, you must be prepared to give clear instructions and conduct the exercise effectively. When you lead the energizer, you are leading and directing the entire class. Plan well and execute professionally, even if the exercise is a "kid's game." Encourage everyone to get involved.

THE EVALUATION TEAM

As a member of the Evaluation Team, you need to review the information in Chapter 10, pages 145–148, before you do anything else. There you will find helpful information on how to conduct your evaluation session. The most important thing to remember is that you are not to judge other people. Your role is to help the class make its own assessment of which practices worked well today and which didn't.

- *Your Ultimate Goal*: to assess group (or class) members' team-building skills.

- *Your Interim Goals*: to (1) assess the levels of disclosure, sharing, and reliance within the group (or class) and (2) identify practices in need of improvement.

- *Instructions*: Create an evaluation instrument based on the selected focus behaviours identified in the evaluation goals above. See Chapter 10, pages 146–147, for information on creating evaluation instruments. Figure 10.1 provides an example. Solicit feedback from the class using the evaluation instrument. Use the feedback to discuss the class session with the purpose of identifying improvements that can be made to individual, group, and class performance in future class sessions. Conclude by noting the specific actions that need to be repeated or avoided to make improvements.

REFERENCES AND RECOMMENDED READINGS

Eadie, W.F. (1982). Defensive communication revisited: A critical examination of Gibb's theory. *Southern Speech Communication Journal, 47,* 163–177.

Fisher, R., & Ury, W. (1981). *Getting to yes: Negotiating agreement without giving in.* Boston: Houghton Mifflin.

Gibb, J.R. (1961). Defensive communication. *Journal of Communication, 11,* 142–148.

Robbins, S.P. (1994). *Supervision today.* Englewood Cliffs, NJ: Prentice Hall.

Walton, R. (1987). *Managing conflict.* Reading, MA: Addison-Wesley.

Wilmot, W.W., & Hocker, J.L. (1998). *Interpersonal conflict.* Boston: McGraw-Hill.

USEFUL URLS

About.com Human Resources. http://humanresources.about.com.

Free Management Library. www.managementhelp.org.

MindTools. www.mindtools.com.

Pfeiffer Publishing. http://ca.pfeiffer.com/WileyCDA/Section/index.html.

Team Technology. www.teamtechnology.co.uk.

Your Meeting Resource Center. www.effectivemeetings.com.

Critical Discussion: Generating Ideas in Your Group

8

Follow the path of the unsafe, independent thinker. Expose your ideas to the danger of controversy. Speak your mind and fear less the label of crackpot than the stigma of conformity.

—Thomas J. Watson, Sr., founder of IBM

INTRODUCTION

As an individual, when you make important decisions, it's essential that you "use your head." That means, of course, that you need to get all the relevant facts and you need to think clearly about those facts, drawing logical conclusions. If, for example, you're going to spend $20,000 on a new car, you'll want to compare competitive makes with regard to safety, fuel consumption, comfort, and reliability, among other things. After you consider the pros and cons of each option, you can make an informed decision. We call fact-based, logical reasoning **critical thinking**.

Groups also need to "use their heads" when making decisions. Group decisions require the same critical thinking as individual decisions. However, because several minds are working on the problem, the process is more complex. Teams, like individuals, make the best decisions when they gather the facts and reason logically. Critical thinking, then, is essential when making either individual or group decisions.

In effective groups, critical thinking is shared through critical discussion, the subject of this chapter. Since many groups make poor decisions, we'll first examine groupthink, a form of uncritical thinking that results in bad decisions. The antidote to groupthink is both critical thinking and critical discussion, the kind of discussion that emphasizes conceptual conflict based on facts and logic. After a brief review of conceptual conflict, we'll examine the steps of the critical discussion process, note two benefits of critical discussion, and provide you with eight rules for discussing issues critically in your group.

> ### CHAPTER GOALS
>
> After completing this chapter, you should be able to:
> - Describe and explain critical discussion.
> - Explain *groupthink*.
> - Describe five factors that contribute to groupthink.
> - Identify and explain three illusions associated with groupthink.
> - Define *conceptual conflict*.
> - Identify and explain the six steps of the process of critical discussion.
> - Identify the two benefits of critical discussion.
> - State and explain eight rules for critical discussion.

critical thinking
fact-based, logical reasoning

GROUPTHINK

groupthink
uncritical thinking within a
group

Groupthink is a word coined to describe uncritical thinking within a group.[1] Groupthink can and does occur in groups of all kinds, and most often it is associated with poor decisions that have had disastrous consequences. For example, groupthink has been cited as the cause of failed invasions (US invasion of Cuba, 1961), exploding space shuttles (Challenger Space Shuttle, USA, 1986), and bank failures (Northern Rock Bank, United Kingdom, 2007). In these and other cases, it is argued that small groups made very bad decisions because they were involved in groupthink. Studies point to five factors that contribute to groupthink.

1. *The presence of a strong leader whose views are firmly held and well known to group members.*

   When a strong leader takes a position, members often avoid conceptual conflict and uncritically accept their leader's point of view. If the leader's idea is a poor one, failure may be the consequence. In the examples above, failure meant disaster. So, if your group has a strong leader with firmly expressed views, be on the lookout for groupthink in your team.

2. *The presence of a high level of cohesion within a group.*

   While group cohesion is usually a good thing, sometimes it can be a problem. For example, if group cohesion is so strong that it eliminates critical thinking and critical discussion, then it's a bad thing indeed. That's exactly what happens with groupthink. If your team spirit is so high that members stop thinking critically and avoid conceptual conflict, then your group will suffer accordingly. Groupthink inevitably leads to poor decisions.

3. *Isolation from critics outside the group.*

   Successful groups often invite outsiders to critique their plans, especially if the decision to be made is very important. Because outsiders don't share the group's perspective, they can offer criticism from a different point of view. They are, for example, more likely to be objective. This different perspective can often identify weaknesses or flaws in the proposed course of action. If your group has to make a really important decision, invite outsiders to critique your proposed action. Don't isolate yourselves from outside critics.

4. *The absence of procedural norms within the group.*

   Procedural norms are rules that require a group to proceed in certain ways. They are a group's rules of operation. If a group has rules that require it to give criticism of proposed ideas and courses of action, then critical analysis becomes a natural part of group life. In contrast, a group that has no such procedural norm is less likely to engage in critical discussion. To avoid groupthink, make sure that your group establishes rules that require critical thinking and critical discussion.

---

1   Janis (1972, 1982) pioneered the study of uncritical thinking and decision making in small groups. Some of Janis's important ideas are included in this section.

5. *Insufficient time to properly consider a decision.*

Where there is insufficient time, small groups may run with the first idea that's put forward. But the first idea is not always the best idea. Unfortunately, many groups create their own time problems by wasting time. Instead of dedicating time to decisions properly, they squander it on less important activities. The Distracter that we met in Chapter 1 is sometimes the culprit. See that your team manages its time well, so that time pressures don't lead your team into groupthink.

In summary, five factors contribute to the uncritical thinking that we call group-think: the presence of a strong leader, a high level of cohesion, group isolation from outside criticism, an absence of procedural norms, and limited time. You will do well to ensure that your group is familiar with these factors and that it avoids the pitfall of groupthink.

> *Thinking is skilled work. It is not true that we are naturally endowed with the ability to think clearly and logically— without learning how or practising.*
> —Alfred Mander, author

SYMPTOMS OF GROUPTHINK

Research indicates that there are at least three symptoms that indicate the presence of groupthink. These symptoms are misconceptions that the group has, and we call these misconceptions illusions. An illusion is a false perception or false interpretation of an event. If you're under an illusion, you think that things are a certain way but they are not. Magicians thrive on creating illusions. Let's look at three misconceptions associated with groupthink.

1. The **illusion of unity**. In this illusion, individual members keep any doubts or criticisms they may have to themselves. They keep silent because they believe, mistakenly, that nobody else has any doubts. They believe that everyone else is in agreement. They perceive unity in the group, when, in fact, it does not exist. Under this illusion, individuals censor their own criticisms. "If everyone else agrees," they say to themselves, "I'm not going to object."

illusion of unity
the mistaken belief that everyone is in agreement on an issue

2. The **illusion of invulnerability**. To feel invulnerable is to feel unbeatable or unstoppable. Here, members believe that their team cannot possibly fail in its tasks. They take the view that their ideas are so good that only success awaits the team. Unfortunately, their confidence in their ideas keeps them from critically reviewing their plans. In competitive situations, members under the illusion of invulnerability say things like, "We can't be beaten" or "We're unstoppable."

illusion of invulnerability
the mistaken belief that one's team cannot fail

3. The **illusion of superiority**. In this third illusion, the group believes that it is morally superior to its opponents or critics. They believe, for example, that they are better people than their opponents. In this case, the belief in moral superiority blinds them to the reality that others are probably their equals, morally and otherwise. Under the illusion of superiority, soldiers on one side in a battle may say, "We can't lose because God is on our side." In all likelihood their enemies on the other side say the same thing.

illusion of superiority
the mistaken belief that one's team is on the side of right

When uncritical thinking takes over in a group, then its members are likely to feel that they are all of one mind (unity illusion), that they simply cannot fail (invulnerability illusion), and that they are better people than their adversaries (superiority illusion). In medicine, an antidote is a substance that counteracts a poison. In group situations, the antidote to groupthink is critical thinking and critical discussion that employs conceptual conflict.

CONCEPTUAL CONFLICT

In Chapter 6, we discussed four forms of conflict that can seriously harm group unity. In particular, we described *personality conflict, resource conflict, power conflict,* and *status conflict.* We began that chapter, however, by describing another form of conflict that should be promoted and encouraged within groups. That form of conflict is *conceptual conflict,* and it lies at the heart of critical discussion.

More precisely, conceptual conflict is a disagreement or controversy about ideas, opinions, or points of view. As noted previously, it is a battle of ideas, not a battle of personalities. When group members don't understand the nature of conceptual conflict, it frequently degenerates into personality conflict, and the group suffers a loss of both cohesion and productivity.

Properly understood, conceptual conflict is desirable, and the reason for this is simple. When there is disagreement over ideas, your group is more likely to make good decisions. If your group uses conceptual conflict that is fact-based and logical, your critical discussions will lead to the best decisions possible.

THE PROCESS OF CRITICAL DISCUSSION

In the introduction to this chapter, we explained critical thinking. We said that it was a fact-based and logical way of thinking. When you and your teammates think critically about an issue, you also need to employ a process whereby you can discuss your ideas. One such process is called **critical discussion**, and it is a six-step process that promotes conceptual conflict within a group. This process ensures that any decisions that your team makes will be well thought out, using the best ideas that the group has to offer. The six steps of the process of critical discussion are listed below.[2]

critical discussion
a six-step process designed to encourage group members to engage in conceptual conflict

Step #1: Research

When faced with important decisions, your group should get individuals or subgroups to research different possibilities. If, for example, your group has to purchase a new computer, then you should have different members do research on different computers. Some can investigate Apple's Mac while others look into Dell's PC. For ease of illustration, we'll talk about only two computers; in reality, your group might research more.

Regardless of how many computers are being researched, each individual or subgroup learns as much as possible about its assigned computer, noting all its

---

2   Johnson and Johnson (1997, pp. 307–311) present a six-step process of constructive controversy based on the earlier work of Johnson and Johnson (1987). This section and the next, "The Benefits of Critical Discussion," rely extensively on their work.

pros and cons. In this step, different members gather the facts about both the Mac and the PC. Only with the facts in mind, can you think critically and discuss intelligently.

Step #2: Presentation

After their investigation is complete, the researchers in our example present the merits and drawbacks of each computer to your whole group. All the pros and cons of each computer are presented, and members take careful note of the strengths and weaknesses of each. In step 1, researchers collected the facts. Here, they are sharing them.

Step #3: Discussion

In a systematic way, your whole group should critically discuss the merits of both the Mac and the PC. Those members of your group who have not served as researchers should now freely enter into the discussion along with the researchers. In all cases, criticism is directed not at the *persons* presenting their views, but toward the respective *merits* of the two computers. The debate is about ideas, not personalities. This conceptual conflict is, as we noted elsewhere, the heart of the critical discussion process. In this step, critical discussion makes the pros and cons of each computer clearer.

Step #4: Reflection

When the merits of the two computers have been presented and challenged, it is important to allow time for members to reflect on the pros and cons of both computers. Persons who first favoured one computer may now experience second thoughts. They may see advantages in the other computer that they weren't aware of previously. This time of "second thoughts" is often a time of conceptual conflict *within* the minds of individual members. However, by using fact-based, logical reasoning the team as a whole moves closer to a decision.

Step #5: Reconsideration

The conceptual conflict that develops in steps 3 and 4 can now continue in a reconsideration of your group's options. All members of the group have received the research results, they have had the opportunity to reflect on the information received, and they have together reconsidered their options. Consequently, everyone is in a position to make an informed choice. Critical thinking and critical discussion have been central to the process throughout. Now it's time for a decision.

Step #6: Decision

Having heard the merits of both computers, debated the pros and cons of each, explored some competing ideas, and taken time to rethink the matter, your group is now ready to decide. Your members' critical thinking has been shared through critical discussion, and you are in an excellent position to make a quality decision.

THE BENEFITS OF CRITICAL DISCUSSION

Research shows that groups that use critical discussion enjoy two benefits. First, despite the fact that critical discussion is time consuming, it ultimately leads to better decisions and greater productivity. As groups become more experienced at discussing issues critically, they become more efficient at making high-quality decisions. This results in greater productivity, as teams get better at doing their various jobs. In summary, one benefit of critical discussion is greater effectiveness in achieving *task goals*.

> *Honest disagreement is often a sign of progress.*
> —Mahatma Gandhi, political reformer

Second, groups tend to experience an increased sense of cohesion, mutual respect and attraction, and increased individual self-esteem. These are all benefits associated with the social and emotional dimensions of group life. Healthy relationships are developed and maintained as groups become teams. The second benefit, then, is greater success in accomplishing *social goals*.

THE RULES OF CRITICAL DISCUSSION

Earlier in this chapter, we presented six steps of the critical discussion process. Here we present eight rules that should be observed throughout all six stages of the critical discussion process. The six steps of the critical discussion process are like your road map and the eight rules below are the rules of the road.

Rule #1: Criticize Ideas, Not People

Conceptual conflict is about ideas, not personalities. The first rule of critical discussion reminds you of this important point, a point that has been made a number of times previously. If you critique ideas while supporting people, then you can identify the best ideas your group has while assuring members that they count, even when their views are rejected.

Rule #2: Encourage Win–Win Approaches

Successful teams emphasize cooperation and avoid competition among members. They encourage a win–win attitude among members who will "sink or swim together." This rule directs you to avoid win–lose approaches. After healthy conceptual conflict, everyone on your team will be a winner because you have together made the best decision possible. Always focus on making the best decisions. Never focus on beating fellow members in an idea game.

Rule #3: Encourage Everyone to Contribute

This rule applies to group life at any time, but it is particularly important when decisions are to be made. Sometimes a quieter member of the group has a great idea but is reluctant to share it. Perhaps the individual is shy or believes that his ideas aren't very good. If you encourage the reluctant member to contribute his ideas, then your group can benefit from them. If there is no encouragement, the ideas may be lost to the group.

Rule #4: Listen Actively

Encouraging contributions is vitally important. Equally important is listening to those contributions. This rule encourages you to listen actively to all who contribute to the discussion. Active listening, you will recall, involves conveying your intention to listen, listening with your whole person, and paraphrasing the speaker to ensure understanding. Often in groups, people listen only half-heartedly or not at all. Your team should listen actively to everyone's contribution.

Rule #5: Think Critically

All too often, people are ready to go with the first idea or the quickest solution that is presented to a group. Successful teams take the time to gather all the information necessary to make good decisions, and they use logic to draw conclusions from the facts. They think critically and become informed. This rule reminds you that critical thinking is an essential ingredient in critical discussion.

Rule #6: Present Clearly

When you present your ideas to others, remember to present them clearly. Use first-person pronouns, convey your frame of reference, present your ideas concisely, describe your feelings, don't be judgmental, and ask for feedback. In sum, when you discuss issues critically in your group, use your best communication skills.

Rule #7: Understand All Points of View

Your team can make high-quality decisions when it has considered all points of view on an issue. An individual who has understood a particular point of view and found it to be weak can give informed support to an alternative and wiser point of view. When the members of your group have a good understanding of alternative points of view, then you are in a position to make the best decisions.

Rule #8: Change Your Mind If the Facts Dictate

The process of critical discussion allows time for individual members to reflect on the facts before them. Members need to be flexible in their thinking and they need to change their minds if the facts dictate. Too often, individuals remain stuck in their original point of view, even when an objective analysis suggests that they should change their minds. To be most effective, the members of your group should be open-minded and flexible, ready to change their positions if the facts support a change.

If your group follows these rules of critical discussion, it will experience the two benefits noted earlier—namely, greater cohesion and increased productivity. In Chapter 9, we'll examine several methods that your group can use to make its decisions as it attempts to solve the problems that come its way.

CHAPTER SUMMARY

In this chapter, we began our study of critical discussion by explaining that critical thinking is a fact-based, logical kind of reasoning, while groupthink is a form of uncritical thinking. We noted that groups that engage in groupthink fail to do the critical thinking and discussing that is necessary to make informed and wise choices. Instead of thinking things through critically, members mistakenly assume that they all agree, believe that they are invincible, and feel that they are superior to their competitors. We called these mistaken beliefs illusions of unity, invulnerability, and superiority. We then reviewed conceptual conflict, a desirable form of conflict that is at the heart of the process of critical discussion. Next, we described the six steps of the critical discussion process—namely, research, presentation, discussion, reflection, reconsideration, and decision. Then we pointed out that increased productivity and greater cohesion are benefits of critical discussion. Finally we presented eight rules of critical discussion that require group members to criticize ideas constructively, to adopt a win–win attitude, to involve all members in discussion, to listen actively, to think critically, to present clearly, to understand all points of view, and to change their minds if they have good reason to do so. conceptual conflict

KEY TERMS

critical discussion   illusion of invulnerability
critical thinking   illusion of superiority
groupthink   illusion of unity

MASTERING THE MATERIAL

Now that you have read this chapter, use the following guides to ensure that you have mastered the material.

1. What is critical thinking?

2. What is groupthink?

3. Identify and explain five factors that contribute to groupthink.

   a.

   b.

   c.

   d.

   e.

4. Identify and explain the three illusions associated with groupthink.

   a.

   b.

   c.

5. What is conceptual conflict?

6. What is critical discussion?

7. From memory, list and explain the six steps of the critical discussion process.

   Step #1:

   Step #2:

   Step #3:

Step #4:

Step #5:

Step #6:

8. What are the two benefits of critical discussion?

   a.

   b.

9. From memory, list the eight rules of critical discussion.

   Rule #1:

   Rule #2:

   Rule #3:

   Rule #4:

   Rule #5:

   Rule #6:

   Rule #7:

   Rule #8:

PRACTISING YOUR GROUP SKILLS

PURPOSE OF THIS SECTION

The purpose of "Practising Your Group Skills" and the ultimate purpose of this book is to help you become a more effective participant in the groups to which you belong. This section is designed to provide opportunities for you and your fellow students to practise your group skills in a structured environment.

TEAM RESPONSIBILITIES

A description of the team responsibilities for each of five different teams—the Executive Team, the Lesson Review Team, the Teaching Team, the Energizer Team, and the Evaluation Team—can be found in Appendix B, pages 177–180. Your professor may have chosen to use from one to five of these teams to conduct the teaching and learning activities of your class. Units 2 and 3 of the Teacher's Guide provide your professor with additional information on the responsibilities of these teams.

INDIVIDUAL ROLE RESPONSIBILITIES

A description of four individual role responsibilities—those of Leader, Recorder, Reporter, and Participant-Analyst—can be found in Appendix B, pages 180–182. Your professor may have chosen to use from one to four of these roles within teams to give individuals experience leading, recording, reporting, and analyzing. Units 2 and 3 of the Teacher's Guide provide your professor with additional information on these individual role responsibilities.

SPECIFIC TEAM ASSIGNMENTS

Specific team assignments for this chapter appear immediately below. Specific team assignments for each of the subsequent chapters can be found in "Practising Your Group Skills" in each chapter.

CHAPTER 8 TEAM ASSIGNMENTS

THE EXECUTIVE TEAM

- *Your Ultimate Goal*: to provide leadership to your classmates for your class session on Chapter 8.
- *Your Interim Goals*: to facilitate the class session by (1) ensuring a good classroom setup, (2) welcoming the class, (3) introducing the lesson topic, (4) coordinating activities, and (5) bringing the session to a close.
- *Instructions*: Ensure that the classroom is set up to accommodate today's class activities. Post an agenda for the session. Welcome people to class and announce the topic, "Critical Discussion: Generating Ideas in Your Group," in a creative and interesting way. Remind the class that the topic includes both the dangers of groupthink and the importance of critical discussion for group success. Introduce and thank all speakers when appropriate. Coordinate the day's activities and bring closure at the end of the class. If necessary, return the classroom to its original configuration.

THE LESSON REVIEW TEAM

- *Your Ultimate Goal*: to review Chapter 7, "Cohesion: Building Your Group into a Unified Team."

- *Your Interim Goals*: to provide a review of (1) the experiential exercise, (2) the three actions associated with trust, and (3) the six rules for creating a climate of trust in a group.

- *Instructions*: As the Lesson Review Team, you have the freedom to choose how you will do the review. You can be as creative as you wish, but you must achieve the review objectives. Remember that your time is very limited, so don't try to re-teach last chapter's lesson.

THE TEACHING TEAM

- *Your Ultimate Goal*: to understand and demonstrate effective critical discussion skills in a small group setting.

- *Your Interim Goals*: to describe, explain, and demonstrate (1) groupthink, (2) the six steps of the critical discussion process, and (3) eight effective practices (rules) for critical discussion.

- *Instructions*: As the Teaching Team, you have the freedom to choose how you will teach your lesson. You can be as creative as you wish, but you must achieve the lesson goals above. Your experiential exercise is called "Critical Discussion" and you'll find it described fully in Appendix C, pages 197–198. Make sure that you refer to it when you teach and explain your lesson goals. The exercise should also be included in your lesson when you describe and explain the five conflict styles and the six rules for managing conflict effectively. If time allows, you can also use exercises from "Mastering the Material" to teach your lesson.

THE ENERGIZER TEAM

- *Your Ultimate Goal*: to motivate your classmates by conducting an energizer activity.

- *Your Interim Goals*: to facilitate the energizing of your classmates by (1) planning an energizer activity and (2) implementing the plan at an appropriate time in the class session.

- *Instructions*: Your team doesn't have a specific, assigned activity to conduct. Rather, the team should remember its energizing purpose and conduct an activity that will provide a break in the class learning routine. Popular games like Simon Says, Heads Up Seven Up, and Murder Wink usually work well. So do various mixers and ice breakers. (Your professor's Teacher's Guide identifies a number of sources of energizer exercises.) Whatever you decide on, you must be prepared to give clear instructions and conduct the exercise effectively. When you lead the energizer, you are leading and directing the entire class. Plan well and execute professionally, even if the exercise is a "kid's game." Encourage everyone to get involved.

THE EVALUATION TEAM

As a member of the Evaluation Team, you need to review the information in Chapter 10, pages 145–148, before you do anything else. There you will find helpful information on how to conduct your evaluation session. The most important thing to remember is that you are not to judge other people. Your role is to help the class make its own assessment of which practices worked well today and which didn't.

- *Your Ultimate Goal*: to assess group (or class) members' critical discussion skills.

- *Your Interim Goals*: to (1) assess the group's (class's) understanding of the critical discussion process and the level of their critical discussion skills and (2) identify practices in need of improvement.

- *Instructions*: Create an evaluation instrument based on the selected focus behaviours identified in the evaluation goals above. See Chapter 10, pages 146–147, for information on creating evaluation instruments. Figure 10.1 provides an example. Solicit feedback from the class using the evaluation instrument. Use the feedback to discuss the class session with the purpose of identifying improvements that can be made to individual, group, and class performance in future class sessions. Conclude by noting the specific actions that need to be repeated or avoided to make improvements.

REFERENCES AND RECOMMENDED READINGS

Janis, I.L. (1972). *Victims of groupthink*. Boston: Houghton Mifflin.

Janis, I.L. (1982). *Groupthink*. Boston: Houghton Mifflin.

Janis, I.L., & Mann, L. (1977). *Decision making*. New York: Free Press.

Johnson, D.W., & Johnson, R. (1987). *Creative conflict*. Edina, NY: Interaction Book Company.

USEFUL URLS

About.com Human Resources. http://humanresources.about.com.

Free Management Library. www.managementhelp.org.

MindTools. www.mindtools.com.

Pfeiffer Publishing. http://ca.pfeiffer.com/WileyCDA/Section/index.html.

Team Technology. www.teamtechnology.co.uk.

Your Meeting Resource Center. www.effectivemeetings.com.

Decisions: Solving Problems in Your Group

The problem is not that there are problems. The problem is expecting otherwise and thinking that having problems is a problem.
— Theodore Isaac Rubin, psychiatrist and author

INTRODUCTION

A light bulb burns out in the reading lamp next to your favourite chair. What do you do? Most of us head for our supply of replacement bulbs, select a bulb of appropriate wattage, return to the lamp, unscrew the dead bulb and replace it with the new one. Problem solved.

If we analyze this simple problem and its solution, we find that several decisions were made to solve it. Normally, we don't even stop to think of these decisions. We just act according to a well-established pattern of problem-solving behaviour. In fact, in the case of a light bulb change, we act according to habit. However, consider for a moment some of the decisions involved in the solving of this problem.

There was the decision to replace the bulb. There was the decision to go to a particular room where the replacement bulbs are stored. There was the decision to take a 100-watt bulb rather than a 40 or 60. There was the decision to return to the lamp, not another place. Then there was the decision to unscrew the old bulb and the decision to install the new one. How many decisions does it take to change a light bulb? Several, it would seem.

In this chapter we examine the best practices to employ when you're in a group and it has decisions to make in order to solve problems. We'll first define the words "problem" and "decision," clarify the relationship of one to the other, and describe the steps of the problem-solving process. Then we'll examine six factors that improve the quality of group decisions. Last, we'll describe eight different methods for making decisions in a group.

PROBLEMS AND DECISIONS

problem
any situation that requires
consideration and a solution

In its most general sense, a **problem** is any situation that requires consideration and a solution. A problem can be big or small, routine or extraordinary. To solve problems of any kind, we have to consider certain information, formulate possible solutions, make choices among those possible solutions, and take actions to ensure that the chosen solution really is a solution.

decision
a choice made between
competing options

A **decision**, of course, is a choice made between competing options. In our efforts to solve problems, we have to make choices among alternatives. This is true because problem solving and decision making are inseparable activities. The light bulb example above illustrates this simple fact.

When problems have simple solutions, we don't even think of the decisions that we make to correct them. Many problems, however, are complex. They require a great deal of thought and often we don't make decisions easily. Correcting your long-time overspending habits, for example, is not as easy as changing a light bulb.

Another important point to consider is that when you make decisions and solve problems as an individual, the process is simpler than when you do so in a group. In a group several people have to agree on the nature of the problem and on the decisions to be taken to solve the problem. If the problem is a burned-out light bulb, the solution may be easy. If the problem is more complex, however, then the group may become involved in a difficult and frustrating process.

Thankfully, the problem-solving process is well established and provides a systematic way for groups to try to solve the problems that they face. The complexity of group problem-solving does not arise because of the problem-solving process itself. Rather, the complexity lies in the fact that there are several different decision-making methods that groups can use. We'll examine the problem-solving process next, and later we'll describe several different methods that your group can use to make decisions as you work through the process.

THE PROBLEM-SOLVING PROCESS

Human experience at solving problems has produced a standard approach that can be used to solve almost any problem that one might face. The steps of the problem-solving process presented below are the same basic steps that scientists follow when they seek to understand something or try to find a practical solution to a particular problem. A variety of different labels are used for these steps, but they share a common process.

Step #1: Definition

Many experts have said that defining the problem is the most important step in the process. A problem clearly defined is a problem on the way to a solution. In contrast, a problem poorly defined is likely to result in wasted energy and time, not to mention frustration. The clearer the definition or description of the problem, the more likely it is that a solution will be found.

Clear definition is critical regardless of whether the problem is being worked on by an individual or a group. A group's definition of a problem, however, requires the agreement of several minds. Although getting such agreement is sometimes difficult, it is always essential. Hopefully, as your group deals with its problems, you and your teammates can agree upon definitions that are both clear and accurate. That is the first step to solving your team's problems.

Step #2: Research

A problem well stated is a problem half solved.

—Charles F. Kettering

Having defined the problem, it is essential to gather relevant information. This research may be conducted formally or informally. Often, with smaller problems, the data gathering can be done informally with good results. If, however, the group is faced with an important issue, formal investigation may be required. The following example illustrates the point.

A community is struck by a tornado that causes loss of life and serious property damage. After the disaster, the community establishes a task force to develop an improved emergency response plan. The task force consists of citizens, health care personnel, firefighters, and police officers.

No doubt, the task force would have to do a great deal of formal research before recommending a plan. Among other things, it would have to research the existing plans of other similar-sized communities in order to gather relevant information. In this case, formal research is clearly a necessity.

You may never be in a group that has such important responsibilities as those of our imagined task force. Nevertheless, research is vitally important in gathering information that is relevant to finding a solution to any problem, regardless of its seriousness. Make sure that your team does formal or informal research as it attempts to solve its problems.

Whenever a theory appears to you as the only possible one, take this as a sign that you have neither understood the theory nor the problem it was intended to solve.

—Karl Popper, philosopher

Step #3: Alternatives

Once the relevant information has been collected, discussed, and analyzed, it is necessary to consider all feasible solutions to the problem. The more alternatives one has, the harder it may be to choose from among them, but any such difficulty is outweighed by the greater likelihood of arriving at a good solution. When many alternatives are formulated, the chances are greater that those alternatives will include an effective solution. The best way to have good ideas, it has been said, is to have many ideas.

In our example of the task force and the emergency response plan, we can imagine research leading to a number of possible approaches. A variety of alternatives would likely emerge from the differing perspectives of the citizen representatives, paramedics, doctors, nurses, firefighters, and police. While a variety of alternatives may be proposed, one approach must ultimately be chosen.

Step #4: Decision

Each of the alternatives from the previous step must be scrutinized, and a careful review of the pros and cons of each one must be undertaken. At this stage, your group should continue to think critically and engage in critical discussion to sift through the information associated with each of the alternative solutions. Conceptual conflict will ensure that the best ideas prevail. At some point, of course, you must make a decision.

Hopefully, if the best ideas have surfaced and the drawbacks of the various proposals have been identified, you will make the best decision possible. However, at this point, you should consider your solution to be only a *proposed* solution. As we will see in the final step of the problem-solving process, all solutions are tentative and subject to review. Only time will tell if your proposed solution truly is the right one.

Step #5: Implementation

A proposed solution to a given problem requires a plan for implementing the solution. If the problem under consideration is a major one, as in our earlier example, a very detailed implementation plan will be required. Often, with minor issues, the plan is quite simple. Whether simple or complex, your plan should be clear, and it should include four essential elements.

First, it should identify the scheduled start and finish times. Second, it should describe the details of the plan. Third, it should identify those responsible for implementation. And, fourth, it should indicate how success or failure is determined. In other words, your team should be able to answer the following questions: *When* will we start and finish the project? *What* exactly is our game plan? *Who* is responsible for the plan? *How* will we know that we've succeeded? You recall that these are exactly the same questions that we noted in our examination of goal setting in Chapter 4.

Step #6: Evaluation

After the plan has been implemented, the situation has to be monitored to determine if, in fact, the proposed solution is effective. Often it is immediately clear that a good solution has been found. Sometimes, however, this is not the case. Ongoing monitoring and evaluation of the plan are essential.

If the evaluation is favourable and the "how" question of step 5 (*How* will we know that we've succeeded?) can be answered clearly, then a solution is in place. If the evaluation is unfavourable or the "how" question cannot be answered, then the problem is not yet solved. The plan may have to be modified, or perhaps even scrapped. In the latter instance, it's "back to the drawing board."

When faced with a problem, then, your team needs to define it very clearly, gather information relevant to a solution, formulate alternatives, decide on a course of action, develop a plan and implement it, and, finally, evaluate the results.

FACTORS THAT IMPROVE THE QUALITY OF GROUP DECISIONS

There are six factors that will increase your team's chances of making high-quality decisions as you work at solving the problems that you face. As with many things in life, there are no guarantees. Groups that include the following factors in their deliberations, however, will improve their chances of making the best decisions possible.

1. Participation

As always in your group life, encourage everyone to participate in the decision-making process. When member participation is high, your group is more likely to make good decisions. This is particularly true when members function as Idea Sharers, Idea Seekers, Comprehension Checkers, Progress Summarizers, Direction Suggesters, and Group Motivators. These are, of course, the basic task roles first studied in Chapter 1.

2. Cooperation

Groups that establish goals and norms that promote cooperation will create win–win attitudes in the minds and hearts of their members. This cooperative spirit is extremely valuable when solving problems and making decisions. As we saw in Chapter 7, competitive win–lose approaches weaken group cohesion and are ultimately counterproductive. Groups that establish cooperation as the norm are far more likely to make good decisions than those that don't. As your group makes its decisions, try to ensure that it adopts a cooperative win–win approach.

3. Heterogeneous Makeup

Groups that have a heterogeneous makeup are more likely to make better decisions than homogeneous groups. The word **heterogeneous** means having variety and the word **homogeneous** means lacking variety. When groups are homogeneous, members may be too much alike and, consequently, may not engage in critical discussion. They may be inclined to fall into groupthink.

heterogeneous
having variety

homogeneous
lacking variety

In contrast, heterogeneous groups—for example, those comprising both men and women, and persons of different ethnic backgrounds—are much more likely to have a variety of points of view on any given issue. Your group should, whenever possible, encourage a healthy mix of members who offer a variety of viewpoints as the group makes its decisions.

Notice again the point that we made about guarantees at the beginning of this section. We said that there are none. If a team, for example, has a difficult mathematical problem to solve and the team has a heterogeneous makeup—women, men, Blacks, Aboriginals, Asians, Hispanics, Whites, etc.—but none of the members has any math skills, then heterogeneity is of no value.

It would be better to have a homogeneous group—all women, all men, all Blacks, all Aboriginals, all Asians, all Hispanics, all Whites, etc.—of people with math skills than to have a heterogeneous group without math skills. In summary, if people have the requisite skills to do a job, then heterogeneous makeup is more desirable than homogeneous makeup.

4. Critical Discussion

The use of critical discussion and conceptual conflict, as we noted in Chapter 8, will help to prevent a group from falling prey to groupthink. This is especially important for homogeneous groups. While it might be desirable to have a mix of people on a team, this is not always possible. Because relatively homogeneous groups are frequently the reality, it is essential that they engage in critical discussion in their decision-making sessions. Criticizing ideas while supporting the persons who offer them is the best way to ensure that your group will generate many ideas that, hopefully, lead to the best decisions.

5. Use of the Problem-Solving Process

Conscious use of the problem-solving process will assist your group in staying on track as it deliberates. Proven by its success in the sciences, the six-step method is a tool that effective groups use regularly. The strength of the process lies in the fact that it provides a structure for dealing with issues. That structure ensures that your group will cover all the necessary steps in a systematic manner.

If your group uses the process, it will have a structured way to deal with the problems and tasks that it has to face. As described earlier in this chapter, your group will define the problem, research relevant information, formulate alternative solutions, decide on a course of action, implement the proposed solution, and evaluate the results.

6. Use of the Eight Decision-Making Methods

An understanding of the various decision-making methods and their strengths and weaknesses will help your group as it makes its decisions. A thorough grasp of these methods will equip you with a number of options. For example, requiring consensus on very important matters is more likely to result in a better decision than moving quickly to a vote. Your group should understand the pros and cons of each method discussed in the next section and use the most appropriate method for the circumstances that your group faces at any particular time. Let's look at group decision-making options now.

GROUP DECISION-MAKING METHODS

As an individual, when you make a decision on your own, you are limited to two general approaches. First, you can do your own research and then, on the basis of your personal standards, decide what you want to do. Second, you can flip a coin or otherwise let the fates decide for you.

In contrast to these individual decision-making options, groups have many more ways of making choices. We'll examine eight methods[1] in this section. Each method has its strengths and weaknesses, and we'll point them out as we survey the different approaches. We'll begin with the ideal method, consensus.

1. Decision by Consensus

Consensus means unanimous agreement. When all members of your group agree on a decision, you have consensus within your group. Whenever possible, your group should decide matters this way. Sometimes groups arrive at consensus easily, but at other times it takes a great deal of time to achieve. The fact that reaching consensus can be very time consuming is one of the criticisms that can be brought

---

1   This review of decision-making methods elaborates on the summary provided by Wilson (1999, pp. 89–91).

against it. Your group, for example, may not have the time to critically discuss an issue because members have other obligations that they have to meet.

When you do have time, however, you should decide by consensus. The strength of consensus lies in the fact that it requires everyone to participate and allows everyone to contribute. In the end, there is no disagreement. Commitment to implementing the decision will be very strong. Both maximum participation and commitment make consensus the ideal method for group decision-making.

2. Decision by Majority Vote

Majority vote is probably the most popular method for making group decisions in our society. **Majority** vote means that 51 percent or more of eligible voters in a group support a particular course of action. This very popular method is sometimes confused with consensus, so note immediately that most of the time they are not the same. The example below will illustrate this point.

majority
fifty-one percent or more of voters in a group

In a democratic society like ours, we learn early in life to respect the vote of the majority. Even when we disagree with the result, we are expected to abide by the decision. Federal, provincial, and local elections are conducted on this basis. So, too, are the decisions of countless groups in society. We are very familiar with this way of making a decision.

Majority vote can work well within your group if three conditions are met. First, all members must have an equal chance to speak to the issue at hand. Second, the vote itself must be conducted fairly. Third, members must support the decision whether they agree with it or not. If these conditions are met, then majority vote can work for your group. Sometimes, however, the conditions aren't met. Consider the following example.

Your group has to decide on how to spend a $35 000 surplus—but some members want to renovate your group's offices while others want to purchase a new van. If a vote is taken on the renovation proposal and 51 percent are in favour, then the renovation proposal passes. That could mean, though, that 49 percent are opposed to the renovation project. If 49 percent feel very strongly about the need for a van, they may not be committed to working on the winning project.

If your group uses majority vote, you could end up with close to half your members opposed to a decision that you've voted on. The majority vote could split your group into winners and losers, and the losers might not be committed to implementing the decision.

Despite this danger, majority vote can work well. As noted above, if you ensure that all points of view are expressed and considered, that the voting process is fair, and that everyone is committed to supporting the decision of the majority, then majority vote can work for your team. In fact, if 100 percent vote for the same action, you will have consensus within your team.

3. Decision by a Minority

Often in small groups, a minority of members makes decisions for the majority. A **minority**, of course, is 49 percent or less of group members. In many organizations, the executive members may make decisions on behalf of the whole team.

minority
forty-nine percent or less of voters in a group

Taking a Vote

The following steps are done in sequence, under the direction of the chair. For more information, see Appendix A, "Meetings: Conducting Business Effectively in Your Group."

1. Somebody makes a motion (formal proposal).
2. Somebody else seconds the motion to show support for it.
3. Debate (critical discussion) is restricted to the current motion.
4. Debate includes equal opportunity for all to speak for or against the motion.
5. A vote on the motion is taken to accept it or reject it.
6. The result is announced and recorded.

For example, in a group of ten, the executive members—the leader, reporter, and the recorder—may make decisions for everyone. Three people decide for ten.

If your group authorizes its executive to act on its behalf, there can be real advantages for the group. For example, the executive can make decisions on routine matters, sparing the whole group the need to meet and deal with every last detail of business. Authorized minority decisions can be very practical and a real benefit to the team, especially when dealing with routine matters.

However, if an unauthorized minority makes decisions for the majority, problems are very likely to arise. If, for example, a minority on your team tries to manipulate a situation to further their personal agendas, then the rest of your group may very well be upset. Such "end runs," as they are sometimes called, are unfair and fly in the face of the democratic process.

Needless to say, if an unauthorized minority tries to decide matters without majority approval, the majority has a right to be upset. Unfortunately, this inappropriate minority action can and does occur. All your team needs, for example, is to have a couple of Rescuers (Chapter 1) assume that they have to save your team from disaster and you will experience an unauthorized minority at work. If this happens, you'll have to confront the self-appointed saviours and find out why they think there's a disaster looming and why they feel that they are the ones to rescue the group.

Authorized minorities can work well for your group, provided that the minority stays within its authorized limits. Unauthorized minorities almost always lead to trouble.

4. Decision by a Leader Without Discussion

Sometimes a leader will make a decision for her group without discussing the matter with other members. If the decision is a relatively minor one and the leader has the confidence of the group, this method can be effective. It can be a very practical way to get things done. But, if the leader makes an independent decision on a matter of importance without authorization from the group, problems are likely to arise.

Also, if some members of the group do not support the leader, an independent decision on even a minor matter may cause conflict. Needless to say, decision by a leader without discussion is effective in only a very limited number of instances in groups that value democracy. Autocratic leaders (Chapter 2) are the ones most likely to take action on their own. If you have a tendency to lead in an autocratic manner, you should pay close attention to the risks inherent in this particular method.

5. Decision by a Leader After Discussion

This method, for obvious reasons, is much less likely to result in conflict. In this case, a leader discusses a course of action with the group before making a decision on an issue. If the decision reflects the views of all or a majority of group members, difficulties are not likely to arise. If, however, some members of your group disagree with the decision and they don't support the leader, then problems may occur.

If leaders discuss issues with members prior to making decisions, then that discussion is often seen as the group's authorization of a leader's subsequent action. If you need to use this method as leader of your group, discuss issues with members and ask for their support for whatever decision you eventually make. If you have such support, then the decision that you make is, in effect, pre-authorized by your group.

6. Decision by a Leader Based on the Most Frequently Expressed Opinion

This method is a special one that looks, at first glance, like majority vote. It's not the same, however, and the following example shows why. Imagine that a group leader has to reply to someone outside the group—a salesperson, for example—and the leader doesn't have time to bring the group together to have members make a decision. The outsider has submitted three prices on three different models of copier and needs a quick answer if the group is to benefit from a time-limited special.

If the team leader telephones the individual members and asks whether they support model A, model B, or model C, she might get the following responses: of the ten group members, four support model A, three support model B, and three support model C. Obviously, the group is split almost equally. If the leader decides to reply to the salesperson on the basis of *the most frequently expressed opinion*, she will purchase model A. Four people supported model A, while models B and C each got support from only three members. The leader in this case has decided on the basis of the most frequently expressed opinion, not majority vote.

A potential problem is obvious. Since six members support models B and C, the leader is acting on the opinions of a minority, the four who voted for model A. If the issue is minor, there may be no ensuing difficulty in the group. If, however, the issue is more important, problems are likely to develop. In groups strapped for time, this is a tempting method for leaders to use. It should be applied cautiously, however, for the reason noted.

7. Decision by an Expert Member

Sometimes a decision is best left to an expert within the group. Imagine a group in which there is only one person who is very knowledgeable about computers. If a computer is going to be purchased for group use, it makes sense to ask the most knowledgeable individual to decide which computer to purchase. If the group wants this and the expert is willing to do the job, this method is likely to work.

If, however, the expert is self-appointed, or if some members do not support the expert, problems may develop. In either case, it's possible that a good computer will be purchased, but interpersonal problems may occur. If you are the expert in a given situation, you will want to ensure that everyone supports you as the decision maker. You may also want to point out that while you are an expert, you are not necessarily infallible.

8. Decision by an Arbitrator

arbitrator
an unbiased third party who makes a decision for a group that cannot reach a decision on its own

When a group is divided and group members cannot come to an agreement on an issue, the group may ask an **arbitrator**, an unbiased third party, to make a decision for the group. The ideal arbitrator is someone respected by all parties and considered to be a fair dealer. The arbitrator hears the reasoning of all parties, gives careful consideration to the differences, and makes an independent determination in the matter.

Sometimes, as in union–management negotiations, the arbitration is legally binding on the parties involved. In many groups, however, adherence to the arbitrator's decision will be voluntary and not legally binding. This fact underscores the importance of having an arbitrator who is accepted by both parties as being a fair dealer.

Our review of these eight methods of decision making has included an appraisal of the strengths and weaknesses of each method. As suggested earlier in this chapter, these decision-making methods are designed to assist you when making decisions in democratically oriented work groups. Hopefully, they will also benefit you in the many situations in your personal life in which you will contribute to group decisions.

CHAPTER SUMMARY

We began this chapter by defining the terms *problem* and *decision*, and showing the connection between problem solving and decision making. We then examined the six steps of the problem-solving process developed by scientists in their pursuit of knowledge and practical solutions to human problems. The steps, in order, are definition, research, alternatives, decision, implementation, and evaluation. Next, we presented six factors that can improve the quality of the decisions that a group makes. The factors include maximizing participation, promoting cooperation, ensuring helpful heterogeneity, using critical discussion, employing the problem-solving process, and using a variety of decision-making methods. Finally, we described eight methods by which groups can make decisions, noting some of the benefits and limitations of each. We held up consensus as the ideal method. The other methods included decision by a majority vote, by a minority, by a leader without discussion, by a leader after discussion, by a leader using the most frequently expressed opinion, by an expert member, and by an arbitrator.

KEY TERMS

arbitrator   majority
decision   minority
heterogeneous   problem
homogeneous

MASTERING THE MATERIAL

Now that you have read this chapter, use the following guides to ensure that you have mastered the material.

1. Define *problem*.

2. Define *decision*.

3. From memory, list the six steps of the problem-solving process.

   Step #1:

   Step #2:

   Step #3:

   Step #4:

   Step #5:

   Step #6:

4. In step #4 of the problem-solving process, group members are encouraged to challenge one another's ideas while remaining supportive of one another. Members are encouraged to engage in _____ discussion that generates _____ conflict.

5. What four questions are essential in the implementation plan of step #5?

   a.

   b.

   c.

   d.

6. Identify the six factors that improve the quality of group decisions.

   a.

   b.

   c.

   d.

   e.

   f.

7. Name and describe the eight methods of making decisions in groups.

   a.

   b.

   c.

   d.

   e.

   f.

   g.

   h.

8. The ideal method for making decisions in a group is _____.

9. Define *consensus*.

10. Majority vote is one of the most common methods of group decision making. What is the main weakness of this popular method?

11. What is an arbitrator?

12. An arbitrator should have the _____ of both parties, and he or she should be a _____ dealer.

PRACTISING YOUR GROUP SKILLS

PURPOSE OF THIS SECTION

The purpose of "Practising Your Group Skills" and the ultimate purpose of this book is to help you become a more effective participant in the groups to which you belong. This section is designed to provide opportunities for you and your fellow students to practise your group skills in a structured environment.

TEAM RESPONSIBILITIES

A description of the team responsibilities for each of five different teams—the Executive Team, the Lesson Review Team, the Teaching Team, the Energizer Team, and the Evaluation Team—can be found in Appendix B, pages 177–180. Your professor may have chosen to use from one to five of these teams to conduct the teaching and learning activities of the class. Units 2 and 3 of the Teacher's Guide provide your professor with additional information on these responsibilities of the teams.

INDIVIDUAL ROLE RESPONSIBILITIES

A description of four individual role responsibilities—those of Leader, Recorder, Reporter, and Participant-Analyst—can be found in Appendix B, pages 180–182. Your professor may have chosen to use from one to four of these roles within teams to give individuals experience leading, recording, reporting, and analyzing. Units 2 and 3 of the Teacher's Guide provide your professor with additional information on these individual role responsibilities.

SPECIFIC TEAM ASSIGNMENTS

Specific team assignments for this chapter appear immediately below. Specific team assignments for each of the chapters in the book can be found in "Practising Your Group Skills" in each chapter.

CHAPTER 9 TEAM ASSIGNMENTS

THE EXECUTIVE TEAM

- *Your Ultimate Goal*: to provide leadership to your classmates for your class session on Chapter 9.

- *Your Interim Goals*: to facilitate the class session by (1) ensuring a good classroom setup, (2) welcoming the class, (3) introducing the lesson topic, (4) coordinating activities, and (5) bringing the session to a close.

- *Instructions*: Ensure that the classroom is set up to accommodate today's class activities. Post an agenda for the session. Welcome people to class and announce the topic, "Decisions: Solving Problems in Your Group," in a creative and interesting way. Remind the class that the topic includes instruction on the problem-solving process and a variety of decision-making methods. Introduce and thank all speakers when appropriate. Coordinate the day's activities and bring closure at the end of the class. If necessary, return the classroom to its original configuration.

THE LESSON REVIEW TEAM

- *Your Ultimate Goal*: to review Chapter 8, "Critical Discussion: Generating Ideas in Your Group."
- *Your Interim Goals*: to provide a review of (1) the experiential exercise, (2) groupthink, (3) the six steps of the critical discussion process, and (4) eight effective practices (rules) for critical discussion.
- *Instructions*: As the Lesson Review Team, you have the freedom to choose how you will do the review. You can be as creative as you wish, but you must achieve the lesson review goals above. Remember that your time is very limited, so don't try to re-teach last chapter's lesson.

THE TEACHING TEAM

- *Your Ultimate Goal*: to understand and demonstrate effective problem-solving and decision-making skills in a small group setting.
- *Your Interim Goals*: to describe, explain, and demonstrate (1) the six steps of the problem-solving process and (2) the eight decision-making methods that groups can use when solving problems.
- *Instructions*: As the Teaching Team, you have the freedom to choose how you will teach your lesson. You can be as creative as you wish, but you must achieve the lesson goals above. Your experiential exercise is called "Comparing Decision-Making Methods" and you'll find it described fully in Appendix C, pages 198–199. Make sure that you refer to it when you explain your lesson goals. The exercise should also be included in your lesson when you describe and explain the problem-solving process and the decision-making methods. If time allows, you can also use exercises from "Mastering the Material" to teach your lesson.

THE ENERGIZER TEAM

- *Your Ultimate Goal*: to motivate your classmates by conducting an energizer activity.
- *Your Interim Goals*: to facilitate the energizing of your classmates by (1) planning an energizer activity and (2) implementing the plan at an appropriate time in the class session.
- *Instructions*: Your team doesn't have a specific, assigned activity to conduct. Rather, the team should remember its energizing purpose and conduct an activity that will provide a break in the class learning routine. Popular games like Simon Says, Heads Up Seven Up, and Murder Wink usually work well. So do various mixers and ice breakers. (Your professor's Teacher's Guide identifies a number of sources of energizer exercises.) Whatever you decide on, you must be prepared to give clear instructions and conduct the exercise effectively. When you lead the energizer, you are leading and directing the entire class. Plan well and execute professionally, even if the exercise is a "kid's game." Encourage everyone to get involved.

THE EVALUATION TEAM

As a member of the Evaluation Team, you need to review the information in Chapter 10, pages 145–148, before you do anything else. There you will find helpful information on how to conduct your evaluation session. The most important thing to remember is that you are not to judge other people. Your role is to help the class make its own assessment of which practices worked well today and which didn't.

- *Your Ultimate Goal*: to assess group (or class) members' problem-solving and decision-making skills.

- *Your Interim Goals*: to (1) assess the group's (class's) use of decision by consensus, decision by majority vote, and decision by minority and (2) identify practices in need of improvement.

- *Instructions*: Create an evaluation instrument based on the selected focus behaviours identified in the evaluation goals above. See Chapter 10, pages 146–147, for information on creating evaluation instruments. Figure 10.1 provides an example. Solicit feedback from the class using the evaluation instrument. Use the feedback to discuss the class session with the purpose of identifying improvements that can be made to individual, group, and class performance in future class sessions. Conclude by noting the specific actions that need to be repeated or avoided to make improvements.

REFERENCES AND RECOMMENDED READINGS

Frey, L.R., & Barge, J.K. (Eds.). (1997). *Managing group life: Communicating in decision-making groups.* Boston: Houghton Mifflin.

Gordon, W.W.J. (1961). *Synectics.* New York: Harper & Row.

Hirokawa, R.Y., & Poole, M.S. (Eds.). (1986). *Communication and group decision-making.* Beverly Hills, CA: Sage.

Janis, I.L. (1989). *Crucial decisions: Leadership in policymaking and crisis management.* New York: Free Press.

Wilson, G.L. (1999). *Groups in context: Leadership and participation in small groups.* Boston: McGraw-Hill.

USEFUL URLS

About.com Human Resources. http://humanresources.about.com.

Free Management Library. www.managementhelp.org.

MindTools. www.mindtools.com.

Pfeiffer Publishing. http://ca.pfeiffer.com/WileyCDA/Section/index.html.

Team Technology. www.teamtechnology.co.uk.

Your Meeting Resource Center. www.effectivemeetings.com.

Evaluation: Improving Your Group's Performance

10

Where performance is measured, performance improves.
Where performance is measured and reported, the rate
of improvement accelerates.
—Thomas S. Monson, spiritual leader

INTRODUCTION

Performance evaluation is an important fact of life for most people. This is true for both individuals and groups of people. In this book about group work, we have focused on the best practices of successful groups. Our last topic is the evaluation of group performance. An **evaluation**, you know, is an assessment of the quality of something. Before we go into detail about evaluating group performance, consider what an individual needs to do to improve performance. Let's take an athlete as our example.

A person who runs the 100-metre dash and wishes to get better at it has to do many things. One of the most important things involves the stopwatch. The runner must time himself repeatedly to see whether his performance is getting better or worse. He may also monitor many other factors—diet, temperature, wind speed, track surface, and time of day, for example—in the overall effort to improve performance. The stopwatch is, in a sense, the most important factor because it gives the most important feedback. Is all the training achieving its goal or not?

To ensure that it is performing at its best, a team must monitor various aspects of its efforts. Just like the individual runner, the group must take account of various factors in its life. This chapter starts with a review of the two basic goals of group life and then provides some rules for evaluating and improving team performance. It concludes with a review of the areas that need to be evaluated. Not surprisingly, these areas are those that we have been studying throughout this book. Each area of performance evaluation that we will note has been the subject of a chapter of this book. Let's begin, now, with a review of the two basic goals of group life.

CHAPTER GOALS

After completing this chapter, you should be able to:

- Explain the difference between describing behaviours and judging people.
- Describe the difference between formal and informal evaluation.
- Design and create an evaluation instrument.
- State and explain five rules for conducting formal group evaluations.
- Describe ten aspects of group work that should be evaluated regularly.

evaluation
an assessment of the quality of something

TASK GOALS AND SOCIAL GOALS

The twin goals of an effective group have been prominent throughout our discussions. Those twin goals are task accomplishment and team development. Every group has as one of its goals the goal of getting the job done, whatever that job might be. This is the group's *task goal*. Every effective group also has a second goal, that of building and maintaining good relationships among its members. This is the group's *social goal*.

When trying to improve your group's performance, you should look at the degree to which you are completing your tasks and the degree to which members feel good about being on the team. In this chapter, we will focus our attention on the various steps that your group can take to measure and improve its performance in both the task and the social dimensions of its life. While these two goals are very general, we will see that there are many specific aspects of your group's activities that require ongoing evaluation if performance is to be enhanced.

THE CHALLENGE OF EVALUATION

challenge
a test of one's abilities

challenge of evaluation
test of one's ability to describe behaviour without judging character

Before we turn to the specific areas of group life that require evaluation, we will review a critically important point that we first made in Chapter 5 and have repeated a number of times since. A **challenge** is a test of one's abilities, and the **challenge of evaluation** is the test of one's ability to describe a group member's behaviour without judging the person's character. When you disagree with a person's behaviour, can you describe that behaviour while still supporting the person in question?

If we describe behaviour and refrain from making judgments about people or their character, we contribute to the development or maintenance of a supportive climate in which group performance can be assessed and improved. If Ned, for example, is late for three consecutive meetings, we can describe the fact of his lateness without making judgments about the reasons for his lateness. We can stick to the facts and avoid attributing his behaviour to laziness, lack of interest, or some other personality factor.

Throughout our study of group dynamics and interpersonal relationships, we have repeatedly made this important point. In Chapter 5, for example, the fifth rule for sending messages effectively is *"Describe the behaviour; don't judge the person."* In Chapter 7, we noted that trust is built and maintained when judgments are avoided. There, the sixth rule for building a supportive climate is *"Be supportive, not judgmental."* Also, in Chapter 8, the first rule of critical discussion directed us to *"Criticize ideas, not people."*

Your group's evaluation of its performance will be most effective when your members *describe the actions* of group members that prevent the group from accomplishing its task goals, *without attributing motives* to those persons. The same is true when your group looks at how well it is doing in terms of building a team—that is, accomplishing its social goals. Supportive environments free of personal judgments are the best environments in which to measure and improve group performance. When assessing your team's performance, the members of your group should describe behaviour and avoid judging people.

FORMAL EVALUATION

Effective groups use both *formal* and *informal* evaluation on an ongoing basis. We'll describe the formal evaluation first. The performance evaluation sessions of professional sports teams illustrate the formal evaluation process well. A professional football team, for example, meets the day after a game to review videotapes of the game just played. The coaching staff have viewed the tapes, and they have some specific points to make. They have isolated key plays to highlight a particular problem, or they have noted specific plays that were especially successful. Two things make this kind of review a **formal evaluation**. One is that it is a scheduled part of the team's overall operations, and the other is that it focuses on predetermined and specific aspects of the team's play.

formal evaluation
a scheduled assessment of predetermined focus behaviours

To enhance your team's performance, your group should schedule regular times for evaluating its performance, just as professional sports teams do. Setting time aside for regular performance assessment is the first step toward improving performance. The second step is to identify specific aspects of performance to review and assess. The professional football team, we said, zeroes in on specific plays that were a failure or a success. You and the other members of your team should do the same. Later in this chapter we will identify the areas that need to be evaluated, but for the moment let's detail the basic steps of the formal evaluation process.

> *Few individuals can fulfill their destinies or realize their potential without knowing themselves well, or without a sense of their own capacities and motivations. Self-awareness is a difficult concept for many individuals because it involves coming to grips with where you are now and what you are about.*
>
> —Ric Charlesworth, sports performance consultant

Steps of the Formal Evaluation Process

To evaluate and improve its performance, your team should take the five important steps described below. Each step covers a key aspect of the formal evaluation process.

Step #1: Identify the Focus Behaviours

If you want to be able to improve your group's performance, then you need to be very specific about what needs to be reviewed. To say, for example, "We were awesome!" is very positive and will no doubt motivate team members to some degree. But, because the evaluative remark is very general, it doesn't isolate or highlight specific things that the group should repeat in order to be awesome again next time.

Similar remarks are relevant to the negative evaluation, "We were lousy!" The first thing that needs to be done in evaluation, then, is to identify the specifics to be examined by the group. **Focus behaviours** are the specific practices or skills that a group wants to concentrate on and evaluate. Decide, for example, that you will evaluate how well members *give feedback* (specific) rather than how well members *communicate* (general).

focus behaviours
the specific behaviours to be evaluated by a group

Suppose that your team wants to evaluate how your members participate in a critical discussion. Since participation is a very general concept, you will want to be much more specific. The six task roles from Chapter 1, for example, are quite specific, and they could become your focus for evaluation purposes. Do your members share their ideas? Do they seek the ideas of others? Do they check to see that "everyone is on the same page?" Do they summarize the group's progress? Do they suggest directions that the group might take? Do they motivate one another to complete the task at hand?

To continue with this example, your group might list these specific behaviours as the focus behaviours or skills that you will evaluate at a future meeting:

- Shares ideas
- Seeks ideas
- Suggests direction
- Summarizes progress
- Checks comprehension
- Motivates others

When you create a list such as this one, you have identified precisely what you want to evaluate. In other words, you have created a list of focus behaviours.

Step #2: Create an Evaluation Instrument

evaluation instrument
a tool used to observe and rate group performance

This step involves the creation of an **evaluation instrument**, a tool that provides questions or statements that members use to rate group performance. Often it is a single sheet of paper that identifies the focus behaviours to be assessed. In the example from step 1, the six task roles were identified as the focus behaviours. An evaluation instrument designed to help assess these task roles would include the specific task roles, the names of group members, and a rating scale. A **rating scale** is a range of values used to measure performance.

rating scale
a range of values used to measure something

Figure 10.1 provides an example of a simple assessment tool that takes this approach. The main purpose of the instrument is to identify focus behaviours so that the group can rate performance, discuss possible improvements, and set goals for improvement. When doing formal evaluations, your group should always create an evaluation instrument to guide the assessment process.

Step #3: Use the Instrument to Observe and Rate Performance

Having included the focus behaviours on your evaluation instrument, it is now time to observe members in a discussion to see how often and how well they perform their task roles in a critical discussion. Remember that the task roles are only one example of what might be evaluated. If necessary, all members are reminded of the particular focus behaviours before the discussion begins. At the end of the discussion, the evaluation instrument is distributed and members are given time to rate everyone with respect to their contributions to the discussion.

observers
group members who are assigned to watch the group's performance

Another approach involves the appointment of **observers** who have the special task of observing the discussion, making note of who contributes what to the dis-

Figure 10.1   Sample Evaluation Instrument

INSTRUCTIONS: Using the scale below, rate member performance in the critical discussion.

  1 = minimal
  2 = good
  3 = very good
  4 = excellent
  5 = exceptional

TASK-ROLE SKILLS	Pia	Milo	Sue	Rav	Dana	Nate	Julio
Shares Ideas							
Seeks Ideas							
Suggests Direction							
Summarizes Progress							
Checks Comprehension							
Motivates Others							

cussion, and then rating everyone's performance using the evaluation instrument. Since the observers do not participate in the discussion, they can be much more attentive to the contributions of each participant. One of the main benefits of having observers is that participants do not have to concern themselves with observation. They can simply get involved in the discussion.

Another approach employs **"secret" observers**, identified long before a particular evaluation session. They secretly make their observations and report them at an appropriate time after the discussion has concluded. To ensure that this method isn't an unethical and unwanted intrusion into the lives of members, the entire team should agree to this kind of approach well in advance of implementation. In other words, if there is consensus on using this approach as one of a number of evaluation strategies, then it will not be ethically offensive when it is employed.

Regardless of the method you use to observe the focus behaviours, the point of the exercise is to get data on the contributions of your members so that those contributions can be discussed by your team to improve the team's performance. As we'll see in the next step, the purpose is not to judge individuals. The purpose is to collect information by observing the focus behaviours, the specific aspects of the group's dynamics to be evaluated.

"secret" observers
group members who have a group's permission to monitor member performance at times that are unknown to the group

Step #4: Discuss the Observations and Ratings

After identifying the focus behaviours, creating a tool for rating them, and observing the focus behaviours, your group is in a position to assess its performance. The rating scale on the evaluation instrument becomes particularly relevant at this point. Using the rating scale, your team can arrive at some numbers that represent your evaluation results. The numbers, however, should be viewed only as a starting point for the discussion and goal setting that takes place in step 5.

In the sample instrument in Figure 10.1, the scale ranges from "minimal" contribution through "very good" to "exceptional" contribution with numbers ranging from 1 to 5, respectively. While evaluation instruments frequently use numbers in their rating scales, other approaches can be used. The ever-popular "happy face," for example, can represent the highest rating on a scale where the equally popular "sad face" represents the weakest performance.

Regardless of whether the tool uses numbers or symbols, the ratings are only a starting point for group discussion. Your group should never, for example, average a bunch of numbers, announce the result, and end the assessment session. You should always use the ratings to focus discussion on ways that your team can improve its performance. The ratings are just one more step in the overall process that leads to the setting of goals for performance improvement.

Step #5: Set Goals for Improvement

The last step in the formal evaluation process is devoted to goal setting. The critical discussion that takes place at this stage is dedicated to setting specific targets for team improvement. Since performance evaluation identifies both strengths and weaknesses, your team can establish goals that encourage the repetition of strong performance and the elimination of weak performance.

When your team sets goals for performance improvement, you should seek consensus among members. Critical discussion of your performance that leads to consensus will help to ensure commitment to improvement. Having had their say and having agreed upon improvement goals, all members of your team are likely to work toward the achievement of those goals.

Throughout the formal evaluation process, but particularly in steps 4 and 5, it is vitally important for your team to follow the primary rule of group evaluation: *"Describe behaviours; don't judge people."* In a supportive climate of trust, your group can take the steps necessary to become the very best. Like a professional sports team, you can work regularly on getting better at what you do.

INFORMAL EVALUATION

informal evaluation
a spontaneous assessment
of performance

The steps described above outline the formal evaluation process. Often, however, evaluation takes place informally. In many cases, informal evaluation can be as effective or more effective than formal evaluation. An **informal evaluation** is a spontaneous, unscheduled assessment of performance. For example, when the coach behind the bench gives immediate feedback to a player returning to the bench after a play, such informal feedback can be very helpful. The returning player will be clear on the specific action or aspect of performance that needs to be repeated or changed.

In group meetings, informal evaluation can occur at any time, and it should occur regularly. For example, words of praise and support that are given to another member for making a particular contribution are a type of informal evaluation. Furthermore, group members can take a time out at virtually any point for informal evaluation of specific aspects of their performance. Effective teams encourage informal evaluation at any time, and schedule formal evaluations on a regular basis.

EVALUATING SPECIFIC AREAS OF GROUP WORK

In the previous section, we described *how* to evaluate performance. Now we will examine *what* to evaluate. Because group work is complex, there are many possible aspects to assess. It's possible, however, to narrow things by homing in on the basic areas of group experience that we have studied. Let's return to these topics to highlight the essential aspects of group work requiring regular evaluation, both formal and informal. Note that the areas are described in fairly general ways. In any area that your team chooses to evaluate, you will need to get very specific. Each of the following broad areas includes many specific focus behaviours that you can assess.

1. Member Roles

Your group should monitor **member roles**, the helpful task roles and social roles that contribute to team success. These roles were the subject of Chapter 1. In the area of task accomplishment, your group should evaluate idea sharing, idea seeking, comprehension checking, summarizing, direction suggesting, and motivating. In the area of relationship development, you should evaluate participation encouragement, the support and praise of member contributions, communication facilitation, process observation, stress relief, and conflict mediation. These 12 roles were identified as the essential member roles in an effective group and they should be evaluated regularly.

member roles
helpful task and social roles that contribute to team success

2. Leader Roles

In Chapter 2, we studied **leader roles**, the part played by those who give direction to others in a particular situation. We pointed out that different situations may require different styles of leadership. Recognizing this fact, your group should regularly evaluate the appropriateness of its leadership actions. For example, is your leader becoming overly task-oriented and neglecting the social needs of the group? Or, in contrast, is she encouraging team development at the expense of team productivity? Is there a healthy balance between concern for tasks and concern for people? Regular evaluation of leadership is necessary to improve your group's effectiveness. In evaluating leadership, as with all areas of group performance, describe behaviours and avoid judging people.

leader roles
the parts played by group members who give direction to others

3. Norms

In Chapter 3, we defined *norms* as the rules of the group and noted that they may be established by outside authorities or determined by the group itself. Usually both conditions prevail—some norms being imposed and others being developed from within. All norms over which your group has any influence should be the subject of regular evaluative reviews. As conditions change within your group, norms may need to change as well. Just as societies sometimes retain outdated laws on their books, so do groups. The old objection, "We've always done it this way," is an appeal to the rules that have governed the past. Adherence to such rules may well inhibit group progress. Consequently, your group needs to be aware of the norms that continue to serve it well and those that are in need of change. Regular evaluation of group norms is essential for healthy group development.

4. Goals

Goals, the subject of Chapter 4, are the targets at which a group is aiming, We noted that some goals are final or end goals. These we called *ultimate goals*. Other goals were called *interim goals* because they must be achieved in order to reach your ultimate goal. Both types of goals need to be stated clearly in specific terms. And, of course, your team's goals should be evaluated regularly. Are the established targets still appropriate? Are they in need of revision in the light of changing circumstances? Answers to such questions are most important. When your goals are appropriate, they serve as benchmarks for assessing your group's performance. Goals that are stated clearly allow you to determine whether you have hit your targets or not. They are essential points of reference for evaluating your team's performance.

5. Dialogue

In chapter 5, we examined several rules for speaking, listening, and giving feedback effectively as you communicate your ideas and feelings in *dialogue* with others in your group. Your team can improve its communication if you dedicate time to ongoing evaluation of your dialogue practices. Do you speak clearly to one another? Do you listen attentively to one another? Do you give one another constructive feedback? These are the kinds of questions you must ask, as you evaluate the communication skills within your team.

6. Conflict

Chapter 6 made the point that conflict within your group is inevitable. A *conflict* is an interpersonal dispute. We noted that the important thing is how your team handles conflicts when they do occur. Are constructive solutions being found to the disputes that arise? Are relationships among members strengthened through effective conflict resolution?

Conflict management is an important subject for group evaluation, and effective groups regularly examine their strategies for dealing with conflict. Some build "gripe sessions" into their agendas so that members will have an opportunity to air their concerns about the group. While the label "gripe session" is not particularly positive, the concept of regularly providing time to assess interpersonal relationships is a good one. If your group evaluates its conflict-resolution abilities and regularly provides members with a chance to vent their feelings, you will establish a supportive climate in which conflict can be dealt with constructively.

7. Cohesion

Team spirit is another focus for periodic evaluation. In Chapter 7, we defined *cohesion* as a group's sense of unity or togetherness. There we emphasized the importance of trust, affiliation, influence, respect, and the creation of a supportive climate. In addition, six rules for creating a supportive climate were reviewed. These rules can, for example, serve as a focal point for assessing the climate in your group. Are your members cold and neutral or warm and empathic? Do you treat one another as equals? Are members cooperative? Are members genuine and honest, refraining from manipulation? Are members open to new ideas? Are they supportive and non-judgmental? Work to ensure that, among other things, your group keeps examining its climate and its sense of cohesion.

8. Critical Discussion

To generate the best ideas possible, your group needs to engage in critical discussion, the subject of Chapter 8. *Critical discussion* is a six-step process that encourages conceptual conflict. A regular review of your use of critical discussion can prevent members from falling prey to groupthink. Conceptual conflict is a fundamental ingredient in effective problem solving, because it encourages a group to make good decisions based on critical analysis of its members' suggestions. In your strategies for assessing your performance, make sure that your group includes evaluations of its critical thinking.

9. Decisions

Effective decision making, as described in Chapter 9, is essential for solving the many problems that your group faces. A *decision* is a choice between options, and your team will make choices regularly as it completes its tasks. Consequently, your team needs to evaluate its decision-making practices and its successes and failures in problem solving. Does your group employ the problem-solving process? Does it take time to define the problem, research it, formulate alternative solutions, consciously decide on a solution, implement the solution plan, and evaluate its success? In addition, does your group use effective decision-making methods? Does it, for example, know when to use majority vote and when to use consensus?

10. Evaluation

It may seem redundant to suggest evaluating the *evaluation* practices of a group. Isn't this overkill? Not really. If, for example, your group has poor evaluation strategies, then your assessments are not likely to produce much improvement. It's possible for a group to evaluate regularly yet do so ineffectively. This could happen if your group neglects to assess specific aspects of its performance and deals only in generalities. Analysis of your group's evaluation practices is, therefore, absolutely necessary.

We have now reviewed the many subjects that require regular evaluation within small groups. Obviously, evaluating them all at one time or in one session would be impossible. All of your group's time would be expended in evaluation, none in performance. Effective groups will consider one aspect at one time and other aspects at other times. Sometimes circumstances will dictate the subject for evaluation. At other times, a well-planned agenda will do so. Your team is more likely to succeed in all these areas if you evaluate your performance regularly.

When it comes to evaluation, your group will want to develop a checklist to ensure that all major areas of its experience are evaluated. Your checklist should include all of the following broad areas:

- Member roles
- Leadership
- Group rules
- Group goals
- Dialogue skills
- Conflict strategies
- Team building
- Critical discussion
- Decision making and problem solving
- Performance evaluation

CHAPTER SUMMARY

We began this chapter by reviewing the fundamental distinction between task goals and social goals, the two broad areas in which performance evaluation is essential. Having made that distinction, we underscored the cardinal rule of group evaluation: "Describe behaviours; don't judge people." Next, we described both formal and informal evaluation, pointing out the similarities and differences, and emphasizing the importance of both. We then presented five steps for effective formal evaluation. Groups should identify the focus behaviours, create an evaluation tool, use the tool to observe and rate performance, discuss the observations and ratings, and set goals for improvement. Finally, we described the ten areas of group experience that require regular evaluation if a group wants to be an effective team, improving its performance throughout its life. Each of these areas, we pointed out, has been the subject of 1 chapter of this examination of interpersonal and group dynamics.

KEY TERMS

challenge	informal evaluation
challenge of evaluation	leader roles
evaluation	member roles
evaluation instrument	observers
focus behaviours	rating scale
formal evaluation	"secret" observers

MASTERING THE MATERIAL

Now that you have read this chapter, use the following guides to ensure that you have mastered the material.

1. The two basic goals of an effective group are _____ accomplishment and _____ development. These goals are called the _____ goal and the _____ goal.

2. Define *challenge of evaluation*.

3. The critical skill of describing the behaviour of others without judging them personally underlies three specific rules presented in various chapters throughout this text. Identify the three rules.

    a.

    b.

    c.

4. Name and describe the two types of evaluation discussed in this chapter.

    a.

    b.

5. Define *focus behaviour*.

6. From memory, list the five steps of the formal evaluation process.

    Step #1:

    Step #2:

    Step #3:

    Step #4:

    Step #5:

7. What is an evaluation instrument?

8. What is a rating scale?

9. Explain the role of observers.

10. What is a "secret" observer?

11. Name and describe the 10 areas of group work that require regular evaluation.

a.

b.

c.

d.

e.

f.

g.

h.

i.

j.

PRACTISING YOUR GROUP SKILLS

PURPOSE OF THIS SECTION

The purpose of "Practising Your Group Skills" and the ultimate purpose of this book is to help you become a more effective participant in the groups to which you belong. This section is designed to provide opportunities for you and your fellow students to practise your group skills in a structured environment.

TEAM RESPONSIBILITIES

A description of the team responsibilities for each of five different teams—the Executive Team, the Lesson Review Team, the Teaching Team, the Energizer Team, and the Evaluation Team—can be found in Appendix B, pages 177–180. Your teacher may have chosen to use from one to five of these teams to conduct the teaching and learning activities of your class. Units 2 and 3 of the Teacher's Guide provide your teacher with additional information on the responsibilities of these teams.

INDIVIDUAL ROLE RESPONSIBILITIES

A description of four individual role responsibilities—those of Leader, Recorder, Reporter, and Participant-Analyst—can be found in Appendix B, pages 180–182. Your professor may have chosen to use from one to four of these roles within teams to give individuals experience leading, recording, reporting, and analyzing. Units 2 and 3 of the Teacher's Guide provide your professor with additional information on these individual role responsibilities.

SPECIFIC TEAM ASSIGNMENTS

Specific team assignments for this chapter appear immediately below. Specific team assignments for each of the chapters in this book can be found in "Practising Your Group Skills" in each chapter.

CHAPTER 10 TEAM ASSIGNMENTS

THE EXECUTIVE TEAM

- *Your Ultimate Goal*: to provide leadership to your classmates for your class session on Chapter 10.

- *Your Interim Goals*: to facilitate the class session by (1) ensuring a good classroom setup, (2) welcoming the class, (3) introducing the lesson topic, (4) coordinating activities, and (5) bringing the session to a close.

- *Instructions*: Ensure that the classroom is set up to accommodate today's class activities. Post an agenda for the session. Welcome people to class and announce the topic, "Evaluation: Improving Your Group's Performance," in a creative and interesting way. Remind the class that the topic includes instruction on five steps of the formal evaluation process. Introduce and thank all speakers when appropriate. Coordinate the day's activities and bring closure at the end of the class. If necessary, return the classroom to its original configuration.

THE LESSON REVIEW TEAM

- *Your Ultimate Goal*: to review Chapter 9, "Decisions: Solving Problems in Your Group."

- *Your Interim Goals*: to provide a review of (1) the experiential exercise, (2) the six steps of the problem-solving process, and (3) the eight decision-making methods that groups can use when solving problems.

- *Instructions*: As the Lesson Review Team, you have the freedom to choose how you will do the review. You can be as creative as you wish, but you must achieve the lesson review goals above. Remember that your time is very limited, so don't try to re-teach last chapter's lesson.

THE TEACHING TEAM

- *Your Ultimate Goal*: to understand and demonstrate effective group evaluation skills in a small group setting.

- *Your Interim Goals*: to describe, explain, and demonstrate (1) the 5 steps of the formal evaluation process and (2) the 10 areas of group experience that require evaluation.

- *Instructions*: As the Teaching Team, you have the freedom to choose how you will teach your lesson. You can be as creative as you wish, but you must achieve the lesson goals above. Your experiential exercise is called "Creating Evaluation Instruments" and you'll find it described fully in

Appendix C, pages 199–201. Make sure that you refer to it when you teach and explain your lesson goals. The exercise should also be included in your lesson when you describe and explain the formal evaluation process and the areas that need to be evaluated. If time allows, you can also use exercises from "Mastering the Material" to teach your lesson.

THE ENERGIZER TEAM

- *Your Ultimate Goal*: to motivate your classmates by conducting an energizer activity.

- *Your Interim Goals*: to facilitate the energizing of your classmates by (1) planning an energizer activity and (2) implementing the plan at an appropriate time in the class session.

- *Instructions*: Your team doesn't have a specific, assigned activity to conduct. Rather, the team should remember its energizing purpose and conduct an activity that will provide a break in the class learning routine. Popular games like Simon Says, Heads Up Seven Up, and Murder Wink usually work well. So do various mixers and ice breakers. (Your professor's Teacher's Guide identifies a number of sources of energizer exercises.) Whatever you decide on, you must be prepared to give clear instructions and conduct the exercise effectively. When you lead the energizer, you are leading and directing the entire class. Plan well and execute professionally, even if the exercise is a "kid's game." Encourage everyone to get involved.

THE EVALUATION TEAM

As a member of the Evaluation Team, you need to review the information in pages 145–148 of this chapter, before you do anything else. There you will find helpful information on how to conduct your evaluation session. The most important thing to remember is that you are not to judge other people. Your role is to help the class make its own assessment of which practices worked well today and which didn't.

- *Your Ultimate Goal*: to assess group (or class) members' team evaluation skills.

- *Your Interim Goals*: to (1) assess group (or class) knowledge of and use of the formal evaluation process and (2) identify practices in need of improvement.

- *Instructions*: Create an evaluation instrument based on the selected focus behaviours identified in the evaluation goals above. See pages 146–147 of this chapter, for information on creating evaluation instruments. Figure 10.1 provides an example. Solicit feedback from the class using the evaluation instrument. Use the feedback to discuss the class session with the purpose of identifying improvements that can be made to individual, group, and class performance in future class sessions. Conclude by noting the specific actions that need to be repeated or avoided to make improvements.

REFERENCES AND RECOMMENDED READINGS

Coffey, R.E., Curtis, W.C., & Hunsaker, P.L. (1994). *Management and organizational behaviour*. Burr Ridge, IL: Austin Press/Irwin.

Harris, E.T., & Sherblom, J.C. (1999). *Small group and team communication*. Needham Heights, MA: Allyn & Bacon.

Robbins, S.P. (1994). *Essentials of organizational behavior* (4th ed.). Englewood Cliffs, NJ: Prentice Hall.

Wilson, G.L. (1999). *Groups in context: Leadership and participation in small groups*. Boston: McGraw-Hill.

USEFUL URLS

About.com Human Resources. http://humanresources.about.com.

Free Management Library. www.managementhelp.org.

MindTools. www.mindtools.com.

Pfeiffer Publishing. http://ca.pfeiffer.com/WileyCDA/Section/index.html.

Team Technology. www.teamtechnology.co.uk.

Your Meeting Resource Center. www.effectivemeetings.com.

APPENDIXES

Meetings: Conducting Business Effectively in Your Group

INTRODUCTION

Meetings are a fact of life and, like so many life experiences, they can be exciting and productive or boring and a waste of time. Frequently meetings are unproductive because people aren't properly prepared, don't understand the purpose of the meeting, or don't understand their role in the proceedings. In addition, time is often mismanaged.

Fortunately, there are many things that you can do to make your meetings more interesting, informative, and productive. Successful meetings require timely notification of participants, an accurate record of previous meetings, a clear agenda for the pending meeting, skillful conduct of the proceedings at that meeting, timely conclusion of the meeting, and appropriate followup.

Sometimes people meet solely to share information, sometimes they meet solely to make decisions, and sometimes they meet solely to solve problems. However, most of the time when people meet to conduct business, they do all three things. They share information, make decisions, and solve problems.

In this appendix, we'll first describe the two key documents that are essential for meeting success. We'll then describe certain rules of order for conduct at a meeting and explain the roles of chair, recorder, reporter, and attendees. Next we'll note the things that have to be done before, during, and after a typical business meeting. We'll also note the importance of time management.

After studying the face-to-face meeting, we'll look at two types of electronic meetings that are conducted routinely in some organizations. Let's start with the face-to-face business meeting.

THE BUSINESS MEETING

A *business meeting* is a meeting that is held to share information, make decisions, and solve problems. A *face-to-face meeting* is a business meeting in which people are physically present in the same room, whereas an *electronic meeting* is one in which attendees are not physically gathered in the same room but are linked together by electronic means.

Among the largest face-to-face meetings are those of national parliaments, where hundreds of people attend. When such large numbers meet to make important decisions, they need an orderly way in which to discuss and decide issues. Consequently, meetings of parliament follow strict procedures to ensure that elected representatives conduct the business of a nation in an orderly manner.

Small groups in schools and in the workplace also conduct face-to-face business on a regular basis, and they also need a systematic way in which to meet, discuss, and decide issues. Your group will conduct successful meetings if you include the following essentials in your business meetings.

BUSINESS MEETING ESSENTIALS

To hold a successful business meeting, you have to give careful consideration to a number of essentials. First, you have to prepare two *key documents*, the record and the agenda. Second, you have to have *rules of order* in place to guide your actions during the course of your meeting. Third, you need to have individuals at the meeting who will fulfill key roles in the conduct of your meeting.

KEY DOCUMENTS FOR YOUR BUSINESS MEETING

The key documents that are essential for conducting successful business meetings are the record and the agenda.

The Record

Traditionally, the official record of a group's meeting has been called the "minutes." More recently, however, the word "record" has gained in popularity. Both words mean the same thing and either can be used. In this book, we refer to the record as the official account of a group's deliberations and decisions.

Keeping an accurate record of a group's reports, discussions, and decisions is extremely important because memories can fade quickly, leaving group members in confusion or disagreement regarding what was decided at previous meetings. A properly prepared record provides a clear and accurate statement of past group actions, as time moves on and memories fade.

The record should follow the order of business in the agenda, and it should note all the decisions that your group makes, identifying individual responsibilities and deadlines for each action item. The following items are essential in the record:

1. The date, time, location, and length of the meeting.
2. The names of attendees and absentees.
3. The chair's name.
4. The recorder's name.
5. Reporters' names and summaries of their reports.
6. The decisions that the group makes (action items).
7. The names of those responsible for each action item.
8. The deadline for each action item.

SAMPLE RECORD

The Association of Canadian College Students
Record of the Meeting of May 23, 2012
Excelsior College, Albright Room 123

Attending: Nancy Kwan (Chair), Larry Singleton, Jose Pablito, Dominic Forte, Ahmed Mahood, Wilma Nguyen, Paula Broxton (Recorder)

Absent: Rodney Upton

1. Call to Order: N. Kwan called the meeting to order at 9:00 a.m.

2. Approval of the Agenda: A. Mahood moved that the agenda be accepted as distributed. L. Singleton seconded the motion. Voted and passed.

3. Approval of the Record of May 23, 2012: D. Forte moved that the record be approved as distributed. J. Pablito seconded the motion. Voted and passed.

4. Unfinished Business: There were no items of unfinished business.

5. Reports: A. Mahood reported for the Communications Committee, indicating that discussions with Universal TV have begun. His report is attached.

6. New Business
   a. L. Singleton moved that the chair, Nancy Kwan, attend the tuition fee protest rally to voice our opposition to the proposed fee increase. J. Pablito seconded the motion. Voted and passed. ACTION: Singleton and Kwan. DEADLINE: June 30.

   b. W. Nguyen moved that the Association hold its annual picnic at the Maidstone Quarry. A. Mahood seconded the motion. Voted and passed. ACTION: Nguyen and Mahood. DEADLINE: July 15.

7. Evaluation: D. Forte thanked the chair for conducting business efficiently. Everyone agreed.

8. Closure: The chair announced that the next meeting is set for July 23 at 9:30 a.m. in Excelsior, Room 123. The meeting adjourned at 10:50 a.m.

Recorder: *Paula Broxton* (signed)

Written reports and other documents that are introduced at a meeting can be attached to the record. Such items should not be edited. They should appear exactly as they were presented at the meeting. See the sample record and sample agenda boxes above and on the next page respectively.

The Agenda

The *agenda* is a list of the items of business to be considered at a particular meeting. It serves as the official schedule for conducting business, allowing attendees to deal with business in a systematic way. In most instances, a group's recorder and chair prepare the agenda.

The agenda has two parts: the heading and the schedule.

The *heading* should appear prominently at the top of your agenda in a distinctive font. It should include: the name of your group, the meeting date and time, and the meeting location.

SAMPLE AGENDA

The Association of Canadian College Students
Annual Meeting
Excelsior College, Paxton, NB
Albright Building, Room 346
May 23, 2012
9:00 a.m. to 11:00 a.m.

1. Call to Order

2. Approval of the Agenda

3. Approval of the Record

4. Unfinished Business

5. Reports
   - Finance
   - Presidential Liaison
   - Communications
   - T-Shirt Design and Sales Plan
   - Online Meetings Software

6. New Business
   - ACCS Response to College Presidents
   - Possible Alberta Faculty Strike
   - Provincial Meeting Schedules

7. Evaluation
   - Next Meeting

8. Closure

The *schedule* includes the following items of business, with items numbered for ease of reference during a meeting:

1. Call to Order

2. Approval of the Agenda

3. Approval of the Record

4. Unfinished Business

5. Reports

6. New Business

7. Evaluation

8. Closure

While agendas are often distributed at the time of a meeting, it is a much better practice to distribute them in advance of a meeting—that is, at the same time that the record is distributed. This may not always be possible, but, if it is, it will put the schedule of business into the hands of members well before a meeting, giving them time to prepare.

RULES OF ORDER FOR YOUR BUSINESS MEETING

Rules of order are procedural norms that require a group to conduct its business in a particular way. Historically, rules of order developed in national parliaments in order to facilitate discussion and decision making in large, elected bodies. Parliamentary rules are very formal and quite complex because they're designed to maintain order when large numbers meet to conduct a nation's business.

In 1876, a US Army officer, H.M. Robert, wrote a book that we now know as *Robert's Rules of Order*. The book was written in an effort to ensure that business was conducted fairly and systematically, and it is still the most widely used set of rules for conducting business in North America. Like the rules of Parliament, Robert's rules are complex and they require that very specific, formal procedures be used when conducting business.

Because of the formality and complexity of Robert's rules, many small groups adopt the *spirit* of his rules, but not all the *details*. That's the approach we'll take. While our approach is less formal, it still provides a fair and orderly way for your group to conduct its business meetings.

Some Traditional Meeting Language

Although we are taking an informal approach to the rules of order, we need to be familiar with certain basic language that originates in the traditional, formal meeting. We'll limit ourselves to the following: *motion, mover, seconder, debate,* and *vote.*

A *motion* is a formal proposal to take a particular course of action, and the person who makes a motion is called the *mover*. This person wants to *move* the group to take the proposed action. Sample motions are shown in the box on the following page.

If the mover is the only person who supports the proposal, discussing it would be a waste of time. Therefore, a second person, the *seconder*, must express support for the motion before discussion of the proposal can begin.

Once moved and seconded, the chair indicates that the motion is open for *debate*, the formal word for critical discussion. During debate all can present their points of view for or against the motion, but only in an orderly and respectful way under the direction of the chair.

When a motion has been thoroughly discussed, the chair calls for a deciding *vote*, a poll to see who favours the motion and who doesn't. In most cases, if 51 percent or more vote in favour, the motion passes. If 51 percent or more vote against it, the motion fails.

While these traditional words are used in many meetings, they certainly aren't used in all. If your group doesn't use the words, make sure that it uses the ideas behind the words, because attendees always need to be aware of the items that are being proposed for discussion and decision.

If your group learns to use these five words (and the ideas behind them) in your meetings, you will conduct your business more efficiently. You'll save time, avoid frustration, and enjoy successful meetings.

SAMPLE MOTIONS

Sample Motions from the Association of Canadian College Students Meeting held at Excelsior College, May 23, 2012

Re: Item 2, Approval of the Agenda
Mover: "I move that we approve the record as distributed."
Seconder: "I second the motion."
Chair, after discussion: "All in favour of the motion say 'Yes.' (PAUSE) Any opposed, say 'No.' (PAUSE) The motion passes (fails)."

Re: Item 3, Approval of the Record
Mover: "I move that we approve the record as distributed."
Seconder: "I second the motion."
Chair, after discussion: "All in favour of the motion say 'Yes.' (PAUSE) Any opposed, say 'No.' (PAUSE) The motion passes (fails)."

Re: Item 6a, New Business, Tuition Fee Protest Rally
Mover: "I move that our class attend the tuition fee protest rally to voice our opposition to the proposed fee increase."
Seconder: "I second the motion."
Chair, after discussion: "All in favour of the motion say 'Yes.' (PAUSE) Any opposed, say 'No.' (PAUSE) The motion passes (fails)."

Re: Item 6b, New Business, Annual Picnic Site
Mover: "I move that our class hold its annual picnic at the Maidstone Quarry."
Seconder: "I second the motion."
Chair, after discussion: "All in favour of the motion say 'Yes.' (PAUSE) Any opposed, say 'No.' (PAUSE) The motion passes (fails)."

Rules of Order for Voting

Here are the basic rules that apply when your group has to make a decision. Note that the rules are to be observed in sequence. These rules for group decision-making include the following:

1. Somebody must make a motion.
2. Somebody else must second the motion.
3. Debate must be restricted to the current motion only.
4. Debate must include equal opportunity for all to speak to the motion.
5. The group must decide to accept or reject the motion.
6. The decision must be entered into the official record.

Rules of Order for Individual Attendees

The following rules of order apply to all attendees except the chair during a business meeting. To ensure an orderly and fair meeting, attendees should:

- Speak only with permission of the chair.
- Direct their remarks to the chair.
- Restrict their remarks to the motion under consideration.
- Refrain from impugning the character or motives of others.
- Listen respectfully to the views of others.
- Participate constructively in the decision-making process.
- Support the implementation of the decisions taken.

KEY ROLES FOR BUSINESS MEETING SUCCESS

1. The Role of the Chair

The *chair* or chairperson is the person who has leadership responsibility for conducting the meeting according to the rules of order and the schedule in the agenda.

Effective chairpersons possess the characteristics of a good leader. They are knowledgeable, they communicate well, they are both task-oriented and people-oriented, and they are flexible. In addition, successful chairs are enthusiastic, patient, tactful, courteous, decisive, assertive, and impartial. They are also excellent managers of time.

2. The Role of Recorder

The *recorder* is the person who has leadership responsibility for keeping a clear and accurate account of team meetings. Recorders should record only the essentials of a meeting, keeping the record concise, clear, and accurate.

Recorders need to possess excellent organizing, listening, note taking, and writing skills, because the clarity and accuracy of the record that they produce is vital to team success. The record should be written in grammatically correct sentences that are free of spelling errors, and it should be as concise as possible.

3. The Role of Reporters

A *reporter* is a person who has leadership responsibility for giving a summary account of some aspect of a group's ongoing work, a special research project, or a significant event that the reporter has observed. On important matters, reporters will provide attendees with both spoken and written accounts. Successful reporters produce reports that are clear, concise, and accurate.

4. The Role of Attendees

The chair, recorder, and reporters are *attendees* with special responsibilities. Other attendees have no special duties, but they do share in the responsibility for the success of a meeting. They are, for example, expected to prepare for meetings by reviewing the record, being familiar with the agenda, and studying any supporting documents.

During the course of a meeting, attendees are expected to follow the rules of order, to contribute their ideas and opinions, to listen to the views of others, and to participate constructively in the decision-making process. Members of your group who do all this with respect, tact, courtesy, and enthusiasm will help make meetings a success.

THREE STEPS TO BUSINESS MEETING SUCCESS

Now that we've described the key documents, rules of order, and the key roles that are essential for successful meetings, let's look at the steps that your group should take before, during, and after your team meetings.

Step 1: Preparation Prior to Your Meeting

Successful meetings start with good preparation, which includes notifying attendees, distributing key documents, and readying the meeting site.

Notification and Distribution

All members of your group and any special guests should be notified of the date, time, location, and purpose of your meeting well in advance of the meeting. In addition, they should receive an agenda, the record, and any related documents so that they can study them and come to the meeting prepared to discuss, debate, and decide on the scheduled items of business.

Ideally, notification of the meeting and distribution of the meeting resources will occur simultaneously, well ahead of the upcoming business meeting. Once ready, these documents can be distributed by handout, regular mail, email, or fax. However, you must use a method or methods that ensure that everyone receives them.

In most groups, the recorder is responsible for notifying prospective participants and distributing the resource documents to them. Regardless of who does it, proper notification and distribution is the first step to a meeting's success.

Meeting Site

If people meet in a place that's comfortable and equipped for the work of a business meeting, your chances of having a successful meeting increase. Select a room that is spacious, clean, well lit, and quiet, and ensure that it has ample table space and comfortable chairs. Restrooms should be nearby.

Attendees should be able to easily make eye contact with one another, and they should have a clear view of presenters, monitors, projection screens, and flip charts. Of course, any special needs of attendees, such as wheelchair accommodation, should be met.

In addition to the room itself, you need to provide resources. These usually include paper, pencils, pens, slide projectors, white boards, newsprint pads, and similar tools. Video conferencing and other technology-based meetings will require special equipment that must be readily available and functioning properly. Also, if food and drink are a part of the meeting, you may need a refrigerator, microwave oven, or similar appliances.

Step 2: Conducting Business Skillfully During Your Meeting

You notified your attendees of the meeting time and location; you provided them with the record, the agenda, and supporting documents; and you selected and equipped the meeting room appropriately. Now it's meeting time. How do you conduct a successful business meeting?

The Order of Business

Earlier in this appendix we noted that the agenda is the schedule of items of business to be conducted at a meeting. Using a typical agenda as our guide, we'll now comment on the proper conduct of your business meeting. The chair plays the key role throughout.

In the *call to order*, the chair officially begins the meeting, welcomes the attendees, thanks them for being present, encourages the involvement of all, and briefly indicates the main purpose of the meeting. By showing enthusiasm for the work at hand, the chair sets the tone for the proceedings. Moreover, by starting on time the chair signals the importance of keeping to the schedule.

Next, directing everyone's attention to the *agenda*, the chair asks attendees if there are any additions or changes to be made. Normally, any suggestion that would lead to a *major* refocus of the meeting will be put off to a future meeting. Otherwise, minor changes are made with the consent of all. With approval, the agenda becomes the official order of business for the meeting.

After ensuring that everyone has read the *record* of the previous meeting, the chair asks if there are any changes that need to be made to the record. If there are inaccuracies or omissions, they are corrected with the agreement of all. Once the record is approved, it becomes the official account of the preceding meeting's actions.

Under *unfinished business*, the chair invites discussion and decision on any unfinished business that appears in the record of the previous meeting. This agenda item is sometimes called "old business" or "business arising from the minutes." Here, unfinished business is concluded before the group hears reports and moves on to new business.

Next, the chair asks for *reports*. When recognized by the chair, each reporter speaks on behalf of a subcommittee and presents a summary of some aspect of the committee's work. Reports serve to inform attendees about the work that others in the organization are doing. See the sample report on the following page.

When all the reports have been given, the chair introduces the first item of *new business* and calls for a motion. If the motion is moved and seconded, the chair directs debate on the motion according to the rules of order for voting. Once decided, the item becomes an official action of the group. The chair then deals with each remaining agenda item in the same manner.

Before closing the meeting, the chair or an appointee may conduct a brief *evaluation* session to determine whether changes in the conduct of future meetings need to be made or not. As noted in Chapter 10, evaluation increases the chances of better performance at future meetings.

SAMPLE REPORT

The Association of Canadian College Students
Meeting of May 23, 2012
Finance Committee Report
Reporter: Dominic Forte

As of May 1, 2012, the ACCS has $5,795.57 in its chequing account and $6,452.39 in its reserve account.

All member colleges have submitted their 2012 membership fee, and the finance committee thanks the local treasurers for submitting their fees on time.

The budget committee continues to prepare its report for 2013 and expects to make its report on schedule at the November 2012 meeting.

Reporter: *Dominic Forte* (signed)

The last item on the agenda is *closure*. The chair ensures that the date, time, and location of the next meeting are established, and makes some brief closing remarks that highlight the achievements of the current meeting. The chair then declares the meeting closed.

Step 3: Following Up After Your Meeting

The most important thing to do once a meeting has ended is to follow up on the decisions made at the meeting. Each action item from the meeting will include an assignment of responsibility and a deadline date. At an appropriate time after your meeting, the chair or the recorder should contact the people responsible to remind them of their tasks and to offer assistance if needed. Always be diplomatic when doing this so that you don't give the impression that you don't trust the person or that you're hounding them to do their work.

ELECTRONIC MEETINGS

To reduce the costs involved in holding face-to-face meetings, many organizations have turned to electronic meetings. An *electronic meeting* is a meeting in which attendees are not physically gathered in a room but are linked together by electronic means. These means include hardware such as telephones, televisions, computers, cameras, microphones, and other electronic devices. They also include specialized productivity software, often referred to as groupware. Electronic meetings are also called "e-meetings," "virtual meetings," and "web meetings," among other things. While these meetings have very real costs, they are rarely as high as those for face-to-face meetings where travel, lodging, and meals are involved.

To conduct a business meeting successfully by electronic means, the selected technology (hardware and software) will first have to support the distribution of notices, records, agendas, and resource documents prior to a meeting. Moreover, it will have to allow the chair, recorder, and reporters to fulfill their special roles during the course of a meeting. Furthermore, it must permit attendees to make motions, second them, debate them, and vote on them throughout the meeting. Finally, it must facilitate post-meeting followup.

Some very popular methods of electronic communication are not capable of handling the complex activity that business meetings require. Text messaging, for example, is an excellent way to send and receive short messages, but it isn't suitable for meetings. More sophisticated technologies are required for electronic business meetings, and they do exist. In particular, properly supported video conferences appear to meet all the needs noted earlier.

In this section we'll describe two forms of electronic meetings, the teleconference and the video conference.

The Teleconference

The *teleconference* is an electronic meeting in which attendees are linked together by telephones. It's the oldest type of electronic meeting, and it consists of a network of telephones with one attendee at each phone. At a designated time, the attendees are linked to each other by dialing a given number. When connected, the network is established and the telephone meeting begins.

In a teleconference, attendees can hear one another, but they can't see each other. Strictly speaking, this type of electronic meeting should be called an "audio conference" or "audio-only conference" because attendees communicate only by speaking and hearing, without the benefits of seeing one another.

Because visual cues are non-existent in a teleconference, special procedural rules or *protocols* are necessary to compensate. In a teleconference the chair needs a protocol for acknowledging those who wish to speak. Because prospective speakers can't visually signal their desire to speak, the chair may need a checklist, for example, and use it to ask each attendee to speak to an issue in turn.

While this protocol may work, it can slow proceedings significantly. It can also frustrate an attendee who wishes to make a point but has to wait "at the end of the line" before speaking. Moreover, it does nothing to provide the eye contact that facilitates good two-way communication. Nor does it compensate for another drawback, the inability of attendees to make visual presentations in their meetings.

Continued use of the teleconference demonstrates that it is, despite drawbacks, still a useful meeting format for certain purposes. For example, it can be used successfully for limited information sharing and simple decision making. However, it remains a poor substitute for a face-to-face meeting when it comes to discussing, debating, and deciding complex issues. In this regard, it is also a poor substitute for the video conference.

Teleconferencing is, no doubt, less expensive than holding face-to-face meetings. For many organizations this is an important consideration, and they view the drawbacks that we have noted as being counterbalanced by the dollars and time saved.

The Video Conference

The *video conference* is an electronic meeting in which attendees are linked together by both video and audio technologies. The network in this case consists of attendee stations equipped with video cameras, web cameras, and video monitors for transmitting video images, and microphones, headphones, and speakers for exchanging audio messages.

Because each attendee can see and be seen, hear and be heard, the video conference should really be called the "audio and video conference." Unlike the teleconference, it incorporates both sound and sight. This capability raises the video conference to the level of the face-to-face meeting. When well supported technologically, it can be comparable to a face-to-face meeting.

The video conference is superior to the teleconference for a couple of reasons. Because participants can see one another, the need for special protocols is reduced, which makes the conduct of business easier. Moreover, attendees can share visual aids and make eye contact.

Like the teleconference, the video conference can save both time and money compared with face-to-face meetings, and this makes it an attractive alternative. Complex issues can be discussed, debated, and decided in a video conference. The fact that attendees have both audio and video contact makes the video conference option very attractive.

Video Conferencing on an Intranet

An *intranet* is a local or restricted computer network that serves the internal needs of an organization. A large business, for example, may establish an intranet to further its corporate goals. The network will consist of a number of computers that are connected to a local server.

A local area network is called an intranet because the computers are all *within* the local network. "Intra" means "within," and "net" is short for "network." If the organization wishes to hold video conferences for members who are within its local area network but physically distant from one another, it can purchase special software and install it on its local network server. All computers on that particular intranet will then be capable of accessing the organization's server-based software to facilitate the conducting of electronic meetings.

Video Conferencing on the Internet

Today, both large and small organizations connect routinely to the Internet, the vast network of computers that comprise the World Wide Web. "Inter" means "between" or "among," and "net" is, once again, short for network. When online, the organization's computers are situated *among* all the computers that make up the Internet.

If an organization wishes to hold video conferences for members who are distant from one another, it can turn to the Internet and purchase resources to conduct such meetings. In this case, commercially owned, remote servers employ web-based software that the members of the organization can access via the World Wide Web.

Key Features of the Best Video Conferencing Software

In order to conduct effective web meetings, you must first have the best hardware available for the job. A description of such hardware is beyond the scope of this appendix. A brief word about software, however, is not. We'll now note some of the key features of the best video conferencing software currently available.

Earlier we described the tasks that you need to complete before, during, and after your face-to-face meeting. We'll follow the same sequence now and focus on software features that assist with these tasks. Note that all the functions described are not necessarily available within a single software application. The best web services, however, include most of them.

Prior to a meeting, you can complete the essential task of notification by using *calendars* and *schedulers*. In addition, you can use an *electronic workspace* to house and distribute resource documents, meeting goals, the agenda, and the record.

During a meeting, you can make the key documents readily available on the electronic workspace, and the chair can direct proceedings with *control features* that can, for example, permit a particular attendee to have the floor to give a presentation or make a motion. *Screen sharing* and *interactive white boards* make real-time collaboration possible. You can also use *file-sharing* features to further facilitate the business of the meeting. Moreover, you can set a *timer* to signal that the allotted time for an agenda item has expired. Set the *record* feature and the entire meeting is archived.

After a meeting, you can place all action items on the electronic workspace along with the names of the persons responsible for carrying out the action. Related deadlines can also be included. At the end of a meeting, all information from the notification prior to the meeting through to meeting closure is readily available for distribution. This makes post-meeting followup very easy.

As with the other types of electronic meeting, there are costs associated with this one. Web-based businesses provide the software, setup instructions, and support at a price. In addition, your organization has to buy the hardware and provide an Internet connection for all attendees. As you can imagine, the cost of video conferencing can be high. However, if these costs are lower than those for face-to-face meetings, the web conference can rival the traditional meeting with respect to effectiveness.

The costs associated with any form of electronic meeting are likely to prevent most small groups from conducting meetings this way. However, since this is a textbook about interpersonal and group dynamics in small groups, let's note some possibilities for your small group.

If your small group is interested in holding an electronic meeting, you can visit the websites below. They offer either a free service or a free trial service. Remember that the best video conferencing features come at a price. If you experiment with the resources at the sites below, especially the free ones, you may have to content yourself with less than the best features.

www.gotomeeting.com
www.fuzemeeting.com
www.webex.com
www.adobe.com/products/adobeconnect.htm
www.ilinc.com
www.dimdim.com
http://office.microsoft.com/en-ca/live-meeting
www.skype.com
www.glance.net

APPENDIX SUMMARY

We began this appendix by defining a business meeting as one in which people meet to get information, discuss issues, and solve problems. We then discussed the essential elements of a business meeting, which include key documents (the record and agenda; the rules of order for conducting a meeting and for voting; and the key roles of chair, recorder, reporter, and attendee. Next, we described three steps for meeting success. Prior to a meeting, people must be notified and sent key meeting documents. During a meeting, the chair directs business according to the schedule in the agenda. After a meeting, the chair or recorder follows up on meeting decisions by contacting those who are responsible for implementing them. We then turned to electronic meetings, describing the teleconference and the video conference, and pointing out their strengths and weaknesses. Favouring the video conference, we described video conferencing on both an intranet and the Internet. We completed our work by describing key features of the best software and listed several sites where students can experiment with electronic meetings.

The Experiential Model: Teaching and Learning Group Skills

B

EXPERIENTIAL LEARNING

Practical Learning

Experiential learning is learning by doing. It is practical, hands-on learning that moves from practice to theory, not the other way around. It is the kind of learning that is best suited to acquiring skills. You can't learn to ride a bicycle, for example, by attending classroom lectures and being tested on the lecture material. It requires doing. The student must get on a bicycle and give it a try. Once the learner has mastered some basic skills, then it's a matter of practice, practice, practice. In this regard, learning interpersonal and group skills is much like learning to ride a bicycle.

As its name suggests, experiential learning refers to the acquisition of knowledge and skills through experience. It is experiential learning—learning by doing—that forms the foundation of the learning model that is described below. In each of the 10 chapters of the text, the "Practising Your Group Skills" section is devoted to developing the various skills discussed in the chapter by having students work together in teams to practise those skills.

The material in this appendix explains how "Practising Your Group Skills" can create the experiences from which students will acquire the skills essential to working cooperatively with others in groups. Students practise group skills in a meaningful way as they carry out their various assignments in designated teams. By using student teams in a structured environment, we create a situation in which interpersonal skills can be explained, understood, and practised.

Effective Teachers

Consider, for a moment, the various tasks that an effective teacher performs when teaching a typical lesson in the traditional teacher-centred fashion. First, the teacher welcomes the students to class and reminds them of the lesson topic of the day. He then reviews basic ideas from the last class. Next he presents the new lesson.

APPENDIX GOALS

Upon completion of this appendix, you should be able to:

- Explain experiential learning.
- Describe the experiential model.
- Identify the responsibilities of the teams used in the model.
- Identify the individual role responsibilities used in the model.
- Describe a typical model-based class session.
- Locate specific team assignments.
- Locate more information on the model and how it works.

Somewhere in the proceedings there is time for a break, a time for everyone to get refreshed for the next part of the class session. After break, the lesson continues until the session is close to an end. Before concluding the class, however, the teacher takes a few minutes to summarize the key ideas of the day's lesson. Finally, he reminds students of their homework assignment and wishes them a good day.

Student Teams

Imagine how the dynamics of the class would change if student teams were responsible for the tasks that the teacher normally directs or coordinates—an introduction to the class, a review of the previous lesson, the teaching of the new lesson, the coffee break, and a concluding summary. Imagine the learning experiences that students would have if they were responsible for planning and implementing the class activities that usually fall to the teacher. With the teacher serving as a coach and consultant, student teams can both teach and learn essential group skills as they host one another, review their own lessons, teach one another new lessons, energize one another, and work together to evaluate and improve their performance in the class.

THE EXPERIENTIAL MODEL

The experiential model provides a structure and directions whereby student teams complete the various classroom tasks that are normally done by teachers. In this model, the teacher becomes a consultant who assists the students with the planning and implementation of their assigned tasks. Throughout the rest of the description of the model, I will refer to the teacher as the consultant or the professor. Instead of directing the class in the traditional manner, the consultant coaches and guides the student teams who practise their group skills within the parameters of the model. Professors can choose to employ one or more teams to do the experiential learning prescribed by the model.

If a professor wishes to have classes that are built almost entirely on experiential learning, then she will want to use all five of the teams. In contrast, if a professor wishes to employ the model in a more modest way, then she will use fewer than five teams to help conduct the class and deliver the lessons. As professors become familiar with the teams and their responsibilities, they will see that it's also possible to have one team carry out two different sets of responsibilities. The model allows for a variety of different applications.

Professors who choose to have a group of students rotate through all five of the team functions in the course of a semester will provide that group with five distinctly different sets of responsibilities that require students to practise their interpersonal and group skills on an ongoing basis. On this approach, each group of students functions as the Executive Team at one time, the Lesson Review Team at another time, the Teaching Team at another time, the Energizer Team at another time, and the Evaluation Team at yet another time. In the next section, we'll provide the job descriptions for all five teams.

Note that the group members stay together as a group throughout the course. The membership of each team remains the same, but a team's responsibilities change from time to time according to a predetermined schedule. At any given time, for example, one team will be responsible for teaching while the other teams are responsible for hosting and coordinating, reviewing the last lesson, energizing their classmates, and evaluating class performance.

The model also includes individual role responsibilities for each of four different roles, those of Leader, Recorder, Reporter, and Participant-Analyst. If individual students are required to serve as Leaders, Recorders, Reporters, and Participant-Analysts on their teams, then both teams and individuals will be involved in experiential learning at virtually all stages of the course. This skills-focused, practical approach to acquiring and developing interpersonal and group skills provides powerful motivation for and reinforcement of student learning.

Take note that the time frames included in the "Specific Responsibilities" sections below are based on the assumption that all five teams are working within a two-hour block of time. Consequently, each team has a time limit within which it has to meet its particular responsibilities for the class session.

THE TEAM RESPONSIBILITIES

The Executive Team

As hosts for the class session, the Executive Team begins the class with an appropriate welcome to members of the class. Team members introduce themselves so that the rest of the class knows who the executive members are. They may also wear name tags or dress distinctively to help others recognize them as the hosts for the class session. Then they introduce the lesson topic for the day in some interesting way and, if required, call for reports from each team, including their own team. The reports are very brief updates by each team, describing their progress on the various tasks for which they are responsible. Someone from the Executive Team introduces and thanks each of the reporters. At appropriate times throughout the class session, the Executive Team introduces and thanks all the other teams—the Lesson Review Team, the Teaching Team, the Energizer Team, and the Evaluation Team—as those teams carry out their responsibilities. Finally, the Executive Team brings closure to the class session.

Specific Responsibilities

- Ensure that the classroom is properly set up.
- Provide an agenda for the class session.
- Introduce the chapter topic in a creative way.
- Introduce and thank all teams and speakers.
- Coordinate the class activities.
- Bring closure to the class session.
- Ensure that the classroom is returned to its standard form.

The Lesson Review Team

After the opening welcome by the Executive Team, the Lesson Review Team assists the class in reviewing the previous week's lesson. The team's specific lesson review assignment is found in "Practising Your Group Skills" in each chapter. Team members can choose to do the review in any way they wish, provided that they achieve the learning objectives of the review. Students can be very creative in their review, and their creativity should be encouraged as long as it serves the learning process. While the lesson review is in progress, the Lesson Review Team is in charge of the class. Their leaders give direction to the review process while members of all the other teams participate in the review. When the Lesson Review Team concludes its review, the Executive Team thanks the members and then introduces the next team.

Specific Responsibilities

- Provide a review of the lesson taught at the previous class session.
- Explain the experiential exercise and its purpose.
- Summarize the key topics taught.
- Complete the review in 10 to 15 minutes.

The Teaching Team

The Teaching Team has the biggest responsibility of any team. During the lesson, the Teaching Team is in charge of the class, and team members teach the assigned lesson to the rest of the class. The specific teaching assignment is provided in each chapter of the text in "Practising Your Group Skills." The consultant works with the team to help plan its lesson. Note that the assigned experiential exercise is a very important part of that lesson in that it provides the class with a common group experience. In addition, the Teaching Team uses the experiential exercise to illustrate various topics from the assigned chapter. In other words, the Teaching Team employs experiential learning, the same kind of learning that forms the basis of the entire experiential learning model. When the Teaching Team has conducted the experiential exercise and presented the assigned chapter material, members call on the consultant to clarify or elaborate. The consultant has a chance, at this time, to highlight key points and clarify any misunderstandings. When the Teaching Team has finished the lesson, the Executive Team thanks the members and introduces the next team.

Specific Responsibilities

- Introduce the goals of the assigned lesson.
- Conduct the assigned experiential exercise.
- Explain the assigned chapter material, linking it to the experiential exercise.
- Call on the consultant (the professor) for any necessary clarification.
- Conclude the lesson with a brief summary.
- Complete the lesson in 40 to 60 minutes.

The Energizer Team

The Energizer Team is responsible for conducting a brief, motivational exercise that follows the work of the Lesson Review Team and the Teaching Team. The Energizer Team's motivational exercise may be upbeat and active or quiet and meditative. Team members plan the kind of energizer activity that they feel will best help students with the learning activities of the class session. Often these are ice-breaker activities that get the class members to move around and intermingle. These fun experiences provide a necessary change of pace after the more serious activities associated with the lesson review and the lesson of the day. The Energizer Team is in charge of the class when team members are conducting their activity. Energizer activities must be safe, relatively quiet, and professional. When the energizer is over, the Executive Team thanks the Energizer Team and introduces the next team.

Specific Responsibilities

- Conduct a brief energizer exercise that involves the whole class.
- Choose an energizer that is either active or meditative.
- Ensure that the exercise is safe, quiet, and professional.
- Ensure that the exercise is conducted respectfully.
- Complete the exercise in 10 to 15 minutes.

The Evaluation Team

The last major activity of the class session is an evaluation of the class's performance. Under the leadership of the Evaluation Team, the whole class assesses its performance in the class session and identifies goals for improving performance in future classes. The Evaluation Team facilitates the evaluation process, but it does not stand in judgment of the other teams or of any individuals. Team members are responsible for assisting the entire class in assessing its performance on some specific aspect of the class's experience that day.

The steps of the formal evaluation process are detailed in Chapter 10 and members of the Evaluation Team need to read this material *before* facilitating an evaluation session. In addition, each chapter provides a specific evaluation assignment that is keyed to material in that chapter. The evaluation assignment is found in the chapter's "Practising Your Group Skills" section.

Evaluation teams can depart from the chapter assignment and assess other practices if there is a need to do so. If, for example, conflict arises while the class is studying goal setting in Chapter 4, the need to deal with the conflict may override the assigned evaluation on goal setting. Such overriding will be an exception though, an exception occasioned only by a very important class need.

When the Evaluation Team concludes its task, the Executive Team brings closure to the day's activities in some appropriate way.

Specific Responsibilities

- Create an instrument to evaluate the assigned focus behaviours.
- Collect class input using the evaluation instrument.
- Conduct a class discussion of the input collected.
- Assist the class in identifying the successes of the current session.
- Assist the class in identifying specific things that need improvement.
- Complete the session in 15 to 20 minutes.

THE INDIVIDUAL ROLE RESPONSIBILITIES

Team Leader (The Chair or Chairperson)

Every group needs a leader. In the experiential approach to learning group skills, each student serves as Team Leader at some point during the course. In this setting, Team Leaders are not dictators who boss others around. Rather, they are individuals who demonstrate leadership through the coordination of a group's activities, ensuring that the group's responsibilities are being met. When teams meet to do their planning, the Team Leader plays a key role as chair of the meeting, facilitating discussion and ensuring that the team gets its work done. The Team Leader may also be required to communicate with the consultant by way of a written memorandum, informing the consultant of the team's progress during it meeting. A standard memorandum form is available in the Teacher's Guide. The memorandum can be graded if the consultant desires.

When functioning as chair for your team, you will find it helpful if you review the material in the section Three Areas of Leader Responsibility (Chapter 2, pages 17–18), the section The Role of the Chair (Appendix A, page 167), and the section The Order of Business (Appendix A, pages 169–170).

Specific Responsibilities

- Chair team meetings according to accepted rules of order.
- Encourage individuals to complete their tasks.
- Ensure that the team meets its responsibilities.
- Communicate with other teams as necessary.
- Identify yourself to the consultant before each class.
- If required, send a memorandum to the consultant.

Team Recorder

A written record of team discussion and decisions is very important. From Parliament to courtrooms throughout the country, individuals are responsible for keeping an accurate record of proceedings. Groups of all sizes, in virtually all circumstances, do well to maintain a written record of their meetings. In this experiential model, the Team Recorder performs this function for the team.

A record is kept for all group meetings. Recorders use full, clear, and concise sentences when creating the record. The emphasis is placed on accurately recording both the decisions made by the group and the names of those responsible for implementing the decisions. Not everything said in a meeting is necessary to record. Students who have never served as secretary for a group may need special coaching to be able to identify what should be a part of the record and what should not.

There is an advantage to having individuals record for two consecutive classes. The record from the first meeting can serve as a practice run for inexperienced Recorders. By giving the Recorder feedback on the first effort, the consultant puts the student in a position to write a more polished record on the second effort. A standard record form is available in the Teacher's Guide. One or both records can be graded if the consultant desires.

When functioning as recorder for your team, you will find it helpful if you review the material in the section Three Areas of Leader Responsibility (Chapter 2, pages 17–18), the section The Role of the Recorder (Appendix A, page 167), and the section Key Documents for Your Business Meeting (Appendix A, pages 162–163).

Specific Responsibilities

- Keep a written record of team meetings.
- Include the following in your record
  - □ Your team name
  - □ Your team leader's name
  - □ Your name (printed and signed)
  - □ Date, time, and length of meeting
  - □ Members present and absent
  - □ Team decisions and actions (action items)
  - □ Members responsible for implementing action items
  - □ Deadlines for action items.
- Check the accuracy of your record with team members.
- If required, submit your record to the consultant.

Team Reporter

Written and spoken reports are a fact of group life, and they are required for a variety of reasons. Sometimes it is simply a matter of keeping others informed regarding the work of the reporting group. At other times, the reporting group has been charged with the responsibility of making a recommendation to a larger group. The safety subcommittee of city council, for example, may recommend that city council install street lights in a particular part of town.

In the experiential model, the Team Reporter typically gives a status report to the other groups, highlighting the work that the Reporter's team did in its last meeting. A team that has solved a particular problem, for example, can advise other teams on how to avoid the problem should the other teams face it in the future. Most often, however, the Reporter will simply inform other groups as to the current status of the Reporter's group.

The Team Reporter prepares a written report on the proceedings of her group, and reports orally to the class when the Executive Team requests the report. Usually the report is made early in a class session. Once the report has been presented orally, the Reporter may be required to hand in the written report to the consultant. A standard report form is available in the Teacher's Guide. Both the oral and the written reports can be graded if the consultant desires.

When functioning as reporter for your team, you will find it helpful if you review the material in the section Three Areas of Leader Responsibility (Chapter 2, pages 17–18), the section The Role of the Reporters (Appendix A, page 167), and the Sample Report (Appendix A, page 170).

Specific Responsibilities

- Write a report summarizing your team meeting(s).
- Present your report orally to the class when requested.
- If required, submit the written report to the consultant.

Team Participant-Analyst

Actively involved group members carefully observe their groups in order to assess two important things. They analyze their group's progress regarding tasks to be accomplished, and they analyze their group's social-emotional status. These are the two broad goals of all successful groups: task completion and team development.

To help students learn to analyze their groups from these two perspectives, the experiential model requires each student to be a Participant-Analyst at various times throughout the course. Whenever a student is not the Team Leader, Team Reporter, or Team Recorder, she is by default a team Participant-Analyst.

The word *participant* in the label reminds students that they are to *participate* fully in the activities of the group. Being a Participant-Analyst doesn't mean that the student now has time off from group work responsibilities to observe others doing the work. Analysts participate fully, contributing to all aspects of the team's work.

The word *analyst* captures the additional responsibility of monitoring the group's progress with respect to its task and social goals. By requiring students to keep a record of team progress in the areas of task completion and relationship development, the experiential model encourages group members to monitor these critical aspects of group life. The Participant-Analyst shares her observations with the team and leads the team in an evaluation of its performance. If required, she submits her notes to the consultant. A standard form for a Participant-Analyst's notes is available in the Teacher's Guide. The notes can be graded if the consultant desires.

Specific Responsibilities

- Participate fully in the work of your team.
- Observe and record your team's use of task actions.
- Observe and record your team's use of social actions.
- Lead your team in an evaluation of its performance.
- If required, submit your notes to the consultant.

A TYPICAL CLASS SESSION

- Opening, welcome, and introduction (Executive Team)
- Reports (Team Reporters)
- Review of the previous lesson (Lesson Review Team)
- Teaching of the new lesson (The Teaching Team)
  - □ Part 1—the experiential exercise
  - □ Part 2—the explanation of chapter material
- Motivational activity (The Energizer Team)
- Assessment of class performance (Evaluation Team)
- Closure (Executive Team)
- Team planning time (individual teams working independently)

SPECIFIC TEAM ASSIGNMENTS

Specific team assignments that are keyed to the material presented in each chapter of the text are found in the "Practising Your Group Skills" section of each chapter.

MORE INFORMATION ON THE MODEL

Units 2 and 3 of the Teacher's Guide provide the professor with more information on the experiential model and how it can be put to use in class. Unit 2 gives a general description of the model, and unit 3 presents a detailed account of the model.

The Experiential Exercises

INTRODUCTION

Purpose and Connections

The purpose of Appendix C is to provide members of the Teaching Team with detailed instructions on how to conduct their assigned experiential exercise. The assignments are given in "Practising Your Groups Skills" in each chapter. Unit 8 of the Teacher's Guide provides further information about each exercise. It also includes resources for duplication and use in the conduct of the exercises. Appendix B describes experiential learning in general and provides a detailed statement of responsibilities for the Teaching Team.

Exercise Format

Each exercise in this appendix is presented using a standard format. First, the chapter number and the name of the experiential exercise are identified. Next, the ultimate goal of the exercise is presented, followed by specific interim goals. Then, the necessary resources are listed. The detailed instructions for the exercise then follow in two sections on procedures. A brief statement on general procedure is followed by detailed, step-by-step procedures for conducting the exercise.

Variations

The detailed procedures include time frames for the various parts of each exercise. The entire exercise is, in each case, limited to 30 minutes. The experiential exercise is the first part of the Teaching Team's responsibility, and it has to be time-limited in order to allow for the rest of the Teaching Team's presentation. You may need to vary the time or the content of your experiential exercise to get everything done in the maximum 60 minutes allotted for the total teaching assignment. If your professor isn't using the full experiential model with five student teams, then you may have more time to devote to the assigned exercise and the subsequent presentation. Work with your professor to determine what is best for your circumstances.

Creativity and Fun

While the procedures for each exercise are spelled out in fairly fine detail, your exercise still allows for some creativity on your part. Conduct your assigned exercise as creatively as you can, but always ensure that your creativity helps to achieve the interim goals and the ultimate goal and the objectives of the exercise. Some exercises are more fun than others. You should strive to make your exercise an enjoyable learning experience.

Teaching Tip

Often the experiential exercise requires groups to report to the class at the end of the exercise. Here's a tip. If you tell each individual member of a group to be prepared to report when you request it, you are more likely to get everyone paying attention to the exercise. If participants know in advance that they may have to report, then they are much more likely to concentrate on the activity.

In contrast, if you allow groups to select their own reporters, you are more likely to have some people tuning out because they will not be responsible for reporting. Moreover, you are likely to get the most outgoing and talkative people speaking to the class. They will be happy to talk, and quieter members will be happy to let them do so. Try to involve everyone and be supportive of all who do contribute.

THE EXPERIENTIAL EXERCISES

Chapter 1   Member Roles: Participating Effectively in Your Group

Effective Participation

Your Ultimate Goal: to demonstrate the effects of different member contributions to a discussion within a small group.

Your Interim Goals: to demonstrate the positive effects on discussion in a small group of both (1) task role skills and (2) social role skills.

Time Limit: 30 minutes.

Resources:

NOTE: In lieu of transparencies and overhead projectors in the list below, you may want to use a laptop computer (or computers) with projection capabilities. A software program such as Microsoft's PowerPoint or Apple's Keynote will be required to create the presentation slides. The end product of the exercise must be viewable by the entire class.

- An adequate supply of Member Role Play sheets per group
- An adequate supply of Discussion and Ranking Worksheets per group
- 1 Scoring the "I Am Canadian" Rankings sheet
- 1 Original Survey Results overhead transparency
- 1 overhead projector
- The Teacher's Guide, which provides additional information and resources for this exercise

PROCEDURE

This is a five-step exercise. First, you will randomly divide the class into groups of five or six players each, and locate the teams around the room with as much space between groups as possible. Second, you will instruct group members regarding the roles that they are to play during the discussion. Third, you will give specific instructions for the "I Am Canadian" discussion and then observe the groups as they discuss the topic. Fourth, you will provide the original (correct) rankings and then lead a discussion of the group dynamics within each team. Finally, you will lead the class in a debriefing session.

Step 1: Selecting and Locating the Groups (2 minutes)

Randomly divide the class into groups of five or six members each. Locate them around the room with as much space as possible between groups.

Step 2: Giving the Role Play Instructions (3 minutes)

When the groups are in place, remind them that Chapter 1 describes the six task roles and the six social roles that effective group members fulfill in order to contribute to the success of their groups.

Next, direct the groups as follows, regarding the role play instruction sheets that you distribute to them:

> You are each getting a role play instruction sheet that reviews the six task roles and the six social roles from Chapter 1 and asks you to practise them in the "I Am Canadian" discussion exercise. In the exercise, try to demonstrate the very best group skills that you can. In order to get the most out of today's discussion, please follow your instructions carefully. You are to role play excellence in group member participation.

Distribute the instruction sheets and give each member a minute to silently read her instructions. There is to be no discussion among members at this point.

Step 3: Giving the "I Am Canadian" Discussion Instructions (12 minutes)

Give the following instructions for the "I Am Canadian" discussion:

> Each year Canadians are surveyed to see what's most important to them. In a moment, each team will receive a sheet that lists 15 items from a survey. Using your best group skills, discuss and rank the items in the order of the importance that your group thinks Canadians place on each item in the survey. Do not give your personal ranking or your team's ranking. Rather, rank the items the way that you believe other Canadians ranked them in the original survey. Use the number 1 for most important and the number 15 for least important. Rank all 15 items. Try to decide by consensus (unanimous agreement). The objective is to see how accurately your team can identify the original rankings.

Distribute one ranking sheet to each team and direct them to start the discussion and the ranking. Tell them that they will have 12 minutes to finish the assignment. Observe the groups throughout the discussion session. Call time at the end of 12 minutes.

Step 4: Discussing the Group Dynamics (10 minutes)

Use the overhead slide to show the original survey results. Allow a minute or two to determine which group came closest. Congratulate the group that has done the best job of identifying the original survey results.

Point out, however, that the overall purpose of the experiential exercise is not to identify the original survey results, as interesting as that may be. The purpose is to examine the interpersonal and group dynamics that occurred during the "I Am Canadian" discussion exercise.

Ask the members in each group to comment on the group dynamics within their teams. For example, ask them who spoke most, who spoke least, who fulfilled the task roles, who fulfilled the social roles, etc. Teaching team observers should also comment on the group dynamics during the discussion.

Step 5: Debriefing (3 minutes)

Conclude the experiential exercise by emphasizing the importance of the task roles and the social roles for group success. Point out that the Teaching Team presentation that follows will look at both the 12 helpful roles and the 6 harmful roles.

Chapter 2   Leader Roles: Leading Effectively in Your Group

Leadership Styles

NOTE: The following exercise was created by professor Maureen Murphy-Fricker of Conestoga College Institute of Technology and Advanced Learning and is used by permission.

Your Ultimate Goal: to demonstrate different leadership styles in the process of teaching a lesson.

Your Interim Goals: to demonstrate (1) autocratic leadership, (2) democratic leadership, and (3) laissez-faire leadership in the teaching of lessons to small groups.

Time Limit: 30 minutes.

Resources:

- 4 teaching stations
- Appropriate materials for each station
- 1 timing device
- 1 bell or other signaling device.
- The Teacher's Guide, which provides additional information and resources for this exercise

PROCEDURE

This is a five-step exercise. First, you will identify and prepare the learning stations. Second, you will randomly divide the class into four different groups. Third, you will give instructions for the overall exercise. Fourth, you will signal the start and finish of each round, and coordinate the rotation of groups. Finally, you will facilitate the debriefing session.

Step 1: Establishing the Teaching Stations (1 minute)

Identify four different locations in the room and set up a teaching station at each. Put all necessary teaching materials at each station in advance of the first round.

Step 2: Selecting and Locating the Groups (1 minute)

Randomly divide the class into four different groups. Indicate to each group the station at which they will start the exercise when you give the signal to start.

Step 3: Giving the Overall Instructions (3 minutes)

Tell the class how the exercise will work overall. Indicate that the lesson at each station will be taught by a Teaching Team member and timed by the Teaching Team. Inform the class that you will give everyone the signal to rotate to the next station at the appropriate time.

Step 4: Coordinating the Rotations (20 minutes)

Ensure that the learning groups move from station to station at the appropriate time. Do this four times, once for each station.

Step 5: Debriefing (5 minutes)

After thanking the four teachers and the four learning groups, ask participants to comment on the three different leadership styles used by the teachers at their stations. Remind the class that the three leadership styles are discussed in Chapter 2 and that the teaching presentation that follows will discuss the styles further.

Chapter 3   Norms: Establishing Effective Rules in Your Group

Mutual Expectations

NOTE: The following exercise was created by Professor Maureen Murphy-Fricker of Conestoga College Institute of Technology and Advanced Learning and is used by permission.

Your Ultimate Goal: to demonstrate a process that a small group can use to develop a set of expectations (norms or rules) for its members.

Your Interim Goals: to demonstrate (1) the individual expectations step, (2) the critical discussion step, (3) the consensus step, and (4) the publishing step of a four-step process for establishing effective rules for the members of a small group.

Time Limit: 30 minutes.

Resources:

NOTE: In lieu of transparencies and overhead projectors in the list below, you may want to use a laptop computer (or computers) with projection capabilities. A software program such as Microsoft's PowerPoint or Apple's Keynote will be required to create the presentation slides. The end product of the exercise must be viewable by the entire class.

- 1 Individual Expectations sheet per group member
- 1 Team Expectations sheet per group
- 1 blank write-on, erasable overhead transparency per group
- 1 erasable transparency pen per group
- 1 or more overhead projectors
- The Teacher's Guide, which provides additional information and resources for this exercise

PROCEDURE

This is a five-step exercise. First, you will randomly divide the class into groups of five or six players each, and locate the teams around the room with as much space between groups as possible. (Note: If the class has been or will be working in a number of established teams over an extended period of time, then you should use the established teams for this exercise, rather than randomly creating new teams.) Second, you will instruct group members regarding the completion of the individual expectations sheet. Third, you will give instructions for the critical discussion and consensus steps. Fourth, you will facilitate a session in which each group presents or publishes its results. Finally, you will lead the class in a debriefing session.

Step 1: Selecting and Locating the Groups (2 minutes)

Randomly divide the class into groups of five or six members each. Locate them around the room with as much space as possible between groups. As noted above, if the class has been or will be working in a number of established teams over a continuous period of time, then you should use the established teams for this exercise, rather than randomly creating new teams.

Step 2: Instructing the Use of the Individual Expectations Sheet (8 minutes)

Tell the groups that this step requires individuals to work independently. There is to be no discussion or consultation with others. Provide each individual with a blank Individual Expectations sheet, and allow five minutes for completion.

Step 3: Discussing and Deciding on Team Expectations (15 minutes)

Give each group a Team Expectations sheet. Direct each group to share their individual expectations and to critically discuss what they have produced. Encourage them to reach consensus on the expectations that the team would include in a code of conduct for its members. Ask them to record their mutual expectations on the Team Expectations sheet.

Direct the groups to write a summary of their expectations on an overhead transparency for viewing and discussion by the class. Ask all individuals to stand ready to explain their team's work should you call on them to do so.

Step 4: Presenting the Results (4 minutes)

Take each team in turn, and ask one member of the team to present the team's expectations to the class, using the overhead transparency prepared earlier. Ask for comments from the class and look for the similarities among the statements of the different groups.

Step 5: Debriefing (1 minute)

Conclude the experiential exercise by emphasizing how important it is for group members to know what others in their group expect of them. Point out that the Teaching Team presentation that follows will further examine the role that norms play in the life of a small group.

Chapter 4   Goals: Setting Clear Targets for Your Group

Writing Clear Goal Statements

Your Ultimate Goal: to write clear and concise interim goals that would support the achievement of a stipulated, ultimate goal.

Your Interim Goals: to (1) carefully consider an ultimate goal, (2) write a number of interim goals that would support the achievement of that goal, and (3) create an overhead transparency (or projection slide) of the ultimate goal and its related interim goals for viewing and discussion by the class.

Time Limit: 30 minutes.

Resources:

NOTE: In lieu of transparencies and overhead projectors in the list below, you may want to use a laptop computer (or computers) with projection capabilities. A software program such as Microsoft's PowerPoint or Apple's Keynote will be required to create the presentation slides. The end product of the exercise must be viewable by the entire class.

- 1 blank 8.5 × 11 inch (21.6 × 27.9 cm) sheet of paper per goal per group.
- 1 blank write-on, erasable overhead transparency per goal per group
- 1 overhead, erasable transparency pen per group
- 1 or more overhead projectors
- The Teacher's Guide, which provides additional information and resources for this exercise

PROCEDURE

This is a four-step exercise. First, you will randomly divide the class into groups of three to five members each and locate them around the room with as much space as possible between groups. Second, you will instruct the groups on the steps of the objective-writing assignment. Third, you will facilitate a class discussion of each team's work. Finally, you will lead the class in a debriefing session.

Step 1: Selecting and Locating Groups (2 minutes)

Randomly divide the class into groups of three to five members each. Locate them around the room with as much space between groups as possible.

Step 2: Giving the Goal Objective-Writing Instructions (12 minutes)

Assign each group an ultimate goal statement for their consideration. Remind the group that properly written interim goals must answer the four specific questions discussed in Chapter 4. Instruct each group to use a blank 8.5 × 11 inch (21.6 × 27.9 cm) sheet to draft three interim goals that would support the achievement of their assigned ultimate goal.

Next, direct the groups to transfer their assigned ultimate goal and the interim goals that they have written down to an overhead transparency or projection slide. Tell them that later you will randomly call on a member of the team to explain the team's overhead to the class. All members should stand ready to provide the explanation if called upon.

Step 3: Discussing the Results (12 minutes)

Ensure that you have everyone's attention. Proceed to view the team results, in each case asking a team member to describe the group's thinking and work. Invite class comments on and discussion of each presentation. When all groups have presented, thank them for their work in this part of the experiential exercise.

Step 4: Debriefing (4 minutes)

Choose an example transparency from the class to illustrate the specific details that must be part of a properly written goal statement. The specific details are, of course, captured by the four questions. Point out the relationship between this experiential exercise and the Teaching Team presentation that will follow.

Chapter 5   Dialogue: Speaking and Listening Effectively in Your Group

One-Way and Two-Way Communication

Your Ultimate Goal: to demonstrate the drawbacks of one-way communication and the benefits of two-way communication.

Your Interim Goals: to demonstrate (1) the drawbacks of spontaneous one-way communication, (2) the drawbacks of effective one-way communication, and (3) the benefits of two-way communication.

Time Limit: 30 minutes.

Resources:

NOTE: In lieu of transparencies and overhead projectors in the list below, you may want to use a laptop computer (or computers) with projection capabilities. A software program such as Microsoft's PowerPoint or Apple's Keynote will be required to create the presentation slides. The end product of the exercise must be viewable by the entire class.

- 3 legal-sized file folders, numbered #1 through #3
- 3 different figures, one for each file folder
- 3 overhead transparency slides, one for each figure
- 1 tip sheet, for folder #2
- 1 overhead slide projector
- The Teacher's Guide, which provides additional information and resources for this exercise

PROCEDURE

This is a five-step exercise. First, you will select volunteers and introduce the exercise. Second, you will direct the one-way, unassisted communication exercise. Third, you will direct the one-way, coached communication exercise. Fourth, you will direct the two-way, open communication exercise. Finally, you will lead the class in a debriefing session.

Step 1: Introducing the Exercise (5 minutes)

Tell the class that the experiential exercise is an exercise in oral communication, the subject of Chapter 5. Identify three volunteer communicators who will come forward individually when you ask them. Instruct class members to take out three, blank 8.5 × 11 inch (21.6 × 27.9 cm) sheets of paper and a pen or pencil.

Step 2: Directing the One-Way Unassisted Communication (5 minutes)

Direct class members to get their first blank sheet ready, to await the instructions of the volunteer communicator, and to do so silently.

Direct the first volunteer to come forward to sit in a designated seat at the front of the class that you have positioned to face away from the class. With his back to the class, the volunteer is prevented from making eye contact with the class. Thus, he will not be able to receive non-verbal messages from class members.

Tell the volunteer that he will have to speak clearly and loudly so that everyone can hear him. Give him folder #1, open it with him, and make sure that class members cannot see the figure inside the folder. Tell the volunteer that he is to describe the figure so that the class members can draw (duplicate) the figure on their sheets. The volunteer must not show the figure to the class, or use any gestures or any aids, such as a white board. Do not give the volunteer any further help.

Remind the class that there is to be absolutely no feedback, either verbal or non-verbal. There are to be no comments, no questions, no moans, and no groans. Tell the volunteer to start. When you call time, ask the class members to set aside their first sheet until later.

Step 3: Directing the One-Way Coached Communication (5 minutes)

Direct class members to get their second blank sheet ready, to await the instructions of the volunteer communicator, and to do so silently.

Direct the second volunteer to come forward, to sit in the designated seat at the front of the class, facing away from the class. The procedure for this stage is exactly the same as that for the last stage except for one difference. The exception is as follows. Before the volunteer begins, give her one minute to read silently the tip sheet that is included in folder #2. When she has read the tips, encourage her to follow them when she describes her figure to the class.

Remind the class that there is to be no feedback, either verbal or non-verbal. There are to be no comments, no questions, no moans, and no groans. Tell the volunteer to start. When you call time, ask the class members to set aside their second sheet until later.

Step 4: Directing the Two-Way Open Communication (5 minutes)

Direct class members to get their third blank sheet ready, and tell them to await the instructions of the volunteer communicator.

Direct the third volunteer to come forward, and to sit in the designated seat that you have now turned to face the class. Tell the volunteer that he will have to speak clearly and loudly so that everyone can hear him. Give him folder #3, open it with him, and make sure that class members cannot see the figure inside the folder. Tell the volunteer to describe the figure so that the class members can draw (duplicate) the figure on their sheets. The volunteer must not reveal the figure, or use any gestures or any aids, such as a white board. He can, however, respond to class questions and comments as they arise.

Encourage the class to give helpful feedback to the volunteer, either verbally or non-verbally. Class members should ask questions and make comments as necessary. Tell the volunteer to start. When you call time, ask the class members to set aside their third sheet for a moment.

Step 5: Debriefing (10 minutes)

Project slide #1 onto a screen and invite class members to compare their drawings with the original drawing on the screen. Congratulate the person who has achieved the greatest likeness. Do the same for slides #2 and #3. Thank the volunteer communicators and highlight the different types of communication that they were required to use. Remind the class that the Teaching Team's presentation that follows this exercise will describe the ideal way of communicating orally in a group—namely, through two-way, open communication.

Chapter 6   Conflict: Resolving Disputes in Your Group

Conflict Styles

Your Ultimate Goal: to demonstrate different conflict styles in a small group setting.

Your Interim Goals: to demonstrate (1) withdrawing, (2) forcing, (3) smoothing, (4) compromising, and (5) confronting reactions to conflict in a small group.

Time Limit: 30 minutes.

Resources:

- 1 Role Play Instruction sheet per group
- 1 large bag of wrapped, hard candies
- 1 designated role-play area in the classroom
- An adequate supply of animal masks (optional)
- The Teacher's Guide, which provides additional information and resources for this exercise

PROCEDURE

This is a five-step exercise. First, you will randomly divide the class into five groups, and locate them around the room. Second, you will instruct each group regarding its role-play assignment. Third, you will coordinate the presentation of five preliminary skits. Fourth, you will coordinate the grand finale skit. Finally, you will lead the class in a debriefing session.

Step 1: Selecting and Locating the Groups (2 minutes)

Randomly divide the class into five different groups and locate them around the room with as much space as possible between them.

Step 2: Instructing the Role Play (10 minutes)

When the groups are in place, remind them that Chapter 6 discusses five different styles of conflict. Provide each group with its role-play assignment sheet, and ensure that they understand their responsibilities. Tell them that they have five minutes to prepare their two-minute skit.

Step 3: Coordinating the Preliminary Skits (12 minutes)

Request that all skit preparation stop and get everyone's attention. Randomly select the first team and invite members to present their silent skit in the designated role-play area. When their skit is over, thank them and invite a second team to present its silent skit. Follow the same procedure with the remaining three groups, ensuring that the class is attentive to the efforts of all teams.

Step 4: Coordinating the Grand Finale Skit (4 minutes)

Ask for one volunteer from each of the existing groups to form a new group of five members. Take them aside and provide them with the role-play assignment for the grand finale skit. Give them two minutes to prepare their silent skit, and then invite them to present their silent skit to the class.

Step 5: Debriefing (2 minutes)

Conclude the exercise by thanking all the teams and individual actors. Remind the class that the five conflict styles demonstrated in the skits are commonly used by members of small groups when conflict arises in a group. Inform the class that the five conflict styles will be discussed further in the Teaching Team presentation that will follow.

Chapter 7   Cohesion: Building Your Group into a Unified Team

Cohesion and Cooperation

Your Ultimate Goal: to demonstrate cohesion in a cooperative effort to reach a common goal.

Your Interim Goals: to demonstrate (1) mutual need, (2) mutual trust, and (3) mutual cooperation in the achievement of a common goal.

Time Limit: 30 minutes.

Resources:

- 1 clean, comfortable blindfold per triad
- 1 10-centimetre piece of wide masking tape per triad
- 2 one-metre pieces of string per triad
- 1 deck of 20 word cards per triad
- The Teacher's Guide, which provides additional information and resources for this exercise

PROCEDURE

This is a four-step exercise. First, you will randomly divide the class into groups of three people (triads) and locate them around the room with as much space between triads as possible. Second, you will read the scenario and start the exercise. Third, you will compare and discuss the outcomes of the exercise. Finally, you will lead the class in a debriefing session.

Step 1: Selecting, Locating, and Preparing the Triads (5 minutes)

Randomly divide the class members into triads. Locate the triads around the classroom with as much space as possible between triads. Clear a space on the floor where two members of each triad can complete the exercise.

Identify one member of each triad as A, another as B, and the third as C. A and B are participants and C is an observer. Blindfold A and gently place a 10-centimetre piece of tape over her mouth. (If participants object to the tape, they must promise to remain silent throughout the exercise.) Loosely tie B's hands behind his back with one piece of string, and tie his legs together loosely with the other piece. Do not blindfold, tape, or tie C.

Step 2: Reading the Scenario and Starting the Exercise (15 minutes)

A special deck of cards is used in this exercise. It is extremely important to keep the deck of cards hidden until the signal to start has been given. Once A and B have been appropriately tied, taped, and blindfolded, read the scenario clearly and loudly so that all triads can hear the scenario and the instructions. If everyone understands the rules of the exercise, then shuffle the cards and spread them randomly on the floor in front of A.

Step 3: Comparing Results (8 minutes)

After 15 minutes, call time, remove all blindfolds and tape, and untie all participants. Allow a minute or two to examine the quality and accuracy of the notes that have been created. Next, call on the observers (the Cs) to report on what they observed. Then, ask the players (the As and Bs) to share their experience of the game.

Step 4: Debriefing (2 minutes)

Finally, you will conclude the experiential exercise by pointing out how it provides a metaphor for real life. On every team, different individuals bring different talents to the group. Point out that this exercise relates to the Teaching Team's presentation on Chapter 7 that will follow, particularly to the material on trust and cooperation.

Chapter 8   Critical Discussion: Generating Ideas in Your Group

Critical Discussion

Your Ultimate Goal: to demonstrate mutual support among members of a small group in the discussion of controversial issues.

Your Interim Goals: to demonstrate (1) assertive communication, (2) active listening, (3) criticism of ideas, and (4) personal support in a small group discussion of a controversial issue.

Time Limit: 30 minutes.

Resources:

- An adequate supply of Controversial Issues sheets
- 1 Rules of Critical Discussion sheet per person
- The Teacher's Guide, which provides additional information and resources for this exercise

PROCEDURE

This is a five-step exercise. First, you will randomly divide the class into groups of five or six members each and locate the groups around the room with as much space between groups as possible. Second, you will instruct group members regarding the rules that they are to observe in the discussion of their topic. Third, you will monitor the critical discussion. Fourth, you will facilitate a post-discussion session in which participants share their experience of the exercise. Finally, you will lead the class in a debriefing session.

Step 1: Selecting and Locating the Groups (2 minutes)

Randomly divide the class into groups of five or six members each, and locate the groups around the room with as much space between groups as possible.

Step 2: Instructing the Discussion Groups (5 minutes)

Tell the groups that they will engage in a two-stage discussion of a controversial social issue. In stage one, the discussion will be free-wheeling without any particular rules in force or any set goal to achieve. In stage two, the participants must (1) proceed according to specified rules and (2) try to achieve consensus. Inform the groups that you will interrupt the free discussion after 5 minutes, distribute and explain the rules for stage two, and begin the stage-two discussion that will be limited to 10 minutes. Finally, assist the groups in selecting a controversial topic and begin the free discussion.

Step 3: Monitoring the Critical Discussion (16 minutes)

Observe the free-wheeling discussions for five minutes, allowing participants to discuss the issue as they choose. After five minutes, interrupt the discussion and distribute and explain the rules for stage two. Remind the groups to follow the rules and seek consensus on the issue. Begin stage two and monitor the discussions, ensuring that participants follow the rules of critical discussion that you distributed.

Step 4: Facilitating the Sharing of Experiences (5 minutes)

Facilitate a class discussion of the exercise. Invite participants to comment on both the free-wheeling stage and the rule-governed stage. Offer comments on the Teaching Team's observations.

Step 5: Debriefing (2 minutes)

After thanking participants for their contributions, conclude the experiential exercise by highlighting the importance of critical discussion for group success. Remind the class that both critical discussion and uncritical groupthink will be discussed further in the Teaching Team presentation that follows.

Chapter 9   Decisions: Solving Problems in Your Group

Comparing Decision-Making Methods

Your Ultimate Goal: to demonstrate and compare several different decision-making methods that groups can use when solving problems.

Your Interim Goals: to demonstrate and compare (1) decision by consensus, (2) decision by majority vote, (3) decision by a minority, and (4) decision by an expert with respect to the solution of a common problem.

Time Limit: 30 minutes.

Resources:

- An adequate supply of pencils
- An adequate supply of blank 8.5 × 11 inch (21.6 × 27.9 cm) paper
- 1 Problem Sheet per group
- 1 Role Play Assignment sheet per group
- The Teacher's Guide, which provides additional information and resources for this exercise

PROCEDURE

This is a four-step exercise. First, you will randomly divide the class into four groups of approximately equal size and locate the groups around the room with as much space between groups as possible. Second, you will instruct group members regarding the role play that forms the basis of the exercise and assign the problem to each group. Third, you will observe the groups as they make their decisions using their assigned method. Finally, you will lead the class in a debriefing session.

Step 1: Selecting and Locating the Groups (2 minutes)

Randomly divide the class into groups of five or six members each. Locate them around the room with as much space as possible between groups.

Step 2: Giving the Role-Play Instructions (6 minutes)

When the groups are in place, remind them that Chapter 9 describes several methods by which groups can make decisions. Inform the class that each group will be assigned a particular method to use in solving the problem that you will give them.

Distribute the role-play instructions to each group, give them sufficient time to read them, and ensure that they understand how the method works. Remind them that they are to use the assigned method to decide their group's solution to the problem. All members should be ready to describe their team's assigned method and to comment on how members felt about the process if called upon to do so.

Step 3: Making Decisions (10 minutes)

Give each team a copy of the problem sheet and instruct them to solve the problem as quickly as they can, using the assigned decision-making method.

Observe each team and ensure that it adheres to the assigned method. Keep time and call time at the end of 8 minutes, or sooner if all teams are finished. Collect each team's answer and determine whether it is correct or not.

Step 4: Debriefing (12 minutes)

Get the class's attention, give the correct answer to the assigned problem, and congratulate any successful teams. Having done that, remind the class that the overall purpose of the experiential exercise was to compare different methods of group decision-making, not to solve the given problem. In other words, the exercise was about group dynamics, not word puzzles.

Randomly select a person from each group to describe that team's assigned method and to comment on how members felt about the process. Discuss the strengths and weaknesses of the method. Repeat this process with each team and each method.

Remind the class that these are only four of eight decision-making methods discussed in Chapter 9. Be sure to link this experiential exercise with the presentation from the Teaching Team that will follow.

Chapter 10   Evaluation: Improving Your Group's Performance

Creating Evaluation Instruments

Your Ultimate Goal: to create an evaluation instrument for use in a small group evaluation session.

Your Interim Goals: to (1) design an evaluation instrument, (2) create an overhead transparency of the instrument, and (3) discuss the instrument's value as an assessment tool.

Time Limit: 30 minutes.

Resources:

NOTE: In lieu of transparencies and overhead projectors, you may want to use a laptop computer (or computers) with projection capabilities. A software program such as Microsoft's PowerPoint or Apple's Keynote will be required to create the presentation slides. The end product of the exercise must be viewable by the entire class.

- 1 blank 8.5 × 11 inch (21.6 × 27.9 cm) sheet of paper per group
- 1 blank write-on, erasable overhead transparency per group
- 1 overhead, erasable transparency pen per group
- 1 overhead projector
- The Teacher's Guide, which provides additional information and resources for this exercise

PROCEDURE

This is a four-step exercise. First, you will randomly divide the class into groups of three to five members each and locate them around the room with as much space as possible between groups. Second, you will instruct each group to design and create an evaluation instrument on an overhead transparency. Third, you will facilitate a class discussion of the assessment tools that have been created. Finally, you will lead the class in a debriefing session.

Step 1: Selecting and Locating Groups (2 minutes)

Randomly divide the class into groups of three to five members each. Ten working groups is the ideal but not absolutely necessary. Locate them around the room with as much space between groups as possible.

Step 2: Instructing and Directing the Group (10 minutes)

Each team should have one or more textbooks for use during this exercise. Randomly assign each group a different chapter from the text. The assigned chapter will provide the group with focus behaviours for its evaluation instrument. Each group will probably have to make a choice of focus behaviours from its assigned chapter in order to narrow the scope of their assessment tool. If there are not enough groups to cover all 10 chapters, then assign only as many chapters as there are groups.

Direct each group to use the blank 8.5 × 11 inch (21.6 × 27.9 cm) sheet to design its instrument carefully before transferring the design to an overhead transparency. Once the group is satisfied that its design is of high quality, instruct them to transfer the design to the overhead transparency for viewing by the class in the next step of the exercise. All members should stand ready to explain the team's evaluation instrument if called upon to do so.

Step 3: Facilitating Discussion of the Group Creations (15 minutes)

Ensure that all members of the class are focused for discussion. Remind them that evaluation has been an essential part of each class session from the beginning of the course. Underscore the importance of formal evaluation for the improvement of group performance.

Randomly select a person from one of the groups to come forward, to project her team's instrument on the screen, and to explain the features of the instrument.

The person should do this in approximately one minute. Ask the class to provide constructive feedback on the instrument as an assessment tool. Repeat this process with each of the groups.

Step 4: Debriefing (3 minutes)

Congratulate all groups on the evaluation instruments that they have created, and remind the class that this experiential exercise is an introduction to the Teaching Team's presentation that will follow.

Appendix A   Meetings: Conducting Business Effectively in Your Group

Conducting a Business Meeting

Your Ultimate Goal: to conduct a mock business meeting

Your Interim Goals: to demonstrate how to (1) use the agenda, the record, and the rules of order in a business meeting; (2) make, second, and vote on a motion in a business meeting; and (3) chair a meeting, record the minutes of a meeting, and make a report in a meeting.

Time Limit: 30 minutes.

Resources:

- 1 Model Agenda per student
- 1 Sample Record Sheet per student
- 1 Sample Report Sheet per student
- 1 Sample Voting Procedure Sheet per student
- The Teacher's guide, which provides additional information and resources for this exercise

PROCEDURE

This is a four-step exercise. First, you will introduce the exercise. Second, you will conduct a mock business meeting. Third, you will lead a discussion of the experience. Finally, you will lead the class in a debriefing session.

Step 1: Introducing the Exercise (5 minutes)

Ensure that the room is properly set up for a business meeting. Explain to the class that you are going to conduct a mock business meeting in which they are attendees. Explain further that they are expected to participate fully, under the direction of the meeting chair. Introduce the chair, recorder, and reporter that you have selected from your team to provide leadership at the mock meeting, and then distribute one model agenda to each student.

Step 2: Conducting the Mock Business Meeting (15 minutes)

The chair calls the meeting to order and directs attention to the agenda. Under the leadership of the chair, each agenda item is dealt with in sequence. Observe the general rules of order and the specific rules for voting throughout the meeting. When all other items of business have been completed, the chair demonstrates closure, which is the last agenda item. In the interest of time, the purpose of the Evaluation item can be explained without actually conducting an evaluation.

Step 3: *Leading a Discussion of the Mock Business Meeting (8 minutes)*

Ensure that the class is focused for discussion. Ask attendees to explain the purpose of the agenda, the record, the rules of order, and the leadership roles in a business meeting. The chair of the mock meeting or another designated team member should lead the discussion.

Step 4: *Debriefing (2 minutes)*

Thank the class for participating in the mock meeting and the discussion. Remind them that this experiential exercise is an introduction to the Teaching Team's presentation that will follow.

Glossary

A

accountability
the obligation one has to explain or justify one's actions to others

active listening
a three-fold process that includes the skills of expressing intention, listening with your whole person, and paraphrasing the messages of others

adjourning stage
the last stage of group development marked by dispersal

affective dimension
our feelings and moods

affiliation
a sense of association or connection with others

aggressive person
one whose concern for personal rights outweighs concern for the rights of others

Aggressor
member who intimidates other group members, makes negative judgments about them, and seeks unhealthy confrontation

arbitrator
an unbiased third party who makes a decision for a group that cannot reach a decision on its own

assertive communication
communication between and among disputing group members in which self-respect, together with respect for others, aids in conflict resolution

assertive person
one whose self-interest is balanced by concern for others, who speaks up yet also listens

autocratic leader
a take-charge leader who tells others what to do and sees that they do it

B

behavioural listening
listening with one's whole person, the result of both emotional (affective) and intellectual (cognitive) engagement with another person

C

challenge
a test of one's abilities

challenge of evaluation
test of one's ability to describe behaviour without judging character

charismatic power
power resulting from personal qualities

coercive power
power to punish members in order to influence their conduct

cognitive dimension
our thinking or intellectual side

cohesion
the act of uniting or sticking together

commitment
a willingness to stick with things over the long term

communication
the successful exchange of information and feelings between people in a group

Communication Facilitator
member who uses uses communication skills to build good relationships among members of the team

competitively structured goal
a goal that is achieved only when people compete with one another

Comprehension Checker
member who is skilled at ensuring that the group has a common understanding of an issue or task

compromising behaviour
making concessions to resolve a dispute

conceptual conflict
a disagreement or controversy about ideas, opinions, or points of view; also called a conflict or battle of ideas

conflict
an interpersonal dispute between or among members of a group

Conflict Mediator
member who is skilled at using the best conflict management strategies to assist members in dealing with the inevitable conflicts that arise between and among members of a group

conflict style
the manner in which a group member typically engages in disputes with others

confrontation
the act of facing up to and dealing directly with a problem or difficult situation

confronting behaviour
facing up to and dealing reasonably with others in a dispute

consensus
unanimous agreement within a group

consistency
agreement with

constructive controversy
a third name for conceptual conflict

cooperation
a mutual effort to achieve common goals; also called collaboration

cooperatively structured goal
a goal that is achieved only by cooperative efforts

critical discussion
a six-step process designed to encourage group members to engage in conceptual conflict

critical thinking
fact-based, logical reasoning

culture
the way of life of people in a given society or group

Cynic
member who is pessimistic and does not trust others, individually or in groups

D

decision
a choice made between competing options

decoder
receiver who interprets a message

decoding
interpreting a spoken or written message accurately

democratic leader
a leader who involves all members of a group in the discussion of issues and decision making

designated leader
a leader selected to fill an official position within a group

developed norm
a rule established by a group to govern behaviour within the group

dialogue
a face-to-face conversation between two or more people

Direction Suggester
member who is skilled at making constructive suggestions about the options that the team has at a given time

disclosure
trusting act in which one reveals one's thoughts and feelings to others

disputant
a person who is in conflict with another person or persons

Distracter
member who takes the group away from its task using a variety of techniques

Dominator
member who takes on excessive amounts of work to satisfy personal needs, denying other members the opportunity to make their own contributions

E

emergent leader
a leader who assumes a temporary, unofficial leadership role because of his or her special talents

empathy
feeling what another person feels

encoder
sender who encodes a message

encoding
expressing a message in spoken or written words

equality
the ethical principle of treating all members of a group equally

evaluation
an assessment of the quality of something

evaluation instrument
a tool used to observe and rate group performance

expert power
power resulting from particular knowledge or skill

F

fairness
giving people what they have earned (merit), giving people equal shares (equity), or meeting a person's special needs (need)

feedback message
a return message sent by a receiver to the original sender

focus behaviours
the specific behaviours to be evaluated by a group

forcing behaviour
using intimidating behaviour to get one's way in a dispute

formal evaluation
a scheduled assessment of predetermined focus behaviours

forming stage
first stage of group development marked by uncertainty and anxiety

Fox
conflict style of one who compromises to resolve differences

frame of reference
the context from which a person speaks or listens

Free Rider
member who does not contribute to the group's effort but expects to benefit from the group's work

freedom
the ethical principle of respecting group members' choices

G

goal
a desired state of future affairs; also called objective, end, aim, purpose, or target

goodness
the ethical principle of doing good to others and not harming them

group maturity
includes a group's achievement orientation, level of responsibility, and collective expertise

Group Motivator
member who is skilled at encouraging others to direct their energy to completing the task at hand

groupthink
uncritical thinking within a group

H

heterogeneous
having variety

homogeneous
lacking variety

I

Idea Seeker
member who is skilled at asking others what they think about a given task

Idea Sharer
member who is skilled at sharing his ideas about team tasks with other team members

ideational conflict
a second name for conceptual conflict

identity
a shared sense of sameness

illusion of invulnerability
the mistaken belief that one's team cannot fail

illusion of superiority
the mistaken belief that one's team is on the side of right

illusion of unity
the mistaken belief that everyone is in agreement on an issue

imposed norm
a rule established by an authority outside the group

individualistically structured goal
a goal that is achieved only when people work independently

influence
the ability to affect circumstances and people

informal evaluation
a spontaneous assessment of performance

interim goal
a goal that must be achieved in order to reach an ultimate goal

L

laissez-faire leader
a leader who leaves a mature group alone to accomplish its goals

leader roles
the parts played by group members who give direction to others

legitimate power
power that accompanies designated positions within a group

M

majority
fifty-one percent or more of voters in a group

measurable goal
a goal that is clearly defined or specified; a specific goal

mediation
the process in which a person (the mediator) intervenes between the disputants to help them reach an agreement or reconciliation

mediator
a person who intervenes between or among disputants in order to help them reach an agreement or reconciliation

member roles
helpful task and social roles that contribute to team success

message
the thoughts and feelings communicated by a sender, whether verbally or non-verbally

minority
forty-nine percent or less of voters in a group

model
a simplified description of a process, often expressed as a diagram

N

negotiation
exchange between sender and receiver as they ensure that they understand one another

noise
any physical, physiological, or psychological interference that impedes communication

non-verbal communication
a message expressed by gestures, eye contact, or body posture, but not words

norm
a written or unwritten rule of a group

norming stage
third stage of group development marked by agreement on rules

O

observers
group members who are assigned to watch the group's performance

one-way communication
the sender sends the message and the receiver receives it, without any feedback occurring

Owl
conflict style of one who confronts in order to achieve win–win solutions

P

paraphrasing
the skill of accurately restating another's position in words different from the original

Participant Supporter
member who is skilled at showing support for others when they make a contribution to the work of the team

Participation Encourager
member who is skilled at stimulating all members of the group to contribute to the group's effort

passive person
one who lacks sufficient self-respect to defend his or her rights in a dispute and withdraws from conflict

performing stage
the fourth stage of group development marked by productivity

personality conflict
an interpersonal dispute arising from differing personal traits

physical noise
loud and disturbing sounds

physiological noise
interferences to communication that result from disorders of the body

power
the ability to influence a situation in desired directions

power conflict
an interpersonal dispute arising from the desire to control a group

principles
the standards by which a group evaluates a course of action

problem
any situation that requires consideration and a solution

Process Observer
member who is skilled at noting the emotional interactions among members as the group goes about its work

Progress Summarizer
member who gets the group to stop and reflect on the progress being made

psychological noise
interference that stems from a heightened emotional state, usually a negative one

R

rating scale
a range of values used to measure something

realistic goal
a goal that a group can achieve given its expertise

receiver
the person in the communication process who interprets the sender's words

reliance
trusting act in which one places confidence in another or depends on another

Rescuer
member who does an excessive amount of work, offers solutions prematurely, and makes decisions independently in order to save the group from failure

resource conflict
an interpersonal dispute arising from unequal distribution of resources

respect
honour and esteem, particularly among peers

reward power
power to give benefits to members in order to influence their conduct

role
a set of expectations associated with a particular responsibility

S

sanctions
the punishments incurred if one breaks the rules of a society, an organization, or a family

"secret" observers
group members who have a group's permission to monitor member performance at times that are unknown to the group

sender
the person who begins the communication process by expressing thoughts and feelings in words

sharing
trusting act in which one gives or lends resources to others

Shark
conflict style of one who forces others to do his will

smoothing behaviour
attempting to "rub the rough edges off" a dispute

social goal
the goal of building good relationships among group members

social roles
member roles that help to build and maintain a cohesive team

social skills
the distinctive skills that characterize each of the six social roles

society
a large, identifiable community of individuals who fulfill a variety of differing and interdependent roles

specific goal
a goal that is clearly defined or specified

status conflict
an interpersonal dispute arising from the desire to be recognized within a group

storming stage
second stage of group development marked by conflict

Stress Reliever
member who is skilled at taking steps to reduce the emotional tensions that groups inevitably experience

subculture
a smaller culture within a larger culture

T

task goal
the goal of getting the job done

task roles
member roles that enable a group to get a task done

task skills
the distinctive skills that characterize each of the six task roles

Teddy Bear
conflict style of one who smoothes things over to maintain harmony

trust
the act of placing confidence in another person without full assurance that the confidence is well placed; entails mutual disclosure, sharing, and reliance

truth
the ethical principle of honesty and integrity

Turtle
conflict style of one who withdraws or avoids conflict

two-way communication
when the receiver of a message becomes the sender of a return message and the original sender becomes the new receiver

U

ultimate goal
the final goal in a series of related goals; also called end goal

unity
a shared sense of oneness or togetherness

V

values
whatever is of importance or worth to an individual or a group

verbal communication
a message expressed in words (speech or writing)

W

withdrawing behaviour
avoiding conflict by removing oneself from a dispute

Index